# BRIDGE OVER TROUBLED WATER

# BRIDGE OVER TROUBLED WATER

## MINISTRY TO BABY BOOMERS —A GENERATION ADRIFT

### JAMES BELL

A
BridgePoint
BOOK

Copyediting: Robert N. Hosack
Cover Design: Scott Rattray

**Library of Congress Cataloging-in-Publication Data**

Bell, James (James L.), 1950-
    Bridge over troubled water: ministry to baby boomers: a generation adrift /
by James Bell.
        p.      cm.
    Includes bibliographical references.
    ISBN 1-56476-112-6
    1. Church work with the baby boom generation. 2. Baby boom generation.
3. Baby boom generation — Religious life. I. Title.
BV4446.B455  1993
253 — dc20                                                                    93-3925
                                                                                  CIP

BridgePoint is the academic imprint of Victor Books.

1   2   3   4   5   6   7   8   9   10   Printing/Year   97   96   95   94   93

# CONTENTS

89506

*To*
*Jason, Mark, and Adrian*
*and*
*Lindsay and Courtney*

# FOREWORD

Why did God become man? (*Cur Deus Homo?*) pondered St. Anselm, archbishop of Canterbury at the beginning of the twelfth century. So that a perfect human, Jesus Christ, could render satisfaction to God through his death on the cross, was the answer. This led to a theory of the atonement to the neglect of a theology of incarnation. An atonement for sin which consumes the humanity of Christ consecrates saints, but cleaves the humanity of the world from the humanity of God. We now know how God can forgive sin, but not much about how sinners can find God. It is this latter concern that seems to preoccupy the contemporary church, for better or for worse.

Set adrift upon the unmapped seas of pluralism, relativism, individualism, and hedonism, the generations of humankind chart their own course, sometimes making port calls at landlocked institutional churches and occasionally disembarking to become permanent residents. Seeking to lure these wayward travelers into their harbors, churches in our own generation have resorted to scientific study of these worldly *species* and, armed with cultural insight, sociological analysis, and marketing methods, have found instant success.

Business is booming in the Baby Boomer churches!

Some are concerned that the offense of the cross has given way to a theology of consumerism. Seeker-driven worship services draw the crowds. Market-driven strategy promotes the church. Is success a sign of Gospel relevance or of spiritual decadence? Has the church bridged the gap with a generation set adrift, or has it lost its own moorings in attempting to be all things to all people?

These are some of the questions and issues which James Bell takes up in his perceptive and prescriptive study. This is no kneejerk reaction. With keen insight into the culture and literature of the so-called Baby Boomer generation, he probes the troubled psyche underlying the superficial and rapidly changing expressions of their needs and desires. In so doing, he finds a core of humanity which is searching in new ways for old truths. Through the restless relativism and hyped-up hedonism of individuals seeking community, he perceives an anxiety that seeks to be comforted and a human longing for divine presence.

7

The church need not create bridges of its own design, argues Bell. The incarnation of God did not end with the cross, but continues to be the bridge between God and humans. The exclusivity of Christ is not a religious claim, but a human bridge which reaches into the lonely and anxious heart of every person and creates a connection beneath the cultural forms which separate one generation from another. The transcendent power and truth of Christ is not an offense to reason nor an isolated ghetto amidst a pluralistic world of beliefs and cultures. Rather, through the humanity of Christ as the incarnate reality of the transcendent God, plurality and relativism are drawn toward a center which affirms uniqueness while healing brokenness.

This book is a call to the church to be as sensitive and insightful toward its own generation as Jesus was toward his. This book will challenge the arrogant and self-serving attitude of a church which sets itself up as wiser than its own generation. James Bell helps us to see that the bridge which God created through the incarnation is a two-way thoroughfare. We are reminded again of the exasperation of Jesus who took aim at the religious leaders of his own day for their cultural isolation and worldly indifference when he said, "For the children of this age are more shrewd in dealing with their own generation than are the children of light" (Luke 16:8, NRSV).

We live in a different era than St. Anselm, but the question is the same. Why did God become human? The answer is, to make peace through the blood of the cross and to secure the restless and searching drift of a new generation in the timeless truths of God's redeeming Word. This book will make the reader wiser in the ways of the children of this age and more effective in leading them across the bridge which leads to present joy and life everlasting.

Ray S. Anderson
Professor of Theology and Ministry
Fuller Theological Seminary

# ACKNOWLEDGEMENTS

Research and writing entails many debts on the part of the writer. In particular, I appreciate the helpful suggestions made by my editor, Robert N. Hosack, and for his attention to detail. Above all, I am grateful to my wife, Jill, who not only endured the usual trials and tribulations of a writer in travail, but also read the manuscripts during its various stages, offering positive criticism in lightening the prose and making helpful suggestions in content and style. Moreover, she gave me the inspiration I needed to complete this study of Baby Boomer culture and their unique needs and aspirations. Needless to say, any unintended confusion and infelicities of style are mine and mine alone.

James Bell
Easter, 1993
New York City

# INTRODUCTION

Whether as primitive as a fallen log over a stream, as ornate as a rope bridge made of twisted lianas, or as technically complex as San Francisco's Golden Gate, bridges serve one main purpose—to unite two separate land masses in order to make a crossing possible. For example, the Brooklyn Bridge, spanning the Pacific Ocean for a distance of 1,095 feet, was built over 100 years ago, making it one of the largest and most spectacular suspension bridges in the world. When it opened in 1883, it effectively brought unity to New York by connecting Manhattan to the separate city of Brooklyn.

The title and leitmotiv of this book was inspired by Simon and Garfunkel's all-time hit, "Bridge Over Troubled Water." Written in the summer of 1969, this song won six separate Grammy awards and profited from global sales reaching 5 million. The expression "troubled water" is used in this text as an analogy to describe the turbulent times of today. Great numbers of Baby Boomers, the generation born in the two decades following the end of World War II (1946–64), who once wanted to "have it all" are now showing signs of wanting to be "out of it all." An entire generation simultaneously discovering that acquisitions cannot satisfy, are searching for something more meaningful. Although they traditionally pride themselves as being unique, as they approach middle-age, Baby Boomers are in fact discovering that they have many of the same spiritual, emotional, and physical desires as previous generations. For a substantial number of Boomers, this dawning reality is causing a renewed interest in the church, a place they have been absent from most of their lives.

The "bridge" in our analogy is used not only to describe the incarnate person of Christ, who is ultimately the one to span the great divide between God and the creation, but also as an analogy for the biblical and theological framework from which an authentic ministry to Baby Boomers can be built. Indeed, this book will stress that it is dangerous to the health of the church for its ministry to be based primarily on the immediate pragmatic needs of Baby Boomers. It must first secure that ministry to the firm foundation of Scripture, tradition, reason, and experience in much the same way that the Brooklyn Bridge hangs from the cables that are securely fastened to the towers at each end.

11

Recent studies show that this powerful "lead" generation is consumeristic in its approach to religion. It has specific needs, tends to be finicky, and makes choices first and foremost in accordance with its pragmatic needs. Baby Boomers are seeking a religious experience that will help make sense of their lives, which are often confused, broken, and void of intimate relationships and community experience. Even though it may be tempting for the church to respond to their social, cultural, and spiritual needs by providing Christian faith "a la carte," this book attempts to establish that the modern church can respond with biblical integrity by drawing its model from the paradigm found in the Acts 2 pericope.

This passage provides us with a brief but significant picture of life in the early Christian community. Here, we find that Christianity was not born solitarily in a vacuum, but arose in the midst of a pluralistic society, characterized by religious syncretism. Palestine, with its distinct Judaic backdrop, was the cradle for the emerging Christian faith. In addition, the Mediterranean basin enjoyed a political and cultural unity that resulted in the widespread dissemination of Greco-Roman thought, new philosophical systems of the Hellenistic period, and a wide variety of mystery religions.

Without maintaining a reductionist view of the church that would eliminate any sense of a supernatural explanation of its origin, it is argued that, as with the early Christian community, the church today does not exist in a vacuum, but does exist within a pluralistic society. Indeed, there are some striking similarities in our day to the pre-Constantinian age. Cosmopolitan urban mass culture, combined with the breakdown of community life, rootless individualism, and church/state tensions were as much a part of the ancient Jewish/Hellenistic world as they are a part of ours today. Like the early Christians, the modern Christian community in North America constitutes a "cognitive minority" (a group of people whose worldview differs significantly from that of general society, and who hold a marginal position of influence in society). Like the primitive apostolic community, our religious profile is very diverse, creating a North American culture with no monolithic standard for moral and ethical decisions. Other ideologies abound: pluralism, relativism, individualism, consumerism, hedonism, pragmatism, as well as a variety of other forms of secular humanism.

Amid its cultural, social, and religious diversity, the early Christians developed a pattern of community life and personal transformation that not only attracted people, but managed to sustain and expand growth. How did they achieve this? The apostolic chronicles of the infant Christian church give us a graphic description of the new attitudes and priorities that were evident in people's lives through a doxologically oriented life-style (i.e., loving fellowship, relevant teaching, small group life, prayer, and worship). The Acts pericope reveals a strong sense of community life in Christ where members act responsible for one another's well-being. In a similar vein, these doxological life-style features are relevant today in meeting the needs of our community-starved Baby Boomer generation.

This book is not simply an argument for primitive restorationism or an attempt to turn back the cultural clock, nor is it an effort to impose an ancient culture upon a modern one. Rather, it endeavors to establish that valuable lessons can be learned by this paradigm of community life, as it provides a solid basis for the effective evangelism, nurture, and spiritual formation of the Baby Boomer generation. An attempt is made at contextualizing theological and doxological principles in the light of our contemporary sociological and cultural realities. The cultural ethos of the day is a fact of life that no Christian community can dare to ignore. These are patterns of life which must not be conformed to, but rather, once understood, be adapted, modified, and put to use in the service of Christ.

# PART ONE

# TROUBLED WATER: THE BABY BOOMER MILIEU

# Chapter 1
# A UNIQUE GENERATION

Bridges have radically changed in design, structure, and composition over the years. Each new design, while building upon existing ideas, also challenges established theories resulting in the creation of different bridges for different needs. From the origins of simple timber bridges of a bygone age, fixed and movable bridges built from materials such as reinforced concrete, steel, and structural aluminum have evolved.

Baby Boomers have likewise challenged and changed almost every aspect of North American life. Before examining this evolving subculture, we must first look at the cultural cradle from whence it emerged. Indeed, the Baby Boomer phenomenon cannot be properly understood independent of its historical origins.

Parents of the Baby Boomers, born prior to 1945, endured scarcities and shortages as a result of a national economic depression and World War II. Because of the hardship, people of this period tended to be cautious conservers rather than carefree gratifiers. The underlying ethic of the day was one of "self-denial," similar to the spirit of the pioneers. Although two major events tested the self-denial ethic (the Depression and World War II), the prevailing belief was that dedicated hard work assured financial stability. For most, there was only enough to cover the basic needs of life with very little surplus for luxuries.

## The Calm Before the Storm

The war years (1939–45) were turbulent as the waves of uncertainty crashed upon the shores of Europe, threatening to change forever the liberal democratic societies of many of its countries with militarism and totalitarianism. This conflict of defending democracy killed more people, cost more money, damaged more property, and caused more far-reaching changes than any other war in history. It was considered to be "the war to end all wars." When it was over and the troubled waters subsided to a period of calm, many North Americans felt that the time was ripe to restore their lives and get on with the business of living. In this post-war fervor, many couples committed themselves to purchasing a home and having a family. From 1946–64, an unprecedented number of children were born. However, accompanying the birth of children was the birth of a new philosophy known as "the ethic of self-fulfillment." Many post-war babies, with only a secondhand knowledge of economic difficulties and an inherited determination to not experience their parents' hardships, grew up in an environment of an expanding economy. Daniel Yankelovich suggests that a four-fold pattern emerged. The first was the notion that an individual was entitled to affluence; second, that the economy provided a cornucopia of goods and services; third, that more was better than enough; and finally, that the basic calling of one's life was the fulfillment of self.[1]

## The TV Generation

Baby Boomers prided themselves as unique. Certainly, there was much in their brief history to substantiate this claim. They were distinctive in being the first generation to live under the threat of nuclear war, experience the excitement of space exploration, and be a part of the sexual revolution, propelled by the availability of the birth control pill. They were also the first to explore their psyche through the use of drugs and the first generation to grow up under the influence of television.

Since Baby Boomers were avid TV viewers, absorbing a steady flow of news, politics, world events, fashion, and advertising, we need to consider what effect this form of communication had on their consciousness.

Although there are many aspects of television programming that are wholesome, entertaining, and informative, there are also distressing aspects—the single most disturbing is its ability to create a distorted view of the world. During the Boomer growing-up years, television provided the ideal role models, particularly of family life—the perfect father; the slim, attractive mother; the cute but precocious children; and as a family they dealt with trivial social issues of the day. Seemingly innocent programs such as "My Three Sons" or "The Andy Griffith Show" featured the single parent as widowed rather than divorced. The children from blended families, such as "The Brady Bunch," suffered only minor behavioral problems and were never involved in controversial issues. Thus, the Boomers' TV world fed into a safe, beautiful, and somewhat affluent worldview. It is not difficult to understand why the catastrophic events of the '60s had such a devastating effect on the Boomers' consciousness. How ironic that the very medium that provided this perfect world would now portray the horror of assasinations and war. The disillusioned Boomers, in shock, reacted very powerfully as evidenced by their protests of and retaliation to what they perceived as violent and unnecessary.

Many years later, television still provides its illusionary world, only now reflecting a wide variety of society's social problems. The role models are now no longer always slim, beautiful, and perfect. The most controversial social issues are frequently woven into the plot of many dramas and sitcoms. However, even within these current issues, there still exists the illusionary world. Contrary to what we see on television, not every senior citizen lives the antics of "The Golden Girls," nor do many enjoy wonderful friends in the bar scene like "Cheers," nor is every black family as affluent as the one depicted in "The Cosby Show."

On a more menacing level, consider how violence is portrayed in TV programming. Varying levels of violence have been gradually infused into the daily diet of viewers over the many years since Boomers first engaged with their TV world. Today, not only are many of the drama programs and movies threaded with violent themes, but we are exposed to the reporting of real-life violence on the evening news, which is followed up in greater depth on subsequent documentaries, and further sensationalized by dramatizations in miniseries. This bombardment of violent stimuli over many years has created an apathy and numbness on the part of the viewers. The Boomer TV world has evolved from a safe, perfect, and beautiful world to a frightening, flawed, and ugly one.

Considering the fact that television has been and continues to be North America's primary disseminator of information and advertising, there can be no doubt that Boomers have been profoundly influenced by the TV worldview. TV, no doubt, will continue to be formative in shaping Baby Boomers worldviews, as it provides one of the most affordable forms of entertainment.

## The Turbulent Years

As every schoolchild knows, storms are caused by disturbances in temperature and pressure in the atmosphere and are usually marked by blustery winds, heavy rain, or snow. I suppose, technically speaking, that storms would never occur if the temperature in the air were to remain equal.

The untimely death of John F. Kennedy on November 22, 1963 brought an end to fifteen years of relative calm on the shores of North America, thus causing the water under the bridge to again be turbulent and unsettled. Kennedy's philosophy of America and confidence in its people inspired a belief that poverty and injustice could be eradicated and a human community could be built where democracy reigned. These high hopes and political idealisms were shattered, causing the bubble of national optimism to burst when the president was assassinated. The nation's climate further changed and the pressure continued to build as a result of the assassinations of two more American heroes, Bobby Kennedy and Martin Luther King. The Vietnam War and civil rights issues eventually brought the forecasted storm to a head. A new era marked by a strong and pervasive antiestablishment mood dawned, giving birth to a stormy decade of political and social upheaval.

Most Baby Boomers considered the Vietnam War immoral, perceiving abuse and misuse of political power. It opened many eyes to the dark side of the human heart, even the American one. In a vain effort to control the destiny of a small country, the strongest nation on earth stooped to a level of carnality and wickedness, causing many Baby Boomers to angrily respond by burning draft cards or leaving the country. Many who served in Vietnam never returned. Those who did, returned stigmatized by fellow citizens, and disillusioned by the futility and lack of purpose for their efforts. Conservative estimates suggest that some 50,000 were killed and 305,000 were wounded, causing great numbers of American citizens to experience personal trauma either within their

**20**

family or neighborhood.[2] The net effect of this war was catastrophic, as Landon Jones writes:

> The optimism and hope that the boom generation took into the Vietnam years only made its eventual disenchantment more devastating. They had been young and idealistic and Vietnam made them old and cynical. Their parents had come out of W.W. II with renewed confidence, but the boom generation came out of Vietnam with little to believe in of its own.[3]

If there were hypocrisies abroad in Vietnam, there were also great injustices at home, which caused large segments of the population to protest against a system that permitted racism, social evils, poverty, and the suppression of women's rights. With the support of many white American Baby Boomers, black American citizens, no longer willing to tolerate the segregated conditions of the past, demanded equality and constitutional rights.

## Christianity During the Boom Years

Prior to World War II, Christianity had significant influence in the North American culture. Large segments of the population read the Bible on a regular basis, attended religious services, and upheld an orthodox belief in God and the authority of the Bible as the source of faith and morality. The Roman Catholic Church, with its strong European origins, had a well-founded appeal to the steady flow of immigrants from predominantly Catholic lands. While there was an excitement in the new life that America offered, there was also a comfort in the familiar ritual and history of Catholicism.

Protestant denominational church attendance was also stable, especially among Pentecostals and evangelicals. In 1949, Billy Graham's career began with a tent meeting in Los Angeles, flourishing in the '50s with the formation of the Billy Graham Crusade ministry. His "Hour of Decision" radio program was welcomed into the homes of many Americans. There was a link, however vague, in many people's minds between flag and faith, fundamentalism and right-wing political conservatism, evangelicalism and capitalism, and Christian values and nationalism.[4]

## The Baby Boomer Exodus from the Church

The widespread reaction of the American public to Vietnam and the Civil Rights movement called into question the relationship

21

between faith and nationalism. While being intensely religious, some Christian groups seemed focused on issues related to private prayer meetings, the need for personal conversion, hairsplitting doctrinal controversies, and disputes over morality taboos (e.g., whether a "real" Christian should smoke, drink alcohol, dance, or view movies). By turning a blind eye to the injustices in the social order and by its pervasive desire to maintain the status quo, the church had little or no voice on such issues as the ethics of war, racism, sexism, and other public, morality-related issues. It was James A. Pike who noted that "the eleven o'clock hour on Sunday . . . [was] the most segregated hour in the American week."[5] Likewise, Theodore Roszak described the Christianity of the day as being "privately engaging, but socially irrelevant." Sadly, many sensitive Christians, including Boomers who were still attending church, left the shelter of the fold. Unconcerned with the insecurities of their newfound wanderings in the secular waste-land, they joined the ranks of the growing numbers of secular humanists in denouncing churches as irrelevant enclaves in to-day's world. After all, they claimed, who would want to give allegiance to a deistic God who lived exclusively above the world with its vital concerns and who required individuals to be "separated" from the world?

In the 1960s and into the '70s, there were some theologians who sought to make Christianity relevant in a secular society. Like the Boomers, they too reacted to the church's conventional talk about God, personal salvation, and the abstract issues of the life-to-come. Some years before, the influential German theologian, Dietrich Bonhoeffer, recognized that society was living *etsi deus, non daretur* (as though God did not exist). Following in his foot-steps, the new and radical theologians sought to restore relevance to the Christian message.

During this decade, it became popular among some theologians to refer to Christianity as being a "religion without God," of "man coming of age," and the birth of "secular Christianity." The under-lying idea was that traditional forms of Christianity as expressed in its ritual, orthodoxy, and piety, were a hindrance to faith in a secular world and should therefore be stripped bare, as one would peel bark from a tree. This radical theological movement promoted the secularization of Christianity by the startling but ill-fated "death of God" theology. This movement did not attempt to promote atheism per se, but rather tried to present the idea of God in a more meaningful way to a growing secular generation. These theologians did not presume to pass judgment on whether God was dead or not, but contested that God was absent from the world and therefore as good as dead. For a brief moment in time, the "death of God" theology caught attention in theological circles and in the media. *Time* magazine displayed a funeral-like background on its front cover depicting the death of God, with the headline "GOD IS DEAD."

In 1962, Paul Van Buren, an Episcopal theologian published *The Secular Meaning of the Gospel.* In this book, the author suggested that since it was impossible to speak about "God" to a generation without the presuppositions of metaphysics, it then followed that the word "God" must be abandoned and with it, the notion of "God" as being one whose actions affect people's lives. This was followed by an influential book, *The Gospel of Christian Atheism* (1966), written by the American theologian Thomas J. Altizer, who suggested that the whole notion of God died on the cross and has been dead ever since.

In 1965, the American theologian, Harvey Cox, published his highly influential book, *The Secular City.* Cox viewed the city (where skyscrapers now dwarfed the church steeples) as the dwelling place of God and called on Christians to reject the false dichotomy between sacred and secular, human and divine. Cox analyzed the consequences of urbanization in a secular world and proposed strategies for Christians to meet this new challenge of secularization. These tactics included the necessity for the church to stop talking about God for awhile and for Christians to join hands with like-minded secular humanists in working toward the formation of a better world.

On reflection however, neither pietism, with its emphasis on separation from the worldly arena and its deep abiding suspicion of the social gospel, nor radicalism, with its emphasis on interaction with the world and the importance of building the kingdom of God here on earth, proved to be prophetically relevant or particularly significant in reducing the flow of Baby Boomers leaving the church. To the Boomers, Christian prayer that called upon God "to bring peace to the world" sounded empty, given the fact that the petition was not accompanied by a determination among Christians to work for such peace. Indeed, prayers like "God's will be done" sounded blasphemous to the ears of the Boomers as long as the church was stuck in its ghetto-mentality with little prophetic voice to the human exploitation surrounding it. On the other hand, the "death of God" theology bore too close a resemblance to simple atheism to have significant impact on this generation. This theological movement, comments George Carey, is an excellent illustration of Dean Inge's observation: "He who marries the spirit of the age will be a widower in the next."

The issues of Vietnam, Civil Rights, and the assassinations of three American heroes, along with the muted voice of the church in the public arena, had a dramatic and collective impact on the Boomer generation. Not only was there a profound distrust for those in political authority, but also a repudiation of many other conventionally accepted beliefs, such as the American Dream, the Protestant work ethic, sexual morality, the traditional family model, and the relevance of Christianity. It is tempting to regard the antics and rebellion of the Baby Boomers as the frivolous dramatics of overindulged, middle-class children. However, to do so would be an oversimplification of their feelings of outrage and an underestimation of the trauma and disillusionment brought on by the apparent hypocrisies in the nation's life, both secular and sacred.

Since the church provided little guidance to this generation as to how to improve the world, the humanists filled the vacuum. In 1973, 114 humanists gathered to write the second *Humanist Manifesto II*. This second draft contained a wide range of issues including: civil liberties, equality, democracy, human survival, population, ecological control, war and peace, the building of world community, and a respect for different ethnic and racial origins — issues generally ignored in the evangelical churches of the day. The importance of the *Humanist Manifesto II* was often dismissed on the grounds of the small association membership. However, a further look reveals that these individuals were highly influential in the transmission of humanist ideas to the general public. Its membership included such prominent figures as Frances Crick, Albert Ellis, B.F. Skinner, Betty Friedan, Sir Julian Huxley, A. Philip Randolf.

After Martin Luther King's assassination (1968) and the end of the war in Vietnam (1975), the political and civil rebellions lost their momentum. Many of the street marches and crusades dimin-

24

ished, the campuses quieted down, students graduated, and the zeitgeist of revolt shifted to a spirit of self-gratification. Yippies, before advancing to Yuppies, "dropped out" to become Hippies and embarked upon a period preoccupied with self-examination, self-discovery, and self-fulfillment. After a decade of social action and street demonstrations, a few gains were made through the Baby Boomer efforts to bring about some changes: minorities and women gained some token ground, forcing many universities to rewrite their curriculum, adding black studies and feminist issues. However, when all was said and done, bureaucracy did not die and, with a few exceptions, organizations did not fundamentally change.

## The Inward Retreat

The seemingly innocuous little phrase in the *Humanist Manifesto I* of 1933, "the complete realization of the human personality," proved to have prophetic significance as the Boomer generation moved into the 1970s. In this decade, the Boomers turned inward and sought freedom through sex, drugs, and rock and roll. To aid them in this process toward personal transcendence, they embraced both religion and psychology. Once again, true to form, they proved to be unconventional. During this decade, Eastern religions emerged, gaining respectability and catching the attention of the press, the public at large, and social scientists. Life in the 1970s was diverse, colorful, strange, and exotic. Saffron-robed, head-shaven, middle-class Baby Boomers were seen on street corners, chanting "Hara Krishna." One of the Beatles, George Harrison, sang, "My Sweet Lord" (Lord Krishna), and the ashrams of the Divine Light Mission devoted itself to the ambiguous Guru Maharaj Ji. There was a general interest in various forms of mysticism, Oriental religions, Transcendental Meditation and Yoga, Zen Buddhism, and the syncretic religious cults of Sokka Gakkai. There were, however, also a few Christian movements that attracted some of the Boomers, among them were the Jesus Movement, the charismatic renewal, and neo-evangelicalism, along with some other groups which were nonconventional and somewhat ascetic.

Related to self-discovery through religious experience was the highly influential Human Potential Movement (HPM), an amalgam of religious and psychotherapeutic practices that some termed the "encounter culture." It had considerable appeal to the better-educated, middle-class segment of the Baby Boomers. Members were taught techniques of telepathy and clairvoyance, in addition to the elimination of "negative thinking," which was believed to prevent full human potential. Unlike the Jesus Movement which protested moral relativism, the HPM tended to turn it into a virtue.

In the 1970s, North Americans spent millions of dollars and countless hours attending seminars and workshops, reading books, listening to tapes—all designed to help the individual discover the inner self. This self-discovery was further promoted by the emergence of the New Age Movement in the early 1980s.

## The "Me" Decade

The 1980s marked a time when many Baby Boomers came of age. Leaving the personal quest for transcendence of the 1970s, many left their cenobite communes to venture to Wall Street with a priority toward career building and financial security. After a long day, they retreated to their electronic castles, screening their calls on the answering machine, watching movies on the VCR, cooking dinner in the microwave, and "chilling out" in the Jacuzzi.

In 1984, *Newsweek* declared the "Year of the Yuppie." A healthy, wealthy, and confident image emerged—a free-spending well-dressed individual, driving a "Beemer" fitted with a cellular phone, living in a spacious home with children in designer clothes. This image of sybarite living, for the most part, was not accurate. Many were far from being financially secure, as they perceived themselves as working harder than their parents with less to show for it. Others were not educated adequately to compete in a shifting occupational structure. Growing numbers experienced the trauma of divorce, and with it, the difficulty of maintaining a decent standard of living as a single parent.

This struggle was more acute in the light of an economic recession, persistent high unemployment, and the growing inflation of the mid-1980s. Yet for some, the two-income family became the norm. Fear and anxiety reigned supreme among the Yuppies, who were aware of competition in the job market, thus creating an intense dog-eat-dog atmosphere. This occupational stress brought about a heavy toll in professional burnout and family crisis. The financial anxieties were further fueled by the 1987 stock market crisis, the worst crash since the Great Depression. Furthermore, the decline of Reagan's presidency, the Iran-Contra scandal, and the deadly realities of sexually-transmitted diseases, such as AIDS, continued to mold and shape this generation.

In 1987, *Rolling Stone* magazine commissioned Peter D. Hart Research Associates to conduct a survey on the Baby Boomer tendencies.[6] The resulting data revealed that this generation continued to remain highly self-centered and materialistic, drawing inwardly away from the wider political and globally-related issues to personal concerns of health, financial security, and family-related matters. When asked to name their greatest hopes, 43 percent cited their desire for a happy home life and healthy, successful children. Regarding their approach to the raising of children, 47 percent of the respondents who had children, and nonparents who hoped to have children, thought their approach to parenting would be similar to that of their parents. When questioned about traditionally organized religion, 50 percent said they were less involved than they expected to be. Nevertheless, 90 percent checked off a religious affiliation, with 22 percent describing themselves as born-again evangelical Christians.

## The Rise and Fall of the Yuppie

"Yuppie" is an ubiquitous acronym coined by the writer Tom Wolfe to describe a significant group of Young Upwardly Mobile Professionals, who put their social conscience aside, steered their shiny new BMWs into the fast lane of the nation's consciousness, and headed toward the quest for personal aggrandizement, self-fulfillment, and material success.

These elitist Boom babies, who enjoyed the abundance of the 1960s in an uniquely optimistic period of North American history, had their aspirations shaped by the prosperity of their parents. This generation wanted everything: the best education, reformation of society, careers for women, and personal happiness.

At the outset, Yuppies, more than any other group within the Boom generation, achieved most of these wants at a very early age. By the early 1980s, Yuppies were living more comfortably than their parents and more affluently than others in their generation. Most Yuppies, having a good college education and owning their homes, accounted for 38 percent of the nation's lawyers, 45 percent of its scientists, and almost 50 percent of computer specialists. An average Yuppie in the 1980s lived in a city of 50,000 or more, and had an income of $34,000 with an equity base of $46,000. There were three features which characterized Yuppies:

### Predictable
They were a look-alike generation, dressed in their designer clothes, Gucci shoes, and Rolex watches. They ate gourmet food, drank imported beer, white wine, and Perrier. They read the *New Yorker* magazine, supported a liberalism that sounded like conservatism, were status conscious, worked sixty-hour weeks, and were preoccupied with the acquisition of more.

### Consumers
They were the grand acquisitors of the 1980s. A generation consumed by consumerism, they were the segment of the Boomer society who purchased everything from blue jeans to power suits, from mountain bikes to Volvos. They perceived themselves as celebrities, being fascinated by the lives of "the rich and famous." It is no coincidence that about half of *People* magazine's 23 million readers are between twenty-five and forty-five years of age.

### Disliked
In the early days, the Yuppies were supported by a culture that deemed it acceptable to be greedy, but eventually their visible indulgence became a source of disdain. They were viewed as pretentious, hollow people who had mastered the fine art of taking without giving. Their "in-it-for-themselves" image gave the impression that they were incapable of continued loyalty, either to partners, causes, or organizations. They were perceived as unable to give innovative, risk-taking leadership (in case of losing the job or failing), as unwilling to follow (in order to preserve their individualism), and as a result, they were considered merely copiers.

The beginning of the end of the Yuppie euphoria was highlighted by the scandals of two Yuppie heroes — presidential candidate Gary Hart's disgrace and Ivan Boesky's insider-trading scandals. Shortly thereafter followed a promotional squeeze in the job market, an economic recession, the ever-increasing cost of living, and the stock market crisis of 1987. By the end of the 1980s, a healthy dose of realism caused the Yuppies to acknowledge the limits of a "psychology of non-satiety."

In recent days, some Yuppies are recognizing that in reality

"enough is never enough" and that materialism can be the prover-
bial "opium of the people." Like drinking salt water, the more they
have, the thirstier they become. Greater quantities are required
for satisfaction, and each increment proves inadequate. Nevertheless, in this present decade, the vast majority of the Baby Boomer
generation still remains highly motivated toward the "good life"
with its acquisition of money and consumer toys as status symbols. Peter Hart Associates discovered in their poll that after
health, Boomers consider money their chief concern.[7]

## Back to the Basics

Baby Boomers in this last decade of the millennium appear to be in
a process of dramatic change once again. The driving need to find
success in the marketplace and the constant striving to climb the
corporate ladder seems to be giving way to a new desire in finding
success on the homefront. The notion that true happiness is found
exclusively in material things is losing its persuasion to a new
view that it is found in self-giving and in loving relationships. The
compromise of these values requiring delayed self-satisfaction
seems to be yielding to a new emphasis on the importance of
personal and family values. What is causing these changes?

To begin with, Baby Boomers are getting older, the youngest
now entering their thirties and the oldest, their late forties. In
other words, the Baby Boomer generation is experiencing a collective mid-life crisis. Since successive stages in human life are
marked by significant transitional events, it should not be a surprise that Baby Boomers are going through a change as they enter
the second and more mature stage of their lives. Mid-life can be
typically characterized by a reevaluation of priorities, a redefinition
of values, and a personal reflection on the purpose and significance
of life. The cultural standards of success as defined by the great
American Dream propelled the Boomer generation in the 1980s.
Today, under the scrutiny of a mid-life reevaluation, the self-indul-
gent quest for wealth, power, and prestige is giving way to such
things as simplicity, self-giving, and concern for the less fortunate.
The theme of a '60s Beatle's song that money can't buy love has
come to pass with an almost prophetic insight.

Another factor which contributes significantly to this back-to-
the-basics trend is the attention to Baby Boomers' children. In
contrast to their parents who started their families early in life,

Baby Boomers tended to defer having children until much later, while they concentrated on their careers. At one point, it was common to refer to Baby Boomers without children with the acronym, DINKS (Double Income No Kids). Today, the term no longer applies. The high value given to children of Baby Boomers is evidenced by the growing number of mothers (and in some cases fathers) who are either leaving the marketplace or are involved in job-sharing programs, in order to spend more time with their children. It is interesting to note that many stay-at-home parents are finding life in the home more rewarding than life in the office.

Within the context of the rediscovery of personal and family values, we also find that Baby Boomers are returning to the churches and synagogues they left during their rebellious years against the status quo of the pre-boom days. How ironic that the same *Time* magazine which declared at one point that God was dead, would many years later reveal a cover story on "The Generation That Forgot God: The Baby Boom Goes Back to Church and the Church Will Never Be the Same" (April 5, 1993).

Obviously, the issues connected with mid-life and the importance placed on children are extremely significant in the Baby Boomer return to organized religion. Mid-life transitions invariably invite a more profound and serious examination of such perennial questions considered superficially during the transitional stage of adolescence: "Who am I?" "Does life have purpose?" "Is there a benevolent God with whom I can relate?" and, of course, "How should I spend the rest of my life?" In the hope of finding answers to these essential human questions, Baby Boomers find themselves in church on Sunday morning rather than the golf course, the garden, or the office.

As every parent knows having children brings a new set of responsibilities. In their childhood many Baby Boomers accompanied their parents to church and participated in some form of religious education in Sunday School and youth groups, as well as in the school setting. Although they eventually rebelled against these religious values, few would deny that values were important. Today, in order to ensure that their children are exposed to basic values, the Baby Boomers of the 1990s are returning to religious institutions with their children in hand giving a new dimension to the biblical passage, "and a little child will lead them" (Isa. 11:6).

Still, other factors are causing the Boomer return. As Baby

Boomers get older so do their parents. The death of a loved one has an uncanny ability to cause individuals to confront the deep uncertainties of human life and to face up to their own immortality. Parents, family members, and friends inevitably die, forcing the reality of death to a conscious point. Perhaps because of a fear of death, or as a result of an interest in a spiritual world, Baby Boomers are now unable to escape the realities of their own immortality.

## Summary

In stark contrast to the complexity of contemporary North American society, life in pre-Boom days was rather simple. The significance of the family unit, the church, and the state were clearly recognized. Values were generally honored and recognized as essential for maintaining the common good. As the postwar Boomer generation began to evolve through its unique lifecycle and establish its autonomy, it found itself in conflict with the values of its parents in the '60s. Events both at home and abroad caused them to experience an identity crisis, a widespread distrust in government, and a disregard for the church. Instead of viewing themselves as one generation interlocked with the preceding one, they tried to forge a new way of living where justice and peace would prevail and civil liberties would be honored. Eventually discouraged by the slowness of change, many Baby Boomers, perplexed and bewildered, withdrew to a hippie counterculture which was more passive than the political activism of the '60s, or they set their sights on education and establishing career goals. In the '80s, Baby Boomers reemerged on the scene, this time driven almost obsessively in the pursuit of health, wealth, and happiness. By the '90s, some had achieved financial success while others had not. But the one thing they did have in common was middle-age. Now Baby Boomers are showing an interest in family life and basic values, and in the quest for meaning, they are returning to occupy those absent pews that they left decades ago.

During the long absence, both Baby Boomers and the church have changed significantly. Like two distant strangers who have lived apart in two separate worlds, their reuniting is bound to be rather awkward. In order for the Christian community to welcome this generation back within its doors, it is imperative that it understand the Baby Boomer cultural and personal ethos. The next two chapters are dedicated to this matter.

# Chapter 2
# THE BABY BOOMER CULTURAL ETHOS

As a schoolboy, I was never particularly good at mathematics. To be honest, I detested the subject with a passion. On the elementary issues of $2+2=4$, I could boast some mastery. However, as time progressed and the levels of mathematics advanced to the more abstract theories of higher algebra, geometry, trigonometry, and axiomatic theories, I had to struggle to attain the most basic comprehension. Looking back over the years and contrary to the opinion of my math teacher who stated, "You will never make anything of your life until you master these theories," I have managed to survive with a small measure of success, without an intricate comprehension of math details at my fingertips.

Unlike abstract theories of mathematics, worldviews do make a significant difference in the way we choose to live out our lives. It is a bit like the difference between an *a priori* position in contrast to an *a posteriori* one. The former need not prove from experience that a concept is true, whereas the latter must be able to verify the truth claim in reference to the real world. A "worldview" is a particular system of belief which shapes our convictions, values, and principles about the meaning of life and our place in it. The beliefs which shape our worldview come from a variety of sources: race, character, tradition, education, antiquity, heredity, and in particular our culture and society.

The German word, *weltanschauung,* has become part of our language and helps to describe what we mean by worldview. This term denotes an individual's philosophy of the nature, origin, value, meaning, and purpose of human life. To have a worldview is to have a comprehensive interpretation or philosophy. It is a picture of reality combined with a sense of its meaning—where corresponding actions are consistent with one's worldview.

One of the goals of discipleship, Christian formation, and the process of Christian sanctification is to help individuals develop a truly Christian *weltanschauung.* For the believer, there cannot be another *weltanschauung* alongside his or her Christian worldview, as there cannot be two sets of ethics, morals, or philosophies operating independent of each other—one for the kingdom of God, applied on Sundays and significant other holy days, and another for the kingdom of this world, applied Monday to Saturday in the marketplace. Simply stated, our worldviews embrace the evaluations we make about the issues of life.

The British philosopher Bertrand Russell once commented, "Man is a credulous animal and must believe something; in the absence of good grounds for belief, he will be satisfied with bad ones."[1] Many of Russell's beliefs were in opposition to Christian beliefs, criticizing them as being rationally indefensible. Nevertheless, he was accurate in his statement that we all believe something, and that out there in the real world, people adopt both good and bad worldviews.

We will examine four components of the Baby Boomer worldview, which has been shaped by the philosophical beliefs of the past as well as by individual life experiences. This is not only the side of the bridge where many Baby Boomers live, but also the context in which the church must wrestle—the dialectic between that which is given as both *paradosis* (a tradition to be preserved) and *paratheke* (a deposit to be guarded) with that which has been left open. As there is no such thing as the Gospel in a vacuum, the Christian community must grapple with the knotty issues associated with the relationship between Scripture and culture, revelation and contextualization.

## Pluralism: The Baby Boomer Ethos

Recently, I decided it was time for some R and R. I hopped into my car and paid a visit to the local video store. With a limited time span available, before getting back to more noble pursuits, I wanted to make a quick choice and return home. I examined the drama section, comedies, westerns, epics, golden oldies, new releases, documentaries, musicals, sports, and spies. By this time, I was in a state of frustration over which choice to make. Eventually, after consulting my watch, I took the bull by the horns and chose an old classic that I had seen as a child, *The Great Escape.* Briskly, I walked to the counter, card in hand, only to find to my utter dismay that it was rented. Being a persistent and stubborn Scotsman, I tried again, round and round looking for the right video among endless choices. Eventually, the time gone, I left empty-handed. The problem: simply too many choices. Pluralism is much like my local video store experience; it promises much, but provides so many different choices that it often leaves individuals bewildered and frustrated.

As far back as 525 B.C., the truly extraordinary and wise mathematician Pythagoras stated that all things consist of numbers. Was Pythagoras one of the world's first pluralists? Pluralism, in contrast to monism (a philosophical theory that maintains that there is one, and only one, substance), upholds the view that reality consists of many different spheres without diminishing its essential substance.

The roots of pluralism spread widely. For example, one can refer to philosophical pluralism to signify how individuals fundamentally differ in worldviews regarding such basic things as first principles, the meaning of human life, political ideologies, and religious convictions. In former days, dominant societies and historic religions were characteristically monolithic. They tended to establish the worldview of the general populace and held the monopoly over the legitimation of individual and collective life. Although alternative views coexisted with the dominant ones, most were absorbed, co-opted, or effectively suppressed and segregated. An example of this was seen by the incorporation of early monasticism into church-controlled monastic orders.

After the Second World War, it was clear for most that the Christian era, inaugurated by Constantine in the early fourth century, was at an end. Western-European colonialism in Asia and Africa gradually disappeared. The emergence of these former colonies and the liberal immigration policy of the post-war years helped create the extraordinary multicultural makeup of contemporary Western society. Unlike the former days however, when uniformity was the goal, the pluralistic ethos of the day provided a milieu of freedom and acceptance in which these newly emerging ethnic groups retained their unique cultural identity. They blended into the main stream of society, thus creating the melting pot of modern life without the fear of discrimination and inequality. Today, North America is so cosmopolitan that the average individual meets as many people of radically diverse backgrounds in one week as a medieval person would in a lifetime. Furthermore, society expects each individual to be treated with dignity and respect as a fellow citizen.

One can also speak of social pluralism to describe how these individuals who represent different cultures, values, and beliefs, attempt to live in a harmonious and peaceful coexistence. Those who uphold the value of social pluralism maintain that since society is enriched by the contribution of cultural diversity, no single worldview should be permitted to dominate another nor any single majority group to hold a monopoly over the form of social customs, permissible languages, acceptable values, and religious expressions of the land. To do otherwise, would be considered a form of totalitarian monism, which in turn may lead to the oppression of minority groups and to the violation of basic human rights.

Canadian sociologist, Reginald Bibby, discussing the global nature of pluralism, writes:

Nationwide and worldwide such a policy translates into an emphasis on coexistence versus conquest of assimilation. Pluralism's call for tolerance and respect frequently takes the form of statements about human rights. Expressed nationally, it means that Californians are expected to coexist on U.S. turf with Mexican Americans, that ethnic groups in the Soviet Union no longer need to pretend that they don't exist. . . . It means that minority-group members in Canada no longer need to change their names and cultures if they want to "fit in." Expressed globally, it means that war and the domination of societies are no longer appropriate. Cultural obliteration in the form of both intolerance and alleged enlightening is likewise an unacceptable violation of the norms of planetary pluralism. Customs and languages, worldviews and religions, are not be tampered with.[2]

**36**

Canada and the United States, the birthplace of the Baby Boomer generation, are renowned for their national pluralistic programs. In Canada, three major policies reveal its commitment to pluralism: Bilingualism (1969), Multiculturalism (1971), and the Charter of Rights and Freedoms (1982). In the U.S.A., the First Amendment states categorically: "Congress shall make no law respecting an establishment of religion, or prohibiting the free exercise thereof; or abridging the freedom of speech, or of the press; or the right of people peaceably to assemble, and to petition the Government for a redress of grievances."

However, pluralism is by no means a problem-free doctrine. Obviously, in a society where a multiplicity of philosophies, ideologies, social customs, and religious convictions are encouraged to coexist, painful misunderstandings and bitter conflicts are inevitable. For example, those who sought a Christian hegemony in the United States tested the depths of the pluralistic waters by raising the question of the place of prayer in the public school system. The uproar that followed was due to a tension between the state's pluralistic accommodation of non-Christian, nonreligious minorities and its position of not favoring one particular worldview over another.

Among Baby Boomers, pluralism is regarded as normative, a national treasure to be preserved at all costs and as a vitally essential aspect of North American life. It is significant to note how the mood shifted in Baby Boomer attitudes from that of their parents. In 1947, the House Committee on Un-American Activities began its investigation of communism's infiltration into the United States. One of the issues, as a result of these inquiries, was the difficulty in deciding how much clemency could be safely extended to alleged communists with more pronounced loyalty to the Soviet Union than to the United States. As a result of these investigations over perceived ideological differences, many American citizens faced prison terms, suffered the loss of friends and possessions, or were denied the right to earn a living. It was not until 1970 that many of these individuals were vindicated for standing up (at great personal cost) for their beliefs. The rationale to support these McCarthy witch-hunts was the belief that persons who adopted such a divergent ideology as communism had forfeited the benefits of their democratic birthright. While this view was widely accepted in its day, it was not to be shared in retrospect, by the majority of the Boomer generation. Most Boomers viewed the McCarthy policies as a scandalous violation of basic human rights, far more sinister than the communism it tried so desperately to root out.

If ideological and philosophical clashes are inevitable in a pluralistic society, the question then becomes, how can a multicultural society live in peaceful coexistence in the midst of such a multifarious environment. The consistent answer to this complex question since the Enlightenment is found in the word "tolerance." This word, taken from the Latin *tolerare,* denotes an attitude of forbearance. As applied to society in general, tolerance is considered a sign of the maturity of the culture if it can accommodate the worldviews of others, without seeking to suppress their legitimate expressions, even if they are considered to be questionable and objectionable.

### Christianity and Tolerance in a Pluralistic Society

The early church fathers, having been cruelly persecuted by the Romans themselves, were in favor of religious tolerance as a principle. Yet, not long after Constantine made Christianity a state religion, the pagans who were the persecuted, became the persecutors. However, it should be noted that in this period, Christian repression of paganism never went to the cruel lengths of the Roman repression. The Christian policy of repression escalated in the late Middle Ages to the extent that torture and death were freely administered in an attempt to recover erring souls for God. The rationale was that God was offended by heretical practices, that unorthodox views were a culpable betrayal of one's baptismal promises and an outright revolt against the church's authority. Furthermore, it was believed by those Christians who supported the practices of the Inquisition, that tolerance of heresy led to a state of sin with the likely prospect of eternal damnation in the life to come.

There were many who were outraged by such a policy of repression and persecution. Indeed, one may argue that the roots of pluralism largely resulted from a long process of secularization when intellectuals such as Voltaire (1694–1778), in reaction to the murderous intolerance of the Inquisition, began to advocate religious tolerance as a principle among enlightened people. In 1667, John Locke, a man of deep religious conviction, published his *An Essay Concerning Toleration,* in which he set forth his plea for greater tolerance by arguing that the repression of divergent views was not an effective policy in trying to bring about change. In this work, Locke contended that such pressure swayed a person to go through the outward motions of endorsing a given view, but could not produce a true conviction in the depth of one's soul. Locke argued that coercion produced an ersatz form of belief and that, in the final analysis, such repression became the breeding ground of hypocrisy. This reminds us of the intriguing insight of the Russian theologian Khomiakoff's concept of *sobornost*. This novel concept stresses the fact that neither faith nor obedience can be enforced and that unity should be seen in terms of the unity of many persons within the organic fellowship of the church, where each member retains his or her full freedom and personal rectitude, while at the same time sharing in the common and corporate life of the whole. Eventually Locke's argument for greater toleration was regarded as basic common sense, finding acceptance among both Catholic and Reformed believers.

Another significant exponent of tolerance was the Victorian philosopher John Stuart Mill (1806–73). Following the principles laid down by Locke, with the exception of fewer limitations on tolerance, Mill insisted that the only justification for interfering with anyone's liberty was a reasonable assurance that some danger or threat to the liberty of another was involved. Mill was increasingly concerned with the limitation on human freedom that stemmed from unwritten law — the pressure of convention and public opinion. Mill wanted to see toleration extended from the realm of politics, to that of morals and all "self-regarding actions," as he called them. Contemporary pluralism certainly achieves this goal.

### Pluralism, the Christian Faith, and Other Religions

While it would appear that we are witnessing a tremendous resurgence of vicious religious altercations among Fundamentalist groups — India, the Middle East, and Bosnia — such narrow-minded bigotry, religious or otherwise, is not representative of the vast majority of people who compose the world's religious traditions. Rather, a new spirit of mutual respect is taking hold of the consciousness of a growing numbers of believers.

This new interest and appreciation of other faith groups is largely the result of the closer proximity of the global village. It seems that as our world gets smaller, our worldview gets larger; the closer we get to an object, the clearer our perspective. Closer proximity and wider exposure to different faith traditions has also fostered increased dialogue, not only at the academic level but also at the international and local levels. Having personally participated in such forums, I suggest that there are a number of positive aspects to such interfaith discussions.

First, one soon recognizes that interfaith encounters are not primarily about *doctrine,* but about the *people* who hold the beliefs, often with a great deal of passion and conviction. When we participate in such gatherings, both around the formal discussion table and the informal dinner table, we discover good people — individuals who pray for peace, who seek justice for the impecunious, who reach out to the disenfranchised, and who share a common *weltschmerz* (concern) for the environment and welfare of our fragile planet. It is through such human interaction that friendships develop, causing our imaginary stereotypes to fade.

Second, dialogue invariably produces new perspectives of one's personal faith. Christians should not be unduly alarmed by this, considering that throughout the centuries, the Christian faith has been enriched as it interfaced with the world around it. When Christianity was forced to move beyond the confines of Palestine and enter into the Greek world of Plato and Aristotle, it adapted aspects of these influencial philosophical systems to give further insight into the depth of the Gospel. For example, Augustine, whose insights helped shape the Western theological tradition, was deeply influenced by Neoplatonism. Thomas Aquinas made his lasting contribution to theology by constructing a system of doctrine in tandem with the philosophy of Aristotle.

Third, dialogue often gives new perspectives to the belief of others. We often think of Buddhism, Islam, or Hinduism in comprehensive terms, as though all members of these faith traditions believe the same thing in much the same way. Whereas in relation, these ancient faiths are as fractioned and diverse as Christianity. Furthermore, while we may discover much about the history of a particular faith and collect many facts about the nature of the belief structure, there is so much more to be gained from hearing these beliefs from those who live their faith within their cultural tradition. There are still many nuances of any religion that remain a mystery, even to those who are fully immersed and familiar with their faith tradition.

I strongly recommend that we as Christians take every opportunity to engage in interfaith dialogue with the honesty and openness that good dialogue requires. Personally, I for one have greatly benefitted from the opportunity to read the sacred texts of others, to listen as well as be heard, and to agree or disagree in a spirit of mutual appreciation. If nothing else, such a sharing of faith in this gathered context reinforces the fact that human beings are spiritual beings at their core. This is a message that needs to be heard in a world where science and technology is rapidly undermining spirituality and robbing humankind of its soul.

In general terms, let us now consider the attitude that Christians have taken regarding the status of other faiths. In recent days, it has become customary to classify the relationship between Christianity and world faiths as either pluralistic, exclusivistic, or inclusivistic. We shall briefly examine each view and consider the questions related to religious syncretism.

*Religious Pluralism*
Religious pluralism maintains that adherence to a particular belief is a private matter, each individual is entitled to a personal faith, and religious differences are neither true nor false. In other words it does not really matter which bridge the individual chooses to cross, as God is the architect and builder of the many bridges which exist. The prolific and controversial author, John Hick, is a leading advocate of religious pluralism. In 1973, using an astronomical analogy, Hick suggested a Copernican revolution in the Christian theology of world religions whereby Christians "shift from the dogma that Christianity is at the centre, to the realization that it is God who is at the centre, and that of all religions."[3] Essentially, Hick calls for a shift from Ecclesiocentrism and Christocentrism to Theocentrism, which facilitates a new understanding of religions, whereby old claims of superiority and exclusivity dissolve and a new era of interreligious ecumenism begins.

Hick's latest work[4] calls for yet another paradigmatic shift from Theocentrism to reality centeredness. He argues that all religions are salvific paths to "the Real," with none being better or worse than the other. According to Hick, the plurality of religions arises from the variety of human experiences that exist, linked with the fact that direct knowledge of "the Real" is impossible as it is always mediated through human perceptions and interpretations.

The framework for his thinking is fourfold: (1) the utter transcendence of "the Real"; (2) Kantian epistemology; (3) the soteriological character of all the great world faiths; and (4) the common ethical principle of love and compassion. These presuppositions lead him to the conclusion that "the great world religions constitute different conceptions and perceptions of, and responses to, 'the Real' from within the different cultural ways of being human."[5]

Naturally to those who embrace this view, the term "evangelism" is considered a dirty word, as it smacks of intolerance and pertinaciousness. The proselytizing process is frequently considered a violation of an individual's privacy, and when directed at new immigrants, evangelistic activity is accused of imperialism, exploitation, and disrespect for another person's worldview.

*The Exclusive View*
The strictly exclusive view takes quite an opposite position to the pluralistic. This perspective, while acknowledging that many different bridges exist, maintains that there is only one bridge that leads safely over the tempestuous seas of uncertainty to a true relationship with the living God. Based on such texts as John 14:6 and Acts 4:12, the exclusive view states *extra ecclesiam nulla salus* (outside the church there is no salvation); therefore, those who do not accept Jesus as Lord and Savior will be eternally lost. The worldwide missionary enterprise is strongly motivated by this exclusive view, which is at the root of recent discussion among evangelicals regarding the completion of the Great Commission by the year 2000. The motivation for this missionary activity lies in the belief that the Gospel must be preached throughout the world for people of other faiths to have the opportunity to respond to the claims of Christ. Furthermore, the enthusiasm for overseas missionary work is often connected with eschatology, as it is believed that only until the Second Coming will individuals have the opportunity to hear the Gospel and be converted to a saving faith. Listeners are presented with an either/or decision—heaven or hell, eternity or damnation, saved or lost—before the coming of the Son of Man.

On the home front, those who embrace the exclusive view tend to see it as their Christian duty to convert friends or neighbors from other faiths, such as Jews, Muslims, Hindus, or Buddhists.

The impetus for this desire to proselytize arises from the conviction that Jesus Christ alone is the Savior of the world and that the Christian church is the only pathway to salvation for all humanity.

*The Inclusive View*
The inclusive view not only acknowledges Christ as the only Savior, but also affirms that his saving work extends beyond the bounds of the visible church. In other words, this position purports that God has provided many bridges for those who seek after truth and godliness. As long as seekers are sincere in their search, they will not be disappointed at the end of their pilgrimage. The Second Vatican Council (1962–1965) declares that

> the Catholic Church does not reject anything which is true and holy in those other religions. She regards with sincere respect those practices, views, rules, and doctrines which, however great their difference from what the Church itself holds and proposes, yet may convey a fact of that truth which shines on all.[6]

To some degree, this declaration indicates a significant shift in the church's attitude toward other great religions. From the time of the barbarian invasions, the "there-is-no-salvation-outside-the-church" stance took root. However, after the Jesuit missionaries traveled to the Orient, and after the discovery of America, there evolved a striking awareness of the spiritual qualities of many of these "indigenous peoples." Little by little, the idea grew that men and women of good faith who were not reached by the good news of the Gospel were nevertheless saved by Christ—even if they belonged to another religion. Vatican Council II went one step further by speaking not only of individuals, but also of other religions as being bearers of the truth.

After Vatican II, some theologians suggested that all the great religions be recognized as valid and as having a salvic role. This view is commonly associated with the eminent Roman Catholic theologian, Karl Rahner, and his novel concept of "anonymous Christianity."[7] Briefly, this view maintains that non-Christian religions not only reflect the natural cognition of God (Rom. 1:20) and the natural moral law (Rom. 2:14-16), but also supernatural instances of the grace of God. Rahner believes that individuals who know only their faith traditions, and are not familiar with Christianity, should be considered "believers" and members of a "legitimate religion." After all, there is far more to be said for the status of the person on the bridge than the one floundering aimlessly in the water below. Furthermore, he suggests that God uses these religions as bridges of supernatural saving grace. For Rahner, it was inconceivable that an atheist be categorized with a devout Hindu or Muslim, and he wonders how such historic, verbalized and institutional religion could be considered superfluous.

This view has been highly influential at the general mass level, but among Rahner's peers it has been held in contention. His opinion that non-Christian religions are a sacramental mediation of supernatural grace has not gained conciliar recognition. Although many Catholic theologians recognize that the Gospel should be transmitted in a way that is comprehensible to people of different cultures and that uniquely Western cultural values should not be presented as essential elements of the Christian faith, they nevertheless insist that the message of the uniqueness of Christ and the grace of God must not to be silenced or the message of salvation be obscured.

## Pluralism: A Christian Perspective
Regardless of the complexity of the issues related to social and religious pluralism, it should be noted that from a Christian outlook, pluralism contains both redeeming and corroding qualities.

### Utilizing Pluralism
First and foremost, pluralism is a fact of North American life, and it is here to stay. The church no longer has the power it once had in society to influence policies in such a way as to repress or stifle the expression of unorthodox views, as it attempted to do during the Enlightenment, the Renaissance, the Reformation, and the Counter-Reformation. There may have been a time when North American society was predominantly Christian, when the culture listened if the church spoke on a certain issue. However, those days are over and the church now exists in a post-Christian secular world, where like every other minority group it also has to fight to be heard. For the majority within the North American culture, the church holds no monopoly over what is morally good or evil, true or false. But contrary to popular Christian assumption, pluralism does not require the "exclusion" of the traditional Judeo-

Christian beliefs or ethics in national affairs. Rather, the church, along with other organizations, has its constitutional right to act in accordance with its conscience and to articulate its convictions on policies and trends in public life which it considers sinful, destructive, and dehumanizing. In practical terms, this naturally requires Christians to become more aggressive in the public domain if they want to make a difference in pluralistic society.

Some Christian groups, whose theology requires members to distance themselves from society, or (to continue our analogy) stay on their side of the bridge, view contemporary culture as "worldly" and as a potential threat to Christianity. It would require a major paradigm change regarding the nature of the church for such groups to cross the bridge. This shift would have to incorporate the recognition that the church's divine mandate includes not only the transformation of individuals, but also the transformation of society and culture. Furthermore, if Christians take a purely defensive stand and view the world as a hostile battle zone, then the pluralistic culture of the day will appear a formidable foe, leaving them feeling overwhelmed by many enemies. If, however, they see that pluralism stands for diversity and encourages a variety of opinions, then perhaps pluralism can work positively for Christians by them speaking out on the ethics of the kingdom of God. If the church can muster the nerve to respond to the opportunities that pluralism extends, then its confidence can be strengthened by the fact that the public philosophy of the Judeo-Christian tradition is one that any Christian can be proud to represent. It is rich, profound, and resourceful in resolving seemingly insoluble problems of the modern world.

*Pluralism and Culture*
Secondly, life in the church can only be enhanced by a pluralism of cultural expression and pastoral approaches to ministry and worship. In much the same way that society is enriched by the diversity of many contributions, variations of viewpoint, and a wide spectrum of cultural expressions, so may be the body of Christ. In this regard, it should be remembered that the unity of the church is not achieved by the uniformity of its membership, in the sense that individual believers who are drawn to faith from various backgrounds and experiences are expected to conform to some form of denominational Christian stereotype. Regardless of the sense of

**45**

security of the "herd syndrome," the fact is that God is neither in the duplication business, nor seeking people who are carbon copies of one another. If the church is to proclaim the kingdom of God to men and women from different races, cultures, languages, and to all forms of thought and life, then surely a multiplicity of ways of proclamation, liturgical and devotional forms of church policy, social involvement, and forms of evangelism, are not only necessary but desirable. It is only by such diversity in unity that the church can be enabled to become all things to all people (1 Cor. 9:19-23). Granted, such diversity presents difficulties for rigid traditionalists and some fundamentalist groups. However, in reference to ministry to Baby Boomers, it is doubtful that it would present a stumbling block. This particular generation has grown up in a society with a broad exposure to variety. Cheryl Russell writes:

> Though the baby boom is no monolith, it is united in its tolerance of diversity. The educational level of the baby boom makes it more accepting and even encouraging of individual differences and alternative lifestyles. The result is an increasingly diverse American culture in which single women have children through artificial insemination, avowed homosexuals run for public office, divorced parents have joint custody of their children, and people marry two or even three times without raising an eyebrow.[8]

### The Promise of Pluralism

Thirdly, it seems that the church, along with the rest of the planet, is moving increasingly toward a form of worldwide unity made possible by the pluralistic values of mutual respect, synergism, and cooperation. The tireless work of the ecumenical movement is in the process of bearing the fruit of its long-term effort in developing a greater sense of unity among the Body of Christ. This movement has as its mandate, the idea of unity in diversity and has worked relentlessly, not only to bring Western churches together, who have been estranged from one another for 400 years, but also the Eastern and Western church who have been divided for 900 years.

How does the ecumenical movement perceive this unity? Certainly not through an edict of uniformity nor through the suppression of divergent views on issues of creed, ritual, and policy, but by the time-consuming process of dialogue, bilateral negotiations, interdenominational joint-working groups, and cross-denomination regional councils. The arsiduous negotiators, who pursue the goal of Christian unity, unanimously testify that it is the experience of living and working together with those of different faith traditions which enables them to see beyond the nonessential issues, to become less exclusive toward other traditions by viewing them as authentic expressions of God's revelation, and to be far less defensive in areas where genuine differences in orthodoxy and praxis exist.

Obviously, the task of discerning between essential and nonessential differences is difficult, but surely the process would be infinitely more formidable if attitudes of exclusivism, denominational isolationism, and provincialism were to prevail. Without a genuine willingness of Christians to embrace an attitude of pluralism, in the sense of being open to the wide historical perspectives of the faith and to encounter the broad and perhaps divergent traditions and mores of fellow Christians, there can be little hope for unity in the essential issues of Christian dogma. This is not to say that the concept of orthodoxy is redundant or evanescent. The faith community must seek to be true to the teachings of Jesus Christ and have a critical awareness of the central core of the Christian tradition which has remained consistent throughout history. This would include the doctrines of the trinity, the incarnation, the atonement, and the two sacramental rites of baptism and the eucharist. However, in nonessentials, a pluralism in theological and philosophical expression of faith allows theologians, biblical scholars, and curious members of the Body of Christ to reexamine and critique Christian dogma without fear of being ostracized. The silencing of such theologians as Leonardo Boff, Edward Schillebeeckx, and Charles Curran is a case in point.

Again, in reference to Baby Boomers, such a tolerant and inclusive attitude as advocated here is an important consideration, and if acted upon should prove to be a plus factor in the church's favor. Thus, Doug Murren suggests that seeking consensus on most nonessential issues is a serious mistake. Himself a Baby Boomer, he offers the following advice:

> If you're going to pastor boomers, you won't get away with
> trying to give us processed opinions. If we come to your

**47**

church and it's obvious that we'll be handed opinions on a variety of issues, we'll feel threatened by such an environment. We just aren't interested in anyone giving us processed opinions, as is done in those churches that tell us what to believe about everything — from the Iran-Contra scandal to the number of children we should have. That's one of the reasons we've stayed away so long. . . . Unchurched boomers particularly don't like being told what to think. We will value, instead, a church that is highly appreciative of multiple opinions — a congregation that honours each individual's right to think on his or her own. Baby boomers like this perspective on Christian growth. We simply want to be given the right tools to make good decisions. We don't want our decisions made for us.[9]

## Pluralism and Freedom

Fourthly, pluralism insists on toleration because it maintains that freedom and individuality are important human values and therefore must be preserved at all costs. Fundamental to the North American concept of freedom is the idea that individuals are free to make choices, choosing alternatives without the pressure of coercion from outside sources. In other words, freedom is intrinsically connected to one's internal faculty of self-determination rather than the subtle pressure of constraint from external sources. Thus, truly free individuals are those who are able to choose between alternatives, plan their course of action, make their choices, and decide how they should act in a given situation. Such freedom includes moral freedom (the ability to determine for oneself without being hindered by threats), psychological freedom (the ability to choose as we wish without any psychic pressure preceeding the act of decision), religious freedom (the ability to voluntarily turn toward or away from God), and political freedom (the ability to vote as one chooses). Put succinctly, freedom can only exist when an opportunity exists to allow choice. One of the benefits of a free democratic society is the rights given to individuals for freedom of conscience, religion, speech, and academic freedom, which are encouraged so long as such freedom does not present a danger to society and the values that it is supposed to protect. It was such freedoms and civil liberties that Baby Boomers fought to protect during the 1960s and still cherish today.

Contrary to popular opinion, Christianity has much to say about freedom. It is extremely unfortunate that for many Baby Boomers, the Christian community represents fideism, control, and repression, rather than freedom. Frequently, the church is regarded as an institution which promotes antediluvian ideas, upholding Victorian morality and supporting narrow-minded censorship. No one has perceived this with greater clarity than William Blake in his poem, "The Garden of Love."

I went to the Garden of Love,
And saw what I had never seen:
A Chapel was built in the midst,
Where I used to play on the green.

And the gates of this chapel were shut,
And, Thou shall not' writ over the door;
So I turn'd to the Garden of Love
That so many sweet flowers bore;

And I saw it was filled with graves,
And tombstones where flowers should be;
And priests in black gowns were walking their rounds,
And binding with briars my joys and desires.[10]

I suspect at the root of this closed and static view of reality lies a religious version of hard determinism. Such a view creates theological fatalists, who stress the classical theistic view of God in terms of the divine transcendence, absoluteness, immutability, and impassibility, to the neglect of God's immanence, contingency, and changeability.

The Bible bears witness to a living, active and personal deity who both acts and wills freely without restraint. It speaks of a God who is free from the cramping limitations of time and space, and one who gives grace and love to creation, entirely independent of the merits or demerits of others. The Bible speaks so clearly about a Savior, indeed a liberator, who came into this world of his own accord and who freely laid down his life for others. This self-giving was motivated purely out of his unconstrained love for humankind. It was this same Jesus who stated categorically to his disciples, "If you hold to my teaching, you are really my disciples. Then you will

**49**

know the truth, and the truth will set you free" (John 8:32).

This theme of freedom could almost be regarded as an article of faith in the New Testament. Paul speaks of it as "the glorious liberty of the children of God" (Rom. 8:21, RSV). He passionately exhorts the Christians of Galatia to "stand firm" in their newfound freedom (Gal. 5:1). A study of the term and its forms reveals that the biblical writers used the notions of freedom *(eleutheria)* to place into perspective many of the liberations that affect our consciousness of who we are and what our concerns should be. Seen in the light of our God-intended destiny, we can speak of a personal, psychic, religious, political, cultural, and intellectual freedom. Even the theological opponents of the doctrine of free will (e.g., Luther and Calvin), did not deny such human freedom. In a wonderful and mysterious way, the freedom of God is so infinitely great, that God not only permits finite freedom, but works alongside human freedom without annulling it.

Although we must acknowledge the sinfulness and repressiveness of the darker side of Christianity in such things as the Inquisition *(Inquisitio Heretice Pravitatis)*, the Index of Prohibited Books *(Index Librorum Prohibitorum)*, or the militant absolutism of some aspects of contemporary Fundamentalism, we must also acknowledge the essential nature of Christianity in its tradition of freedom, which liberates the individual from restrictive legalism to a living relationship with Christ.

One of the positive aspects of the freedom of pluralism is religious emancipation for people whose involvement with Christianity is rooted in manipulation or coercion. In 1987, a Canadian professor of sociology, while probing the declining membership of the Canadian church, discovered that for many, the decrease lay in the fact that because religion was a forced issue as a child or young adult, many left when old enough to make a choice.[11] Whatever else evangelism represents, its basic meaning should be "good news." Whenever the Christian faith is associated with intimidation, manipulation, and coercion, it can hardly be perceived of as "good news." Indeed, absolutist attitudes have a blood-stained past in Christian history (e.g., Galileo, a host of martyrs, and so-called dissenters) and rarely produces faith in the biblical sense of the word. A major theme of the Judeo-Christian tradition is that of God calling people to be "sons and daughters," with the freedom to accept full responsibility for the choices made in their lives. Thus, pluralism makes it possible to differentiate between true commitment and dragooning people to belief.

*Pluralism and Choice*

Finally, on a more cautious note, pluralism increases the scope of choice a la carte in the ideological supermarket. This proliferation in options often leads to the decrease in commitment and continuity, which in turn can result in a form of dilettantism and a selectiveness in the way people relate to faith. As far as Christian theology is concerned, theological pluralism is only a legitimate expression of authentic Christianity if it involves diverse expression of the "Christian faith" as seen within the context of Scripture and its historic creeds. A pluralistic church which embraces religious syncretism, compromising the essential aspects of its historic faith and obscuring the uniqueness of the person of Christ, ceases to be a Christian church in the monolithic sense of the word. It is this subtle aspect of religious pluralism which the church must reject, as it seeks to justify a multiplicity of religious convictions by affirming that all truth is relative and that all personal opinions have the same intrinsic value. The only form of pluralism which a Christian can affirm is one that can bear the scrutiny of Scripture, Christian tradition, and the values and ethics of the kingdom of God.

## Relativism: The Baby Boomer Options

Albert Einstein was a brilliant German physicist, whose formation of the special and general theories of relativity laid the foundations of modern physics. When he died in April of 1955, his obituary included the following observation: "When a man sits with a pretty girl for an hour, it seems like a minute. But let him sit on a hot stove for a minute—and it's longer than an hour. That's relativity." This reminds us of the ancient proverb that states: "In the country of the blind, the one-eyed man is king," or the Yiddish proverb that comments: "He is a giant who has many dwarfs about him."

For a number of years, I served as a minister to the Innuit people of North Baffin Island in Canada's Arctic. It was a tremendous experience for me to live among such a wonderful people, learn their language (Inuktitut), and experience their customs and culture. On one occasion, I was visited by an older Inuk man who

**51**

had lost his wife to cancer, leaving him with a handful of children to care for on his own. He had heard through the grapevine that a woman in a neighboring community had lost her husband and that she too had a number of children. It seemed logical to my visitor that the solution to both problems would be marriage, and he asked me to please arrange the details. From my perspective, I found it incredulous that anyone would plan to get married to someone they didn't know, never mind not be in love with. Thus I inquired, "Don't you think that you would want to discover whether or not you could love this woman before you commit yourself to such a final commitment as marriage?" He replied, "There is a difference between your way of viewing love in marriage and mine. For you non-Innuit, marriage often begins hot and then the love grows cold. For Innuit, love may begin cold, but often grows warm over time." Of course, he was correct in his assumption that we had relatively different views on the role of love in marriage.

There are many sorts and senses of relativism, but it is absolutely clear that the impact of relativism is ubiquitously pervasive as far as North America is concerned. The late University of Chicago philosophy professor Allan Bloom writes:

> There is one thing a professor can be absolutely certain of: almost every student entering the university believes, or says he believes, that truth is relative. If this belief is put to the test, one can count on the students' reaction: they will be uncomprehending. That anyone should regard the proposition as not self-evident astonishes them, as though he were calling into question $2+2=4$. These are things you don't think about. The students' backgrounds are as various as America can provide. Some are religious, some atheists; some are to the Left, some to the Right; some intend to be scientists, some humanists or professionals or businessmen; some are poor, some rich. They are unified only in their relativism and in their allegiance to equality. And the two are related in a moral intention. The relativity of truth is not a theoretical insight but a moral postulate, the condition of a free society, or so they see it.[12]

According to Bloom, the education system which has evolved over the last half decade has made a moral virtue out of openness, and it has become the primary reservoir from which relativism flows into the vacant recesses of the American mind. He writes, "Relativism . . . is the only virtue, which all primary education for more than fifty years has dedicated itself to inculcating."[13] According to Bloom, this openness has created a form of American conformism which teaches students that the world is a drab diversity, where values are relative and where individuals can choose their lifestyles in accordance with their worldview and moral philosophy.

The idea that truth is a personal opinion is found in the often heard cliché, "It's all relative." Again, Bloom is insightful when describing the devastating impact which relativism has had on adult education. He observes that today's pupils are simply unable to advocate a perspective on a particular issue because they have precious little passion for truth. Consequently, "The best they can do," writes Bloom, "is point out all the opinions and cultures there are and have been. What right, they ask, do I or anyone else have to say one is better than the others?"[14] This of course implies that if an individual does express a strong conviction on a particular issue, then he or she runs the risk of being considered a segregationist, bigot, supremacist, and an enemy of the common good. Oddly enough, in former days, it was the skeptic and nonbeliever who was considered the public adversary. Relativism, however, has so changed the fabric of contemporary American life that the number one enemy has become those who express their opinions with conviction and passion. Looking at this from the relativist's position, Professor Bloom suggests, "The study of history and of culture teaches that all the world was mad in the past; men always thought they were right, and that led to wars, persecutions, slavery, xenophobia, racism, and chauvinism. The point is not to correct the mistakes and really be right; rather it is not to think you are right at all."[15] Bloom argues, however, that, "It is important to emphasize that the lesson the students are drawing from their studies is simply untrue. History and the study of cultures do not teach or prove that values or cultures are relative. All to the contrary, that is a philosophical premise that we now bring to our study of them."[16]

Having been taught that truth is relative, it is no surprise to discover that Baby Boomers pride themselves in their ability to hold diverse and broad viewpoints. Hans Finzel, who labels himself as a card-carrying Baby Boomer, describes the values of his generation as "clusters of attitudes." He writes:

**53**

Where do we get our values? From our parents, peers, teachers, and of course the powerful media. The world around us shapes our values into what they are at any given time. And yes, they are fluid and dynamic, ever changing; however, most of us form our basic value system in our early years of life, say before we reach 25. That is why baby boomers, especially the early crop, have values that still linger from the turbulent 1960s.[17]

Following, we shall examine the effect of cultural, ethical, and religious relativism in contemporary North American life. Broadly speaking, relativism may be defined as an ethical companion of pluralism, which professes that there is no ultimate truth. In its extreme, relativism asserts that truth is not the exclusive property of a single culture, philosophy, worldview, or sacred text. It maintains that there is no one way, no absolutes, and that all moral and ethical principles stem from the individual's conscience.

### Cultural Relativism

In the latter part of the nineteenth century social scientists, anthropologists, and philosophers became increasingly exposed to the non-European civilizations of India, Persia, and China. As they studied these ancient cultures, it quickly became apparent that these societies not only possessed elaborate and radically different social organizations but long-standing artistic, intellectual, and religious traditions. As a result of such careful study of these civilizations, the "explorers of culture" made some significant observations. *First*, in attempting to classify diverse cultures, they recognized that the former presupposition of judging all cultural phenomena according to European standards was clearly wrong. *Second*, this unconscious prejudice in Western thinking that attempted to raise European culture above others was not only challenged, but was identified as a form of ethnocentrism. *Third*, they promoted the concept that influences other than objective reality worked in the acquisition of human knowledge and suggested that the prime source of reality was the cultural tradition itself. Thus, cultural relativists believed that values were relative to culture in the sense of being a function of and causally dependent on it. In effect, this meant that truth was relative in that it was only valid for a given person, in a given society, and at a given time, but not necessarily valid truth for another. Therefore, cultural relativism abandoned the principle of a universal validity of truth by making it culture bound. Cultural relativists also suggested that the source of many disagreements which exist in a pluralistic society stemmed from enculturation of different traditions, incongruities in social constitutions, and diversity of personal histories.

As we noted, the development of pluralism within Western society brought the previously accepted concept of a unilinear civilization into question. Pluralism also helped to curb policies that attempted to assimilate other societies into the mainstream of Western culture and indeed went further in suggesting that much could be learned from such groups. In this regard, the impact of cultural relativism in North American life has been extremely beneficial in correcting and softening many previous jingoistic attitudes toward ethnic minorities, as it challenges the belief that one culture is better than another.

In another regard, it could also be argued that the adoption of cultural relativism comes at tremendous cost to democratic societies. Bloom states:

> Cultural relativism succeeds in destroying the West's universal or intellectually imperialistic claims, leaving it to be just another culture. So there is equality in the republic of cultures. Unfortunately the West is defined by its need for justification of its ways or values, by its need for discovery of nature, by its need for philosophy and science. This is its cultural imperative. Deprived of that, it will collapse.[18]

### Ethical Relativism

Most ethical relativists would accept the proposition suggested by the cultural relativists, that values and ethical principles have little objective validity in themselves, but rather have their origins within the individual's cultural conditions. Consequently, it cannot be said that a single "correct" set of ethical principles exists for all people, all the time. Ethical relativism maintains that human values are subject to change depending on the circumstances of a given situation. In practical terms, this means that if an individual decides that it is right (or wrong) to do action A, then it is right (or wrong) for them to do A regardless of the fact that action A may be wrong (or right) for another person in similar circumstances. It would be safe to say that this view is widely endorsed by North

American Baby Boomer culture with its belief that a person should not be condemned morally for doing what he or she sincerely believes to be right.

Some would say that the Episcopalian writer Joseph Fletcher came very close to the position taken by the ethical relativists, in his highly influential book *Situation Ethics* (1966). In this work, Fletcher suggested that proper ethical decision-making be taken from the context in which an ethical decision is made, rather than from any moral system. Situation ethics were founded on the idea that love was the only intrinsically good thing. He argued that no principle of justice can transcend the expediency of a given hour. Right and wrong cannot be dependent on a set of rules, but rather on how people "operationalize" the concept of love in a specific situation. Fletcher also suggested that "nothing is inherently good or evil except love and its opposite, indifference and malice."[19] This love, which Fletcher held as the guiding sentiment, is a "social attitude" which has nothing to do with laws or general principles, and "may be thrown aside if they conflict on any concrete case with love."[20] This reminds us of Niebuhr's famous statement: "Nothing is intrinsically immoral except ill-will and nothing is intrinsically good except good-will."[21] Situation ethics is a healthy corrective against legalism, but some would argue that it has an inadequate understanding of God's love as a guide to loving. It is interesting to note that Fletcher was one of the signers of the *Humanist Manifesto II*. His influence can be seen in the following principle regarding ethics.

> We affirm that moral values derive their source from human experience. Ethics is *autonomous* and *situational*, needing no theological or ideological sanction. Ethics stem from human need and human interest. . . . Reason and intelligence . . . infused by a sense of human caring, is the best method that humanity has for resolving problems. . . . We believe in maximum individual autonomy consonant with social responsibility.[22]

There are many obvious difficulties related to the ethical relativist's position. For example, the sociologist would wrestle with the question as to whether any culture can survive in the absence of shared beliefs, common goals, and collective values.

For the Christian, ethical relativism is in conflict with the Christian concept of moral theology in at least two main areas.

*First,* Christian ethics maintain that since the spiritual person as the image of God, is present in every human being, there must be a universal moral order that binds all people, at least with regard to its fundamental requirements. The idea that different types of morality exist for different people is not only foreign to Christian thought, but would suggest that a Christian's business ethics, social ethics, or even personal ethics may function separately from theological ethics.

However, ethical relativism has made significant inroads into the Christian community, causing a role conflict between the ethical demands of the Christian faith and life in the real world. This lack of consistence causes the fragmentation of faith. Bibby writes:

> Business ethics are frequently incompatible with religious ethics. Sexual inclinations are commonly in conflict with religious expectations. People very often are not particularly responsive to the "nice guy" approach. Many frustrated people have, somewhat defensively, protested that religion is simply not relevant to life as they know it—a simple way of saying that what it frequently enjoins in belief and behavior is inappropriate to or dissonant with the roles one plays.
>
> Fragments, on the other hand, seem to work. For example, retaining belief in God means that one can still have recourse to prayer. Continuing to believe in life after death gives one a measure of hope in the face of bereavement. The use of religious fragments permits one to retain some central elements of belief and practice without requiring a high level of role consistency. Commitment does not resolve the problem of role conflict; fragment adoption does.[23]

Faced with the choice between a fragmented self or a fragmented worldview, many Baby Boomer believers choose the latter. This choice represents a radical departure from historic Judeo-Christian thinking, whereby the individual is linked to a larger reality that gains its unity from God. Again, Bibby is insightful.

> In short, for many people, fragments may, ironically, be highly conducive to integrated role performances. Life is much happier for some Roman Catholics when they can attend Mass every week yet reject the church's position on birth

control as unacceptable and based on questionable authority (e.g., "I don't think the Pope is always right in everything he says"). Some Conservative Protestants are relieved to be able to drink socially despite the wide spread evangelical position of abstinence, using the rationale of showing moderation and being individually "led by the Spirit." Employers and employees in all religious groupings have a weight taken off their shoulders when they distinguish between what they would like to do ideally and what the competitive world of economic life, and their very job requirements, actually calls them to do.[24]

*Second,* Christian ethics maintain that the source of morality has its origin in supernatural revelation, not from the individual, or the cultural environment, as was suggested by relativism. Thus, Christian ethics seek to relate the long-standing tradition of interpretation of the Bible's moral teaching to contemporary thinking and decision-making. Prescinding from revelation, Christians also stress that such ethics are not intended to be merely an exposition and analysis of theoretical doctrines, but a practical guide to living, which may be presented objectively as a catechism with a pedagogical end in view.

### Religious Relativism

In a typical city in North America, all the great world religions are visible and vibrant. Christians go to their churches; Jews to their synagogues; Muslims to their mosques; and Sikhs, Hindus, and Buddhists to their temples. The existence of these many religions side-by-side in the same community has given rise to the popular belief that since all religions are to be considered equally valid in a pluralistic society then so must their particular expression of truth be considered legitimate. In other words, no one particular faith is said to be the authorized way to find God, nor to be the sole bearer of truth.

A further development of this form of religious relativism is syncretism. This concept attempts to combine different faiths in such a way as to blur their distinctiveness. Syncretism is a system of belief which extends beyond the cultural adaptation of the Gospel to indigenous cultures by encouraging the mingling together of religious faiths resulting in a hybrid form of faith. In some Christian circles, it is not uncommon to hear support for syncretism expressed in such statements as: "the dangers of absolutizing Christian faith," "interfaith spirituality," "construction of world theologies," "being open," "broadminded," the "development of syncrestic worldviews," the "hidden Christ in Hinduism," "the time of conversion is over," and the idea of "cosmic Christology" as represented by Henri de Lubac.[25]

Whether syncrestic views flow from the unexamined presuppositions in philosophical anthropology or an eagerness to submerge questions of truth in favor of joint activity, the fact remains that syncrestic sympathies are pervasive and are encouraged both within and outside the Body of Christ. Religious education within the school structure encourages pupils to discover truth by being exposed to a broad number of alternatives, thus enabling them to choose the most convincing religious faith. In a typical North American city, it is not uncommon to hear of festivals of worship and prayer in which Christians, Jews, Muslims, and Buddhists celebrate those "things they have in common." One local newspaper, reporting on a Catholic/Buddhist retreat, stated: "Their goal was identical; only the means were different. The Buddhists were pleased to enter into the experience of western spirituality. The Catholic Benedictines were glad to gain a deeper insight into Zen Buddhist forms of meditation. . . . They were also deeply impressed by the importance of silence in the Buddhist tradition."[26] Furthermore, many churches in North America have a great interest in the assimilation of Native American spirituality into the Christian faith tradition. As a result, there are countless meetings, forums, articles, and books written with the intent of encouraging the intermingling of Indian pre-Christian religion within Christian faith and practice. As to be expected, syncretism has profoundly affected the mission of the church by bringing a lack of confidence in the Gospel and an uncertainty regarding the claims and person of Christ himself. One Catholic author wrote of his commitment to "spiritual mongrelism" in this way.

> Although now a professing Christian, I am still a mongrel, in that I find truth, get help, and take delight in other religions, past and present, in nonreligious spiritual movements, and in religiously unlabeled spiritually-oriented men. I do look everywhere for my light, and I do not find the process confusing

**59**

but, on the contrary, illuminating and edifying. I believe that it is possible and necessary for many of us today in seeking the face of God to look not only at home but abroad. This outlook is rooted in deep conviction. I am stuck with it and, if you read further so are you.[27]

No one has promoted religious syncretism more vigorously than Matthew Fox, the California based Dominican priest and author, who popularized a blend of Catholic mysticism and New Age ideas, which he calls "creation spirituality."[28] Its gist is the celebration of all creation by drawing on science, the traditions of native peoples, the mystical teaching of the Medieval church, feminism, environmentalism, the arts, animals, ecumenism, liberation theology, and aerobics. In this cosmology, all religions are one, and "Mother Earth" is the center of human worship. Fox regards the doctrine of original sin as being less important than the doctrine of the original blessing, where, among other things, sexuality and freedom replaces fear and guilt. In his workshops, a variety of subjects are taught: African dance, massage, aikido, art, T'aichi, Jungian dream interpretation, and mystic environmentalism.

### Relativism: A Christian Perspective
We may sum up our discussion of this aspect of the Baby Boomer worldview by saying that there are both constructive and destructive facets to relativism.

*First,* the insights of cultural relativism may benefit the church in its missionary procedures in recognizing that some human values are "culturally conditioned" and stem from a particular culture rather than inherently belonging to Christianity. It follows that such values and beliefs not be considered universal norms for every Christian regardless of his or her particular cultural setting. Cultural relativism is thus able to help distinguish those things that are fundamental to God's purpose from those things that are simple expressions and vary from culture to culture.

*Second,* religious relativism is correct in recognizing that God is universally present to all of creation and that the whole of humanity has the potential for imaging the deity. It is preposterous to believe on the one hand, that only the "Christian culture" draws from God's creative handiwork. To claim such an exclusive view would be to deny such biblical themes as God's presence within the creation (Gen. 1; Ps. 139); the wisdom of humanity (Prov. 8; Rom. 2:15); the planting of the human search for God within the heart of all people (Acts 17); the divine intention to reconcile the whole of creation (Eph. 1:9-10); and God's *agapic* nature for all creation (John 3:16-21). The call of the relativist to "meet together" is of far greater importance than the exclusivist's desire to stay apart.

*Third,* as Murren observed, to be successful in ministry to Boomers the church must have "multi-type" options and show a profound respect for counter opinions. In effect, he is suggesting that strong absolutist views on issues can be counterproductive in ministry to this generation. It may not be necessary for fundamentalists to insist that the Genesis stories of Creation be taken at face value or treated as science and natural history.[29] It is doubtful that this generation is impressed by the papal claims to infallibility — when the Pope is speaking *ex cathedra* on matters of faith and morals or by the silencing of men such as Hans Küng for challenging traditional views. History suggests that it is dangerous to seek after built-in guarantees of freedom from error or a discovery of absolute truth, whether it be in the form of an individual (the Pope, mystic, sage, guru, or charismatic evangelist); a particular denomination (Roman Catholic, Baptist, Lutheran, or Anglican); or a much loved doctrinal emphasis (biblical prophecy, predestination, free will, or signs and wonders). The truth cannot be stated boldly enough: God is not a fascist. To that end, Murren is wise in his suggestion that in ministry to Baby Boomers, "don't try to force consensus."[30]

*Fourth,* relativism is sequaciously self-destructive. If all truth is entirely culture-specified, then so is the truth of the cultural relativist analysis; hence, it cannot be said to be true. It is this contradiction in terms that we shall return to when we discuss the relationship between relativism and truth. At this point, suffice to say that relativism reduces truth to a matter of personal opinion and social location by emphasizing such things as "viewpoint" and what is "right for an individual," rather than "truth" and being "right." A Christian apologist may ask of the relativist how it is possible to maintain contradictory ideas without feeling that they have to deny any of them. This is the point that Allan Bloom makes when he describes relativism as an attractive philosophy that pursues niceness to the exclusion of truth.

**61**

## Individualism: The Baby Boomer Image

Among the Sophists who lived in Athens, Protagoras of Abdera was the oldest and, in many ways, the most influential. He was best known for his statement, "Man is the measure of all things, of the things that are, that they are and of the things that are not, that they are not." To say that man is the measure of all things meant something different to Protagoras than it means today. For this ancient philosopher, it meant whatever knowledge man could achieve would be limited to his human capacities. In Baby Boomer culture, it is used to denote the pervasive belief that the individual is the central, most important aspect in the universe.

In classical Christian theology, there exists an underlying assumption that humankind's self-knowledge is discovered as a result of its knowledge of God. The Bible asserts that human beings have a fourfold network of relationships as a result of a fourfold vocation: (1) People find their dignity and their magnanimity in loving, serving, and glorifying God. (2) People are social beings, not solitary and as such must enter into interpersonal relationships to find fulfillment. (3) People are intrinsically related to the creation and the world in which they live, to care for it as stewards and to manage as guardians. (4) People stand in relationship with themselves and are responsible for their own actions.

The first major philosopher, apart from Machiavelli, to present an alternative to the classic view was Thomas Hobbes (1588–1679), who by detaching the doctrine of natural law from the Aristotelian framework, developed a picture of human existence which maintained that human nature is essentially individualistic, non-social, competitive, aggressive, and self-seeking. Cynically, Hobbes suggested that even what appears to be an altruistic deed is in one way or another an action of the ego. John Aubrey, in his sketch of Hobbes, tells of an exchange between Hobbes and a priest who had just seen Hobbes give alms to a beggar. The priest inquired whether Hobbes would have given alms if Jesus had not commanded it. Hobbes replied that by giving alms to the beggar, he not only relieved the man's distress but he also relieved his own distress at seeing the beggar's distress![31] It hardly needs to be said that such an egotistical view flies in the face of Christian belief, which asserts that good deeds are to be performed out of gratitude for the gift of God's saving grace and not with an eye to one's own advantage. Thus, "love for one's neighbor" from the

Christian perspective, salvages us from mere sentimental philanthropy (a frequent front for a refined egotism) and from that extravagant altruism which maintains that the only actions which have moral validity are those performed for the good of somebody else.

More recently, a team of social researchers led by Robert Bellah began a study of the American middle class. After five years of study, they produced their results in a best-selling book entitled *Habits of the Heart*. The researchers thought of their work as the continuation of a study of the American character which began in the 1830s with the French social philosopher Alex de Tocqueville. His book, *Democracy in America*, was filled with much admiration for the inhabitants of America, but it also contained many prophetic warnings. In regard to the dangers of individualism, de Tocqueville wrote:

> They acquire the habit of always considering themselves as standing alone and they are apt to imagine that their whole destiny is in their own hands. Thus, not only does democracy make every man forget his ancestors, but it hides his descendents and separates his contemporaries from him; it throws him back forever upon himself alone, and threatens in the end to confine him entirely within the solitude of his own heart.[32]

Bellah and his team suggested that individualism, along with antistatism, populism, and equalitarianism, has always been at the heart of the American creed.

> Individualism lies at the very core of American culture. . . . We believe in the dignity, indeed the sacredness, of the individual. Anything that would violate our right to think for ourselves, judge for ourselves, make our own decisions, live our lives as we see fit, is not only morally wrong, it is sacrilegious. Our highest and noblest aspirations, not only for ourselves, but for those we care about, for our society and for the world, are closely linked to our individualism.[33]

Bellah points out that individualism is a persistent theme in American literature, embodied in two mythical hero figures — the cowboy and the detective.

Both the cowboy and the hard-boiled detective tell us something important about American individualism. The cowboy, like the detective, can be valuable to society only because he is a completely autonomous individual who stands outside it. To serve society, one must be able to stand alone, not needing others, not depending on their judgement, and not submitting to their wishes.[34]

Bellah and his associates assert that excessive individualism is threatening group life—love and marriage, community involvement, and national identification: "What has failed at every level—from the society of nations to the national society to the local community to the family—is integration. . . we have put our own good, as individuals, as groups, as a nation, ahead of the common good."[35] In similar fashion, Christopher Lasch demonstrates in thorough and revealing ways, how infantile narcissism and the North American consumer ethic have combined to impoverish the quality of collective life.[36]

Furthermore, according to Bellah and his fellow writers, individualism is threatening the very freedom of the nation.

It seems to us that it is individualism, and not equality . . . that has marched inexorably through our history. We are concerned that this individualism may have grown cancerous—that it may be destroying those social integuments that . . . [moderate] its more destructive potentialities, that it may be threatening the survival of freedom itself. We want to know what individualism in America looks and feels like, and how the world appears in its light.[37]

Tocqueville identified three specific ways that could keep Americans from self-destructing on individualism: religion, family, and public service. Unfortunately, the last three decades witnessed radical changes in the amount of time and energy individuals are willing to invest in these three areas of life. The influence of secularism has led to a widespread disenchantment with God; and frankly, many people find Christianity no longer compelling. It is not that Christianity is rejected outright, but it has been trivialized or subverted to the status of individual enhancement. Instead of being considered the "queen of the sciences" as it once was, religion has been reduced to just one more column in *Time* magazine!

The quality of family life in North America is becoming optional and commitments a matter of choice. Easy divorce and single parenting are regarded as normal. With longer lifespans, it is considered by many, unreasonable to expect men and women to live together for fifty or sixty years. Bloom writes, "Apart from the fact that many students have experienced the divorce of their parents and are informed by statistics that there is a strong possibility of divorce in their futures, they hardly have an expectation that they will have to care for their parents or any other blood relatives, or that they will even see much of them as they grow older."[38]

In the political realm, the general torpor caused by the sense that nothing ever changes, in conjunction with the hurried lifestyle, the cult of leisure, and the lulling world of television, has profoundly reduced the time people are willing to give in community service. Furthermore, corruption and abuse of office has badly damaged the image of public service in the minds of many Baby Boomers. With regards to the general student population Bloom observes:

> Very few of them are destined for a political life; and if they do actually enter politics, it is by accident, and does not follow from their early training or expectations. In the universities about which I am speaking, there are almost no students born of families that have inherited the privilege and responsibility of public service, for almost no such families remain. Neither duty nor pleasure involves students with the political, and our lives exhibit in the extreme what Burke and Tocqueville said about the disappearance of citizens and statesmen. The petty personal interest of youth — "making it," finding a place for oneself — persevere throughout life. The honesty of this generation of students causes them to laugh when asked to act as though they were powerful agents in world history.[39]

Individualism with all its excrescences is so pervasive that historians and social commentators, such as Christopher Lasch, fear that North American culture has fallen into "narcissism" and that this excessive individualism has become the "faith of those without faith."[40] In reference to the cult of narcissism, Herbert Schlossberg writes, "The individual believes himself to be the measure of both reality and moral principle. Thus, there are no standards, no belief in eternal truth, no objective measure of right

**65**

and wrong; norms or delusions, and self-discipline serves no purpose."[41]

Individualism flourished in the 1970s as a result of the disappointed political aspirations of the Baby Boomers of the 1960s. The extent of an inward focus was so widespread that Lasch and others labeled it as the "me decade." This lack of faith in the future, turned people in on themselves, to the extent that personal well-being, health, and psychic security became the trend. Lasch observes:

> Having no hope of improving their lives in any of the ways that matter, people have convinced themselves that what matters is psychic self-improvement: getting in touch with their feelings, eating health foods, taking lessons in ballet, or belly dancing, immersing themselves in the wisdom of the East, jogging, learning how to relate, overcoming the fear of pleasure.[42]

In a similar fashion James Hitchcock writes:

> Preoccupation with the self became, for many people, a virtual obsession with it. They began spending most of their waking hours pondering ways of improving their personalities and discovering how to get more out of life. The narcissism was both physical and psychological. The American obsession with diet and exercise, while commendable from the point of view of health, has been mainly motivated by a kind of worship of one's own body.[43]

This all-consuming quest for self-fulfillment created an industry of psychiatric care for people who essentially had no serious psychological problems in the customary sense of the term. Psychologist Paul Vitz saw this genre of popular psychology (as represented by men such as Erich Fromm, Carl Rogers, Abraham Maslow, and Rollo May) as feeding narcissism in that "it . . . [taught] self-worship and . . . [was] in fact a religion posing as a science."[44]

### Utilitarian Individualism
Utilitarian individualism is the belief that social good for all can only emerge in a society where each person single-mindedly and passionately pursues self-interest. It is argued that the government's main task is to create the proper condition for fair and open

competition where (in Darwinian terms) "the strongest prevail." As to be expected, this extreme form of individualism affects human compassion. As every clinical psychiatrist knows, a preoccupation with self leaves little room for the needs of others. Here, we are reminded of the ancient Greek myth about Narcissus, as told by the Roman poet, Ovid. In this story, a handsome young man, Narcissus, sees his reflection in a pool of water. He falls in love with the image and becomes so infatuated that he has no room for the nymph, Echo, or for anyone else. This "no room for anyone else" is the frequent result of narcissistic preoccupation.

Utilitarian individualism also tends to concentrate more on personal achievement, such as career advancement with all the recognition, prestige, and financial benefits that come from success in the marketplace. In this area, "self-reliance" is a key term along with characteristic features such as intelligence, credentials, pragmatic skill, and innovation. Put to proper use, these features actualize the elusive dream of unlimited success. Thus, it is hoped that *homo narcissus* leads to *homo economicus.*

The problem with this view, as many North Americans are now realizing, is that success of this nature is an elusive commodity, pursued by many, but achieved by few. Life in the fast lane, driven by the quest for power, wealth, status, and happiness, creates its casualties and ironically causes the "loss" rather than the "discovery" of self-identity. Furthermore, those driven by the need for professional success are often required to move from one metropolitan city to another, according to the dictates of the nationwide job market. This upwardly mobile society reduces the strength of personal relationships and creates a sense of loneliness and rootlessness.

### Expressive Individualism

Expressive individualism recognizes some of the pitfalls of utilitarian individualism and acknowledges that there are things that money cannot buy—one being the freedom of self-expression. In order to achieve the freedom of being "one's self," it is believed that individuals need to break free from the bogus controls imposed on them, whether it be the pressures of business or family responsibility. Thus, many choose to put additional energies toward the pursuit of the "good life." Although the route is different, it should be pointed out that the goal of expressive individualism is

**67**

the same as that found in the more tunnel-vision focus of utilitarian individualism. Key words to achieve the goal of self-actualization are self-discovery, self-exploration, and self-fulfillment. This group of expressive individualists, having satisfied their material needs, are now turning the state of their psyches into the principle preoccupation of their existence. Thus, *homo economicus* leads to *homo narcissus.*

### Individualism in the Christian Community

Before decrying the excesses of individualism evident in North American culture, contemporary Christianity should first examine its own forms of individualism. For example, a walk through a typical Christian bookstore reveals an abundance of books, videos, and tapes on issues related to self-reliance, self-esteem, self-love, and self-fulfillment. Indeed, the emphasis on self-fulfillment seems to have more prominence than the self-negation which Christ regarded as a prerequisite for discipleship.

Other forms of Christian individualism are seen in forms of exclusive denominational loyalties. When conflict arises, whether it be doctrinal or matters of policy, Protestant churches in North America have tended to spawn new denominations, rather than striving for harmony or living with differences in peaceful coexistence. These divisions are often fostered by strong individuals who are either religious "virtuosos," calling the faithful to a return to "truth" (which is often a form of an older tradition), or strong charismatic figures who call the faithful to a new message (on the basis of new authority or new insight). Dismayed by this sectarian individualism, the late Anglican author David Watson wrote:

> Impatient with the mixture of impurities in terms of faith, life or doctrine, (often minor doctrine of secondary importance), some pull out of existing denominations to form another fellowship of like-minded Christians who, for the time being at least, enjoy greater freedom in worship or flexibility in structure. Soon however, another denomination is born; and a little later another visible church, with the same impurities as before, will have come into being.[45]

The incredible plethora of churches and denominations in our culture does bear some significance to the sociocultural reality of individualism. It is not the variety that is harmful to the Body of

Christ, as much as it is the damaging exclusive and excluding attitudes which insist that "we are right and you are wrong." Denominationalism suggests to the world that Christians do not need each other. To the onlooker, the abundance of congregational denominations cannot be viewed as an answer to our Lord's prayer "that all of them may be one" (John 17:21). When Christians say *credo ecclesia* (we believe in the church), the phrase often means little more than a belief in a church created in its own image.

### Individualism: A Christian Perspective

There are some very positive aspects to individualism that a Christian can affirm. First of all, Christian teaching upholds the greatness of the individual as one created in the image of God. Most of the insights from the great thinkers (Montaigne, Pascal, Kierkegaard, de Chardin, and Jung who have probed the human heart and psyche and discovered the complexity and incomparable greatness of humanity) are consistent with Christian teaching. Most Christians would agree with Sophocles' Antigone: "Many great things exist, but nothing is greater than man." The Christian doctrine of humankind, while recognizing humanity's sinfulness *(massa peccatrix)*, also recognizes its uniqueness, as one created for God and in the likeness of God. This concept of the *imago Dei* lifts humankind above all other creatures as one who can think, choose, and create, and who possesses, to use Brunner's terminology, the gift of "addressability" and "answerability" to God. Furthermore, the incarnation of the Son of God who became the Son of Man, is in itself a declaration of the supreme worth and dignity of humanity. It states that individuals, despite their fallenness, are worthy of redemption and are capable of being restored. In this computer age where the uniqueness of the individual can be easily obscured and the potential for dehumanization is ripe, the Christian view of humankind is one that values, upholds, and celebrates this supreme creation of God.

Secondly, Christianity encourages a certain amount of self-examination as part of an individual's spiritual formation. It is widely believed by many Christians that seasons of personal reflection, conducted by the Holy Spirit and fortified by the Word and sacrament, can bring about significant healing and growth toward maturity. Certainly the old model of denial, repression, and reaction has proved to be ineffective in producing personal growth and integration. Christianity also encourages individuals to adopt a solid approach to their self-esteem; and it recognizes that when people do adopt a positive attitude, they often come away with an enhanced self-image, empowered to pursue excellence in all areas of their lives.

There are two main reasons why we as Christians must resist the excesses of individualism. First of all, individualism is bad for our spiritual and emotional health. There is an optimal value beyond which anything can become toxic: oxygen, sleep, psychotherapy, philosophy, love, and individualism. For many years, psychiatrists and psychologists have claimed that the preoccupation with self often leads to loneliness and depression. Recent statistics seem to confirm this by suggesting that large numbers of North Americans deal with personal problems by some form of diversion which often can turn into an addiction. In fact, addiction in the last twenty years has become a cultural phenomena to the extent that it cannot be adequately calculated by statistics. Factor into the following statistics those who are relationship, exercise, money, and compulsive-consumer addicts to get the full picture of the devastation which U.S. individualism brings:

10 million alcoholics
50 million smokers
40–80 million compulsive overeaters
13 million sex addicts
12 million gamblers
12 million workaholics
6 million drug addicts[46]

The biblical antidote to such loneliness is the belief that an individual's fulfillment can be found in relationship with God and in service to others. As previously mentioned, and contrary to the present-day "cult of self-love," Christian belief asserts that individuals find their true fulfillment in compliance with the two ethical requirements of the Golden Rule—to love God and to love one's neighbor. In contrast to the excesses of utilitarian individualism, Christian service to the world should spring from the example that God has given us in Christ—obedient service without thought of personal gain or advantage for ourselves. Since God loves every person absolutely, true love of God is always linked with love of

**70**

neighbor (Mark 12:30-31; John 13:34; 1 John 2:8-10; 1 Cor. 13). Indeed, love of neighbor is the criterion for the genuineness of the love of God (1 John 4:20-21). The love of God that is linked with love of neighbor bestows love, joy, peace, and compassion. It also helps to create a healthy balance between the lonely life of extreme introversion and the busy life of excessive extroversion.

Secondly, individualism is bad for the spiritual health of the Christian community because it reduces it to nothing more than the sum total of individuals. We shall return to this theme later on, but it should be noted that one of the marvelous gifts the church has to offer the Baby Boomer generation is the experience of authentic community. These are extremely dehumanizing times, and there is a hunger in the hearts of many wanting to experience intimacy, cohesion, unconditional love, and acceptance. In their earlier days, there was little time for Boomers to develop significant relationships. As they grew older their values changed. They face a pressing question at this stage in their life cycle: "How can I build lasting friendships, and where can such friendships be found?" Interestingly, it is to the church that many Boomers are turning in hope of finding genuine community.

## Hedonism: The Baby Boomer Life-style

Hedonism is a philosophy of life which maintains that the pursuit and experience of pleasure is the sole and proper goal of human existence. It claims that the art of living consists in maximizing the enjoyment of each moment through the pleasure of the senses. In modern times, hedonists practice the "pursuit of the good life," marked by the trilogy of virtues: health, wealth, and happiness — which incidentally are the watchwords of the prosperity gospel.

Hedonism as an ethic has never been without its devotees. Early advocates include such figures as Democritus, Aristippus of Cyrene, Eudoxus of Cuidus, and the influential Greek philosopher Epicurus, through to John Stuart Mill and Jeremy Bentham who started from the dictum: "Nature has been placed under the governace of two sovereign masters, pain and pleasure."

It is possible to think of hedonism in ethical and psychological terms. Ethical hedonism contends that pleasure, and pleasure alone, is intrinsically good. Psychological hedonism believes that no one, in fact, ever does anything that does not further his or her own pleasure. Hedonism is not simply an abstract theory, but a

**71**

widely accepted worldview practiced by many people who live in step with its ethical and moral principles. Indeed, North American culture extols hedonism and the pursuit of pleasure.

After World War II, the United States became a Croesus-rich country. Most Americans (with the exception of African-Americans and other ethnic groups) experienced a constant and perceptible increase in their standard of living, and with it, more disposable income. Unlike the riches of a medieval prince, this newfound wealth among the American population meant purchasing power — indeed more buying capacity than ever before in history. This offered people a bewildering array of items that were considered luxuries in the previous generation: records, clothes, education, books, kitchen and home appliances, exotic holidays, home entertainment units, cottages, and vehicles.

A subtle but significant psychological process began to take place, whereby people became quite accustomed to having their needs met, so much so that "needs" became almost indistinguishable from "wants." There is a philosophical base to materialism which should not be overlooked. The de-Christianization of society, especially in the last three decades, caused a vacuum in the lives of many Americans. Much of that void was filled with the belief that the highest values and objectives in life were to be found in one's material well-being. According to this belief, reality was measured in material terms, and spiritual and intellectual dimensions were regarded as epiphenomena. Perhaps no subgroup within North American culture better exemplified the priorities of the metaphysical materialists than the Baby Boomers.

### The Prosperity Gospel

Great inroads into the contemporary American religious scene have been gained by the prosperity gospel movement. It is disturbing to find how easily the church incorporated this spirit of materialism. The origins are rooted in society's determination that success is proportional to material wealth. To a large extent, the Christian community also emphasized personal success which included self-realization and financial prosperity as well as institutional success (megachurches and TV ministries). "Name it and claim it!" "God wants you rich!" and "Health, wealth, and success can be yours!" became the slogans of the teachers of this new gospel. Frequently, Jim Bakker would say to his audience: "Don't settle for a Chevrolet, if you want a Cadillac. Pray for a Cadillac!" Bakker was the proud owner of a Rolls Royce, a million dollar salary (plus an enormous expense account), six luxury homes, and the infamous air-conditioned doghouse!

Into the homes of many North Americans came the TV evangelist's message: "God loves you and wants you to be rich." After all, "the cattle on a thousand hills belong to Him," and "God wants the best for you." "What is the desire of your heart? Name it, claim it, and it will be yours! Your Heavenly Father has promised it. It is right here in the Bible!" John Stott cites the following example of this type of reasoning in the literature of a Pentecostal evangelist.

> "There's no better way to insure your own financial security," he argued, all in capital letters, "than to plant some seed-money in God's work. His law of sowing and reaping guarantees you a harvest of much more than you sow. . . . Have you limited God to your present income, business, house or car? There's no limit to God's plenty. . . . Write on the enclosed slip what you need from God—the salvation of a loved one, healing, a raise in pay, a better job, newer car or home, sale or purchase of a property, guidance in business or investment . . . *whatever you need*. . . Enclose your slip with your seed-money. . . . Expect God's material blessings in return. . . ."[47]

This was a movement with key preachers, conferences, massive publications, media ministries, and a distinctive teaching, which proclaimed that the good news of the Gospel promised healing, financial prosperity, and a general well-being for all who believed. The following titles from the leaders of this movement are quite revealing: Kenneth Hagin's *How to Write Your Own Ticket With God* (1979) and *You Can Have What You Say* (1979); Kenneth Hagin Jr.'s *How God Taught Me About Prosperity* (1980); Kenneth and Gloria Copeland's *The Law of Prosperity* (1974) and Jerry Savelle's *Living in Divine Prosperity* (1987); Joe Magliato's *The Wall Street Gospel* (1979); and Elbert Willis' *God's Plan for Financial Prosperity* (1982).

Theological rationale to justify these positions and protect these interests was derived from a belief that the Abrahamic covenant, along with the atonement, opened the door to the material benefits

**73**

of the covenant of grace. It was argued that since material wealth was part of the Abrahamic covenant and since Christ overturned the "curse of the law" (which included poverty), God wanted to bless people with both health and wealth. Further support for this "King's Kids Theology" was derived from such passages as the *King James* rendition of 3 John 2 and the prosperity formula promised in Mark 10:29-30.

There are a number of reasons why the prosperity gospel movement flourished over the last two decades. Most of all, it blended into the general cultural ethos of society and therefore found ready acceptance. Its message rang a bell that lies deep at the heart of the consciousness of the American people. Thus, Robert Bellah writes, "Americans tend to think of the ultimate goals of a good life as matters of personal choice. The means to achieve individual choice, they tend to think, depends on economic progress."[48]

The Scriptures issue many warnings regarding the hazards of the accumulation of wealth. Indeed, it states categorically that "the love of money is a root of all kinds of evil" (1 Tim. 6:10). The innate perils related to success—fame, fortune, and the opulent life-style associated with such "blessing"—are demonstrated in the tragedy of the North Carolina based PTL organization. In 1987, the media reported the lurid details of the sexual and financial debacles of the TV evangelist, Jim Bakker and his weepy, doll-like wife, Tammy Faye. Here was a couple who modeled the American Dream. Rising spectacularly from poverty, they triumphantly embraced a society that honored wealth and fame. They lived the life-style of the rich and famous. They built an organization which, interestingly enough, had a replica of Main Street USA anchored at the center of their theme park. The PTL was a 130 million dollar-a-year business that turned from a TV ministry to a TV miniseries to a TV misery. The world sneered as the press exposed decadence mingled with fraud. One could not help but recall the words of the English author G.K. Chesterton, who wrote, "A man who is dependent upon the luxuries of this life is a corrupt man, spiritually corrupt, politically corrupt, financially corrupt. . . . Christ and all the saints have said with a sort of savage monotony . . . that to be rich is to be in a peculiar danger of moral wreck."

The PTL scandal revealed that the financial ethics of some segments of the church were no different than much of Wall Street. At least Ivan Boesky admitted his theft and never claimed that

**74**

God encouraged or endorsed him! Commenting on the Bakker fiasco, John Gardner asks a searching question, "What is missing in American culture that leaves people so undernourished that even a Jim Bakker could satisfy their spiritual and emotional hunger?"[49]

### Happiness

Happiness *(eudaemonia)* philosophy is considered to be the highest goal that an individual can achieve. Present-day hedonists and eudaemonists likewise, have affirmed that happiness is one of the most important goals of human life, if not the supreme goal. There are, however, different views in determining what will make a person happy. For some, happiness is achieved through sensory pleasure (hedonists). For others, it is to be found in the security of earthly possessions (materialists). To yet another group, happiness is to be found in acquiring knowledge exclusively for knowledge's sake (rationalism); and for others, it is found in any action that results in pleasure (utilitarianism). The one thing that unites all of the abovementioned views is that happiness is circumstantial, based on outward and tangible experiences. Thus, one often hears of happiness being used in conjunction with prepositions. For example, "John is happy *with* his new job." "Mary is happy *about* the birth of her baby." "Peter is happy *at* his progress with the violin."

Baby Boomers certainly seem to exhibit an insatiable desire to find happiness. This can be seen in their quest for the good life. Although Boomers have considerably less leisure time than their parents, they tend to live it to the fullest. Their lives are often crowded with social activities, which include frequent eating out; attending movies, concerts, and plays, or enjoying exotic vacations.

For Christians, the concept of happiness is quite different. Happiness is considered to be less circumstantial and more internal; it is fundamentally connected to human spiritual nature. This was a lesson that Augustine was to learn from his own personal experience. He was an extremely cultured man whose learning went far beyond the standard of the time. At a young age, Augustine began his search for truth and wisdom. He was educated at the University of Carthage, where he studied rhetoric with the goal of becoming a lawyer. As an academic, he was well aware of the philoso-

**75**

phies of his day which, of course, included the pleasure philosophy promoted by Epicureanism. In the early days of his life, Augustine abandoned the Christian education he had received from his mother, took a mistress, and devoted himself exclusively to literary pursuits. It was not until he was thirty-three years old, after a long philosophical pilgrimage, that he was finally baptized, thus beginning his influential career as priest, bishop, apologist, and theologian par excellence. Augustine experienced the Epicurean pleasures of life. If happiness was to be found in such sensory delights, he would have discovered this from his experience. But history tells us that this was not the case. In fact, Augustine's theology of happiness denotes a radical departure from that of Epicurus as he places it clearly in the internal world of humankind's relationship with God.

Augustine's theology of happiness is fairly simple to follow. He maintained that there cannot be a "naturally" happy person since nature did not create human beings, but rather God did. Consequently, people are created to live in relationship with God and therefore instinctively seek after God. "O God, thou has created us for thyself, so that our hearts are restless until they find their rest in thee." It is therefore no accident that people seek happiness to fill the empty void in their lives. This search is simply a consequence of human incompleteness and finitude. Thus, according to Augustine, individuals find their true happiness in God since they were created to be in relationship with the divine.

The radical message Christians have to offer our hedonistic culture is that lasting happiness is not found in temporal pleasure, but in relationship with God. Happiness is not simply a result of external circumstances or a state of mind, but a matter of the heart. This is not to give the impression that Christians find no happiness in the everyday experiences of life or that all pleasures are only to be found in the spiritual realm. It can surely be assumed that Christians find great satisfaction when efforts to achieve turn out favorably, or when they experience the love of a spouse, or the joy of friendship with acquaintances. Christians may also find happiness in sports and play, discover pleasure in art and music, and draw satisfaction in the pursuit of knowledge in literature and the sciences. However, lasting happiness, the happiness that cannot fade away, is found in the relationship with God through Christ as Lord and Savior.

## Health

In antiquity, as in all ages, health was a highly prized possession. However, perhaps no group has been so preoccupied with health-related issues as the Baby Boomer generation. It is not an overstatement to say that Baby Boomers are obsessed by their appearance. This is clearly demonstrated by the importance they place on physical fitness, exercise, health-conscious diets, and the millions of dollars spent on tapes, videos, seminars, and books. Thus, demographic expert Cheryl Russell writes:

> The baby boom will not grow old gracefully. Already, there are signs of hysteria. Despite aerobics, health clubs, home gymnasiums, and triathlons, Americans feel worse about their bodies today than they did in the early 1970s. . . . The baby boom's obsession with fitness is one of the consequences of its aging. Magazines such as *Superfit, Triathlete, Runner's World, Women's Sports and Fitness,* and *Bicycling* soothe the baby boom's fear of losing its looks and physical abilities as it gets older. But the most radical consequence of the aging of the baby boom is the rise in cosmetic surgery. Between 1981 and 1984, the number of cosmetic operations increased by 61%. Plastic surgery is one of the fastest-growing medical specialities in the country, according to *New York* magazine. "It used to be that when people wanted to feel more confident, they'd go to a therapist, or to est. Now they're going to plastic surgeons," says writer Patricia Morrisroe. Nearly half a million people had cosmetic surgery in 1984.[50]

This fixation with health indicates that the need for healing in our society is great. The church's role as a healing community is a subject we shall return to and discuss at some length. However, it should be pointed out that a preoccupation with health can in itself become a form of sickness. Therefore, it is important for the Christian community to respond to the need for healing with a high level of biblical integrity. Even a superficial reading of the Gospels will reveal that healing, primarily motivated out of compassion, was an integral part of the mission and message of Jesus. Likewise healing has played a significant role in the life of the church. However, from a biblical viewpoint, healing was never offered merely as a consumer item to satisfy the requirements of a narcissistic generation.

Recently, while previewing my local newspaper's church direc-
tory, which listed the weekend's schedule of church services, I
was struck by the bold headline: MIRACLE PRAYER EVENT!
RECEIVE YOUR MIRACLE FROM GOD! The advertisement
went on to promise participants "victory in every area: financial,
mental, physical, and spiritual." I have no doubt that many attended this conference and it was a great success. Why? Because the
health gospel, as with the prosperity gospel, being far more influenced by secular worldviews than good theology, touches on two
major preoccupations of North American culture: materialism and
health. To promise health and wealth to all who put their faith in
Jesus Christ, comes very close to the gospel of cheap grace, as
described by Dietrich Bonhoeffer. Apart from being bad theology,
it can also cause people to come to Christ for all the wrong reasons. Michael Green speculates:

> How people would rush to Christianity (and for all the wrong
> motives) if it carried with it automatic exemption from sick-
> ness! What a nonsense it would make of Christian virtues
> like longsuffering, patience and endurance if instant whole-
> ness were available for all the Christian sick! What a wrong
> impression it would give if salvation of physical wholeness
> were perfectly realized on earth whilst spiritual wholeness
> were partly reserved for heaven! What a very curious thing it
> would be if God were to decree death for all his children
> whilst not allowing illness for any of them.[51]

## Conclusion

In this chapter we have identified some of the virtues and vices of
four major features of North American culture: pluralism, relativism, individualism, and hedonism. This is important because it is
the cultural ethos where the church is called to bear its witness to
the good news of God's saving grace in Christ. While I recognize
that there are some Christian traditions that would assert that the
church has no business meddling in the affairs of the world, and
would therefore take every precaution to distance itself from it,
the following chapter will show that this separatist view, while
convenient, stands in opposition to the theology of the incarnation.
The incarnation of Christ teaches that Jesus, the Son of God, fully
and completely identified with the world he came to seek and save.

Therefore, it will be suggested that the church, following Christ's example, must also risk the cost of such engagement with the world, if it is to be God's agent for the transformation of society.

# PART TWO

# GOD PROVIDES A BRIDGE: THE INCARNATION OF CHRIST

# Chapter 3
# JESUS AND THE
# JEWISH WORLD

The construction of a bridge is an extremely complex affair. The architect has countless imponderables to consider before construction can begin. First and foremost, to undertake such a project one must possess considerable experience as an engineer, have an intimate knowledge of science and mathematics, understand the effects of aerodynamic action, and know graphic methods of structural analysis to qualify to calculate the design of a bridge. Furthermore, the designer must consider the issue of weight: the bridge's *and* the traffic using it, as well as unpredictable elements such as the additional weight of a heavy snowfall. Then there is the question of which type of material to use in consideration of fatigue, corrosion, and safety. Finally, the designer must also exercise judgment in his assessment of future traffic developments and at the same time work within budget. With so many minute and unapparent factors to consider, the task must seem overwhelming. Indeed, one of the architects of the Brooklyn Bridge, Washington A. Roebling, was plagued by a nervous disorder as a result of stress from this enormous project — so much so that he was forced to continue supervision from his bed. It is not surprising that the time span between the conception of a bridge on paper and its actual construction can be several years. In the case of the Brooklyn Bridge, it was some fourteen years in the construction process.

In a similar way, the construction of God's divine bridge was conceived in the mind of God long before Christ was made manifest in the person of Jesus of Nazareth. In the Old Testament we see how God acted not only as a divine architect, but also as a master mason, constructing a bridge of divine reconciliation. The early Christian martyr, Stephen, understood something of God's momentous plans. In his defense against the charge of blasphemy (Acts 7), Stephen used a variety of carefully selected texts and well-known stories from the lives of such heroes as Abraham, Joseph, Moses, David, and Solomon. He attempted to inform his audience of how God had laid a succession of building blocks for the construction of an edifice of redemption which culminated in the coming of Christ. In his speech, Stephen pointed out, in no uncertain terms and at great personal cost, that throughout its history, the nation of Israel repeatedly opposed God's master plan, and that such opposition met its climax in the ultimate rejection of the Messiah (v. 52).

From the abundance of Old Testament quotations and allusions in Stephen's speech, Peter's sermons, and Paul's letters, it is clear that the early Christians believed that the Old Testament anticipated and predicted the coming of the Messiah. Consider, for example, the central thesis that runs throughout the letter to the Hebrews—that Christ through his death and resurrection established a new order and that his sacrifice, promises, and covenant were superior. To further prove this point, the author makes the contrast between the insufficiency of the old order with the sufficiency and finality of this new work in Christ. Of particular interest to our discussion and in line with our analogy of the bridge, the author considers the Aaronic priesthood and its ritual as an imperfect shadow of the eternal priesthood of Christ. The writer of Hebrews argues that since the Levitical priesthood could not offer perfection, a new high priest in the order of Melchizedek was necessary. In Christ's reconciling offering as both priest and victim, he removed all obstacles and accomplished a "once for all" eternal crossway to the living God (Heb. 4:14–7:28).

Perhaps because the term "priest" has been associated with clerical Monophysitism, professionalism, or simply because of its lack of usage in the New Testament, many Protestant communities tend to avoid it. While it is true that the Greek word *hierus* is not used in the New Testament to describe the ministerial office,

**84**

priestly language is used to describe both the ministry of Christ (Heb. 5:1-10; John 17) and the Christian community (1 Peter 2:5-9). The word also has a history in the church as it was used by such eminent authors as Tertullian, Hippolytus, Origen, Eusebius, Basil, and Chrysostom in describing the reconciling work of Christ. Further illumination of the meaning of "priest" comes from the use of the Latin word *pontifex* meaning, literally, a bridge builder, suggesting that Christ's eternal priesthood is concerned with linking people to the living God.

As every designer knows, there comes a time when the action must move from the drawing board to the construction site. Once a location is selected, the plans are applied and the construction begins. Likewise, we must move on from our discussion of God's grand plan to the building of a divine bridge over the troubled water of enmity to examine not only the construction site chosen by God, but also the bridge itself.

## Life in First-Century Palestine

To have been born a Jew in the time of Christ meant a person inevitably lived out life within a religious framework. There was the widely accepted belief that an individual belonged to a unique nation, specially chosen by God (election) as an instrument of divine purpose. From Old Testament instruction as taught in the home, the local synagogue, and the temple, the typical Jew (regardless of the level of piety) was aware of the history of the Jewish ancestry and believed that obedience to God's commandments regarded him or her as a "peculiar treasure," a member of a "kingdom of priests," and a "holy nation" (Ex. 19:3-16).

### The Temple

The temple in Jerusalem represented a powerful symbol of Jewish identity and was the official center of Jewish worship until destroyed by the Romans in A.D. 70. Although Jewish theology stressed the transcendence of God, the temple was still regarded as being the divine dwelling place. Here, pilgrims flocked to the major festivals, often traveling vast distances to be present at the Feast of Weeks, Tabernacles, and of course, the Passover.

The sheer size of the temple proclaimed its significance, giving an impression of permanence and power. Even to this day, nothing speaks more eloquently of the dominance of a religious leadership than its physical expression in buildings. Human beings are refractory. Stones stay in place. The connection between social dominance and conspicuous buildings continues, even in the secularized modern world—exemplified by the country houses of the English aristocracy, Stalin's palaces of culture, or the Vatican. By the time of Christ, the temple, which was intended to express the reality of God's invisible presence, was represented by a compromised priesthood who disguised the financial dependence of the offerings of the faithful by demanding sacrifices to the one God whose attention they commanded.

No matter how majestic and beautiful the walls, they could not hide the contradictions and hypocrisies from Jesus. In this context, Jesus predicted the temple's destruction by saying, "Not one stone will be left here upon another; all will be thrown down" (Mark 13:2, NRSV). In a similar saying, Jesus said, "Destroy this temple . . . and in three days I will raise it up" (John 2:19, NRSV). Here we discover innovative teaching that builds upon a foundation of understanding within the culture, as Jesus makes the analogy and contrast between the temple made with hands and the temple made without hands. In John 2:21, the apostle remarks, "the temple he had spoken of was his body." Although John does not say so here, we may understand the new temple to mean the Christian church in the Pauline sense (1 Cor. 3:1ff; 6:19; 2 Cor. 6:16). Thus, the cleansing of the temple in Jerusalem takes on a more profound meaning. Not only was it a demonstration of the improper use of the Lord's house, but it was also a sign that the sacrificial worship associated with the temple had come to an end. The one perfect and sufficient sacrifice was the paschal Lamb of God. As the Gospel replaced the Law, so Jesus replaced the temple with the new temple, that is, the community in which Christ is the living head.

### The Law

At the center of the Jewish faith and nationality was the Law. Not only did it provide an historical foundation for Jewish origins, but represented a tangible expression of God. It was the written basis for Judaism as delivered to Moses on Mount Sinai. Through the passage of years (which included many patriotic struggles), the Law became the symbol and bulwark of the Jewish national spirit. With the decline of the prophetic movement, it eventually occupied the center of the religious scene. As a result, this new spiritual interest focused not so much on the temple but on the Law.

Furthermore, new religious castes, distinct from the priestly, emerged with conflicting interpretations. The Pharisees were a vigorous reform movement, dedicated to faithfully keeping all the commandments. They believed that such obedience was possible through adherence to the oral Torah, which was an interpretation of the written Torah and considered of equal authority. The Sadducees, comprised predominantly of the upper class of Jerusalem, rejected the Pharisaic oral Torah, and concentrated on the sacrificial rites prescribed in the Old Testament Scripture. Finding no clear evidence of the resurrection of the dead and other eschatological doctrines in the Hebrew Bible, they rejected them. The Essenes were more withdrawn from society than other Jewish religious groups. This loyalist, Torah-centered movement had a different interpretation of the Law. (Most scholars identify the Qumran community from the Dead Sea Scrolls as Essene.) They had a strong eschatological orientation, identifying themselves as the faithful remnant of Israel. Essenes accepted the temple cults in principle, but refused to participate in it as long as Saducean priests, whom they regarded as corrupt, officiated. The Zealots, motivated by Torah loyalty and messianic expectation, were an active anti-Roman guerilla movement and, naturally, were regarded as bandits by the Romans.

Rabbi Jeshua bar-Joseph was born into the midst of these conflicting crosscurrents of religious diversity, seething messianic hopes, political maneuvering, and plots against Roman domination. Amongst Jews and as a Jew, Jesus lived his life as an itinerant teacher. His instruction was framed within the Jewish worldview, and his disciples and hearers received his words as Jews. He spoke in the Semitic tongue of Aramaic and conducted his ministry within the culture in which he lived.

## Identification:
## The Essential Meaning of the Incarnation

Christianity is well-described as the most materialistic of the world's religions. Support for this conclusion is found in the doctrine of the incarnation, which affirms the belief that the Lord God Almighty, Maker of heaven and earth, cared so much for the creation that he identified with it to the utmost by being born into this world as *vere deus, vere homo* (very God, very man). Through

**87**

Christ, God entered our world, identified with human frailty, became vulnerable to temptations and pain, bore the sins of the world, and died on its behalf. In other words, God could not have identified with humankind more completely.

There can be little doubt that the doctrine of the incarnation, along with the atonement, constitutes the very heart of Christianity. The doctrine of the incarnation lay at the heart of the great Christological disputes of the fourth and fifth centuries. In A.D. 451 at the Council of Chalcedon, it was formally affirmed that Christ is one person dwelling in two natures, united unconfusedly, indivisibly, and inseparably.

Before the advent of Christ, God's relationship with the human race was significantly more distant. The high priest acted as the chief representative of the Jewish people, functioning as a sacred mediator between God and the chosen people. Under the high priest, there existed an extensive staff of temple priests and Levites who were responsible for the offering of daily sacrifices on behalf of the people. Only within the temple, according to the legislation of Deuteronomy, could sacrificial worship be offered. Additionally, God was further represented by the prophets who spoke forth God's word, thus giving guidance to the nation.

The incarnation introduces a radical concept by which God moves into the center stage of the human arena. This unique difference is illustrated in antidotal fashion in Kierkegaard's *Philosophical Fragments.* In a parable about a king's love for a humble maiden, the king can only win the maiden's love if he lays aside his royal robes and woos her as an ordinary man in her village. There are two points here: the king must do it himself; and secondly, he must do so in a way that does not overwhelm the girl. Of course, this is only a parable for the understanding of the incarnation, and it falls short as far as the king's condescension involving only a change of clothes. However, the main point stands, that there is a difference between God being known indirectly and God coming in the person of Christ. The primary difference is that of personal identification and direct engagement with the world.

Moving beyond the world of fairy tales, we may also perceive why such identification is necessary by human analogies. In the mid-nineteenth century, the Yorkshire missionary, James Hudson Taylor, left the shores of England to begin a historic ministry in Inland China. At first his ministry bore little fruit until he identified with the ordinary people by living with them, speaking their language, practicing their customs, and wearing similar dress. Likewise, this identification was demonstrated by Father Damien in his sacrificial ministry to the lepers at Molokai by such things as constructing their dwellings, changing their dressings, as well as giving them spiritual comfort. Eventually, he died as a result of leprosy. More recently, we see Mother Teresa and her sisters working the backstreets of Calcutta, instead of remaining a concerned but physically uninvolved sympathizer of the plight for the poor and unwanted. This reality of love being incarnate in action to remain true to itself, is beautifully conveyed in the following prayer, which has been adapted from the meditation of Teresa of Avila:

Christ has no body now on earth but a human body;
   in your neighbor you see him.
Your body is Christ's dwelling place.
Your hands are the only hands
   with which he can do his work.
Yours are the only feet
   with which he can go about the world.
Yours are the only eyes
   through which his compassion
   can shine on a troubled world.
Yours are the only ears which can hear his call
   in the cries of the people.
Yours is the only mouth
   which can sing God's praise.
Christ has no body now on earth but yours.

## The Humanity of Jesus

Christ's acceptance of His true and full humanity is seen in two New Testament hymns that were used in worship life in the early church.

Who, being in the very nature God,
   did not consider equality with God
   something to be grasped,
but made himself nothing,
   taking the very nature of a servant,

being made in human likeness
And being found in appearance as a man,
he humbled himself
and became obedient to death—
even death on a cross! (Phil. 2:6-8)

In the beginning was the Word,
and the Word was with God,
And the Word was God.
He was in the beginning with God.
Through him all things were made;
without him nothing was made
that has been made (John 1:1-3).

While these two passages indicate Christ's acceptance of being born into the concrete historical actualities of human life and culture, it would seem that a certain tension existed among His followers concerning this extraordinary phenomenon of incarnation. This discomfort was seen as early as the apostolic period, where an early Christian sect known as the Docetist repudiated the human nature of Christ by maintaining that his humanity was not real and therefore concluding that His suffering was only apparent. This was followed by the Gnostic view that the incarnation was purely an appearance of God, to which the Apostle John replied:

That which was from the beginning, which we have heard, which we have seen with our eyes, which we have looked at and our hands have touched—this we proclaim concerning the Word of life. The life appeared; we have seen it and testify to it, and we proclaim to you the eternal life, which was with the Father and has appeared to us. We proclaim to you what we have seen and heard, so that you also may have fellowship with us. And our fellowship is with the Father and with his Son, Jesus Christ (1 John 1:1-3).

From the first century to the present, ancient and modern writers have consistently endeavored to throw a cloak of divinity over the humanity of Christ. Frequently, he was portrayed as empty of any qualities that would identify him as a human being—void of spontaneous feelings, empty of a distinct personality, and set apart from the human race as some kind of spiritual robot whose divine computer enabled him to bypass serious engagement in human life. However, as we read through the historical accounts of the life of Christ, there is no evidence to suggest that Jesus despised his Jewish heritage, social class, the boundaries of his human personality, nor the historical setting of his birth. Neither is there any hint that he was uncomfortable with his humanity to the extent that he found it necessary to disengage himself from human interaction in order to escape to the desert and join the Essenes. On the contrary, Jesus entered into his own time in history, with full acknowledgment of who he was—personally, spiritually, physically, culturally, socially, and historically.

### The Self-Emptying of Christ

Closely related to the incarnation is the Pauline teaching of the "self-emptying" and "self-disclosure" of Christ. Writing in the context of an early hymn in praise of Christ's acceptance of his humanity and fidelity of his human condition, Paul recorded these words, "Who, being in the very nature of God, did not consider equality with God something to be grasped, but made himself nothing, taking the very nature of a servant, being made in human likeness" (Phil. 2:6-7). According to Paul, the true *kenosis* of Jesus lay not in self-negation, but in self-embrace. The life of Christ reveals that he said a consistent "yes" to all the demands of becoming fully human. Indeed, Paul states that Jesus did not cling *(harpogmos)* to his divinity as one who despised culture, nor did he consider himself to be above and beyond human customs. Neither did he exempt himself from the needs, feelings, desires, struggles, and pain of human existence. Rather, he identified with the human experience by (as the word *kenosis* implies), "pouring" himself into human life.

As we mentioned, the historical accounts of the life of Christ reveal that Jesus embraced the Jewish heritage, social class, and the historical setting of his birth. His entire ministry was conducted within the very culture in which he lived; his instruction was framed within the Jewish worldview; and his disciples and listeners received his words as Jews. In this regard, it would be a mistake to assume that Jesus' teaching was a *hapaz phenomena* (new revelation). His concepts were not entirely revolutionary in the sense that they stood outside and apart from their historical setting. Rather, Jesus employed familiar terms, concepts, ideas,

**91**

and traditions, by adopting, modifying, and indeed transforming them, to embody a new order of reality.

## Implications of the Incarnation

There are many implications to the Christian doctrine of the incarnation. For our purposes, we shall discuss the significance of the incarnation of Christ as a model and example to the church of the need for engagement and identification with the world. First of all, perhaps a clearer distinction needs to be made between the terms "worldliness" and "involvement in the world." Worldliness is that aspect of culture that includes indulgent hedonism, reckless materialism, and selfish narcissism—all of which Christians are emphatically to reject (Luke 9:25; cf. 2 Tim. 4:10). However, when using the term "the world" in the context of what follows I will be primarily referring to the contemporary English usage of the word as "humankind," which includes God's providential and redemptive purpose for the human race.

To aid our discussion, we shall consider five theological positions pertaining to the relationship of Christ to culture and society, as suggested by the late H. Richard Niebuhr. In his book, *Christ and Culture,*[1] Niebuhr argues that there have been five types of relationships between Christ (acting through the church) and culture.

### Christ Against Culture

First, is the Christ against culture view. In this view, Christ is depicted as standing against culture, confronting the world. This characterizes the sectarian position as justified on the basis of such texts as: "No one can serve two masters; either he will hate the one and love the other, or he will be devoted to the one and despise the other. You cannot serve God and mammon" (Matt. 6:24, RSV). Thus, Christ is viewed as Lord of all. There is no middle ground.

This position brings to mind the image of a medieval drawbridge, which was interestingly enough, intended to keep intruders out. In the Middle Ages, a castle was more than a fortress providing protection. It was a living community where servants, soldiers, crafts workers, and the aristocracy lived. Many castles served as centers of local government, complete with dwellings, chapel, bakery, armory, and prison. Within the safety of the castle walls, residents remained secluded from the outside world for long periods of time, choosing when to lower and close the drawbridge. An unwelcomed force attempting to gain entrance quickly discovered a daunting series of obstacles. First, there was the moat, then an outward wall, followed by a heavily barricaded gate. If the castle happened to be a crusader castle, there would be two, perhaps three additional walls to overcome before confronting the primary defensive wall. No doubt at this point, intruders were greeted by the arrows, spears, and swords of those whose task it was to defend the castle.

In a similar way, to many Baby Boomers, the church must appear like a formidable castle, secure within its own community life, insulated from the secular wasteland outside, and protected by the heavy defensive walls of fear and misunderstanding. For those who seek entry, there are many obstacles to overcome before gaining entrance. There are daunting language walls to ascend and presuppositions regarding life-style, sexuality, and vocational issues to mount.

Perhaps the most difficult wall to climb is the wall of acceptance. Let me illustrate. Not too long ago I decided to participate in a recreational sport. As I enjoyed badminton, I joined the local health club. On the first evening, I arrived wearing shorts and a T-shirt ready for a game. When I was joined by other members, I soon realized that a dress code existed for court playing, of which I clearly had not conformed. Overcoming my growing sense of self-consciousness, I decided to soldier on in my quest to play the game. Eventually I was invited to complete a doubles team by joining three others, who while strangers to me, were obviously extremely good friends and used to competing with one another. To my dismay, I soon discovered that my fellow participants were quite advanced and possessed a detailed knowledge of the rules. Very little sympathy came my way as the volleying progressed at a rapid pace. The shots flew fast and furious. Lobs, drops, and smashes came over the net, most of which I was unable to return. When the game was over, we shook hands and parted cordially enough, but it was obvious to me that I remained the outsider. Later that evening, I noticed that the trio, joined by their regular fourth member, were obviously having a marvelous time.

The net result of my experience was that I never returned to the club, as my initial enthusiasm for the game somehow subsided.

My ordeal, however, was not all in vain. Reflecting on this experience, I wondered how many people come to church and soon feel inadequately dressed, awkward in the act of worship, unaware of the community rules and regulations, or intimidated by the closeness of the fellowship among its members. Like me, they might never return, sensing their inability to fit into the mold which is all too often culturally rather than theologically defined. Beatle member, George Harrison, as with many other Baby Boomers in the 1970s, discovered a spiritual side to his being. In searching for a spiritual meaning to his life, he was once asked whether or not he had considered going to a church. He replied that he would find it impossible to join any organization in which millions of people believed the exact same way.

In the early church, Tertullian was a somewhat forceful exponent of this antagonistic view. A rigorist and author of many theological and apologetic works, Tertullian emphasized the belief that Christians, in order to escape contamination from immorality and idolatry, must separate themselves from the world—in other words, raise the drawbridge and close the doors. In the *Apologeticum* (ca. 197), he wrote, "Our tongues, our eyes, have nothing to do with the madness of the circus, the shamelessness of the theater, the brutality of the arena, the vanity of the gymnasium." In a later work, *De praescriptione haereticorum* (ca. 200), he strongly advocated that since Christian revelation contained all truth necessary for salvation, there was therefore no need to dabble in pagan wisdom, nor to tamper with pagan culture. In regard to possible virtues of human wisdom, Tertullian wrote:

> What is there in common between Athens and Jerusalem? What difference between the Academy and the Church? What between heretics and Christians? . . . Away with all projects for a "Stoic," a "Platonic" or a "dialectic" Christianity! After Jesus Christ we desire no subtle theories, no acute enquires after the gospel.[2]

Tertullian was not alone in his view that true Christians must separate from the world. The desert fathers, the Monastic movement, the mystical traditions of the Middle Ages, the Puritans, the Methodists, and some segments of the fundamentalist traditions have upheld this view as a vital ingredient in the process of personal sanctification.

## Christ in Agreement With Culture

Second, is Christ and culture in agreement. This view, and the position previously discussed, are well-illustrated in the medieval conflict between the egocentric Peter Abelard and the pious Bernard of Clairvaux. The issue which caused these two men to lock horns centered on the controversy of whether reason and faith, inquiry and belief, logic and revelation, can live together. Abelard believed that faith was a starting point of spiritual understanding, but that faith should never be forced, nor exist without substance. Rather, faith must seek to understand what it cannot comprehend by itself. For further illumination in which faith may be nurtured, Abelard looked for support from two main sources: reason and natural theology. With regards to reason, he argued that divine revelation is to be reasoned, since it is in our reason that we are made in the image of God. Furthermore, since knowledge about God can be discovered outside the scope of divine revelation (i.e., in natural theology), then there is much to be gained from the study of non-Christian philosophical systems of thought. Far from shunning the wisdom of the past, Abelard welcomed it as a valuable resource for elucidation, as well as for providing additional resources in the apologetic defense of Christian doctrine. One could say that Abelard was attempting to do for theology, what the current Cambridge University genius Stephen Hawking is endeavoring to do for physics in his quest for a theory of everything—that is, a theory that would be nothing short of an explanation of the universe and everything that happens in it.[3] Abelard's position similarly proposed an all-embracing way of seeking truth and tried to avoid the extremes of blind faith and cold rationalism.

Bernard of Clairvaux, like Abelard, was a strong personality. He was known as a man of great devotion and piety and as a passionate defender of orthodox faith. His faith needed no explanation since it was clearly stated in Scripture and tradition. Bernard was closely related to the doctrine of fideism, which maintains that metaphysical and religious truths are inaccessible to human reason and can be grasped only by faith. Abelard saw Bernard's faith as too simple. Bernard, on the other hand, considered Abelard's views as defiling and undermining holy faith. Although Bernard was known for his "spirituality of love," that love turned to fury when he called for the silencing of Abelard at the council of Sens in 1141. Abelard incurred the hostility of Bernard and other traditionalists mainly because they considered theology more for reading in the cloister than for debate in the lecture hall. Metaphorically speaking, Abelard chose to open wide the armored gate and wander freely outside the confines of the castle to investigate the world of reason and natural theology, whereas Bernard was content to stay indoors.

### Christ Above Culture

Third, is the Christ above culture position. Throughout the history of the church, this view has expressed itself by the pursuit of a truly Christian society where natural law is synthesized with the theological virtues. Niebuhr cites Aquinas as an example of one who was able to combine natural law and divine grace. Aquinas integrated Stoic, Christian, and Aristotetlian elements within a comprehensive philosophic system. According to Aquinas, laws are standards of human conduct which have a rational origin and as such, possess a binding or obligatory character. Combining natural law with a teleological concept of nature and culture, Aquinas was able to distinguish an all-embracing, fourfold form of law which could be promulgated for the common good: eternal law (an expression of God's rational ordering of the universe); divine law (which guides individuals toward their spiritual ends); natural law (which guides individuals toward their natural ends); and human law (which regulates community life). Christ above culture signifies the infusion of divine grace into the natural order, assisting society to live up to a high level of morals and ethics fitting for the kingdom of God.

Consider the example of Thomas More. Here was a man well-acquainted with the world, having served society as a lawyer, civil servant, and eventually, the Lord Chancellor during the reign of Henry VIII. More had a vision, which he described in his book, *Utopia* (1516), of a Christian society that would live as one nation under God. For the idealist, More's vision was a truly attractive one. He described the ideal government as exercising the law of the land in a merciful way, ensuring that justice and equality prevailed for all citizens regardless of social status. In *Utopia,* the reader saw how wonderful life could be in a society where its members lived their faith according to the law of God. It is no coincidence that this book was written early in More's career, as some twenty years later he found himself writing another book entitled, *A Dialogue of Comfort Against Tribulation* while languishing in the Tower of London awaiting execution on perjured evidence in a trumped-up charge of high treason. Ironically, the term utopia, derived from the Greek *ou* and *topos,* means "no place." Thomas More discovered his idealism was shattered by his underestimation of the sinfulness and selfishness of the human heart.

Failure to take the inherent dangers seriously, in offering faith "a la carte" to a consumeristic society, may have severe consequences. It is important to remember that Baby Boomers, like no other generation before them, have radically challenged and changed every institution they have come into contact with over their brief life cycle. To understand the Baby Boomer phenomena and to welcome them back to the church is vital, but to conform to Baby Boomer culture, or to seek to synthesize it without discernment, is quite another issue. Many churches and secular organizations discovered to their peril that there is a world of difference between catering to Baby Boomer "wants" instead of meeting their "needs."

## Christ and Culture in Tension

Fourth, is Christ and culture in tension. This position acknowledges the paradox between the exclusive claims of Christ over individuals, and the reality of them living within their culture as loyal members of society. Thus, an inevitable tension exists between the individual's obedience to state and his or her conscience before God. Niebuhr refers to Paul (see Rom. 13:1-7), Luther, and Kierkegaard as examples of individuals unable to reconcile this dilemma.

This predicament of where the individual loyalties lie and to whom obedience should be given has divided Christians from the first century to the present. In former days, when people were concerned with obedience to the Emperor *and* the Pope, the complex issues relating to matters of church and state were very perplexing. Some historians and theologians considered this marriage of temporal and spiritual powers as a serious mistake, which resulted in a paralyzing compromise for the church. For example, the German theologian, Jürgen Moltmann, described the post-Constantinian church as *cultus publicus* (public cult or state religion), in that the church was busy sanctifying the existing political order to safeguard its own being. Other Christians advocated the position developed by Augustine in *The City of God* where he suggested that ecclesiastical power must be superior to secular power because the visible church represented the mystical city of God on earth. Martin Luther, however, offered no systematic political teaching of the right to resist the dictates of the state over conscience. In fact, in his treatise *Of Good Works,* Luther wrote traditional patriarchal rules for submission in a particularly emphatic form. The Protestant Reformation brought a new dimension to this dualistic tension between church and state, as it challenged a Lutheran or Calvinist to obey a Catholic prince. Similarly, a Catholic subject made the same decision regarding a Protestant prince.

This age-old friction resurrects itself in Third World countries where large numbers of people are exploited by greedy foreign investors, multinational companies, and oppressive governments. Some church officials in these underdeveloped countries believe that salvation in this context cannot be distinguished from political liberation and therefore actively work for liberation of the oppressed, the poor, and the exploited. More often than not, these leaders, such as Gustavo Gutierrez and the late Archbishop Romero, find opposition not only from the oppressing governments, but also from those conservative church people, who are more aligned with the interests of capitalism and colonialism than the needs of the poor.

### Christ the Transformer of Culture

Lastly, is the Christ the transformer of culture view. This position takes the reality of human sin seriously. It recognizes that society is under the curse of the Fall and makes no attempt to synthesize faith with culture. Rather, it views the church's role as a transformer of culture by the power of the Gospel. The biblical basis for such a stand is found in Jesus' high priestly prayer. Knowing that his time on earth was brief and his ministry limited, he prayed for his followers not to be taken "out of the world," but "sent . . . into the world" (John 17:15-18).

Before discussing the efforts made by the influential figures mentioned by Niebuhr, we will consider the contribution of that great missionary of transformation, the Apostle Paul. Whereas our previous discourse of the incarnation of Christ kept us within the narrow confines of Judea and Galilee, our discussion of Paul's phenomenal bridge-building ministry will take us to the Hellenistic world. Here, pluralism reigned and the Greek language served as a vehicle for art, music, philosophy, literature, modes of expression, worldviews, and life-styles, as well as embracing many different nationalities. The question which Paul and the later apologists[4] wrestled with was how were they to proclaim an essentially Jewish message in a Hellenistic world. In this regard, let us remember that Paul, prior to his conversion, had been a proud and somewhat arrogant Pharisee, who, along with his fellow Jews, held some strong views regarding the distinctiveness of the Jewish faith and the unique status of Israel as the exclusive people of God. Perhaps a measure of the greatness of this man is to be seen in his willingness to lay aside his religious bias and national pride in order to embrace the greater task of constructing bridges of reconciliation and hope in the Graeco-Roman world.

### The Apostle Paul: Ambassador of Transformation

A good example of Paul's bridge-building ministry is to be found in Acts 17. Here we find the apostle in Athens, participating in an informal discussion with the Greek intellectuals of his day. Athens, of course, was the museum of the classical culture of the Greek world. For Luke, the author of Acts, it was a symbol of the religion and philosophy of the Hellenistic world. It was the center for the two principle schools of philosophy in Paul's day: the Epicureans and the Stoics. To this learned audience he states:

> Men of Athens! I see that in every way you are very religious. For as I walked around and observed your objects of worship, I even found an altar with this inscription: *to an unknown god.* Now what you worship as something unknown I am going to proclaim to you. The God who made the world and everything in it is the Lord of heaven and earth and does not live in temples built by hands. And he is not served by human hands, as if he needed anything, because he himself gives all men life and breath and everything else. From one man he made every nation of men, that they should inhabit the whole earth; and he determined the times set for them and the exact places where they should live. God did this so that men would seek him and perhaps reach out for him and find him, though he is not far from each one of us. "For in him we live and move and have our being." As some of your own poets have said, "We are his offspring" (Acts 17:22-28).

**99**

This passage provides us with a sample of how the apostle was able to build bridges into the hearts of his listeners, by the careful use of their concepts and the acknowledgment of the scholars and poets that they held in high esteem. Thus, he quotes the thoughts of Epicurus, "God needs nothing from men"; Epimenides, "In him we live and move and have our being"; and Aratus, "We are his offspring." Paul also echoes the Stoic belief that "God is the source of all life." Once acknowledging these insights, the apostle goes on to announce, "In the past God overlooked such ignorance, but now he commands all people everywhere to repent. For he has set a day when he will judge the world with justice by the man he has appointed. He has given proof of this to all men by raising him from the dead" (Acts 17:30-31).

Granted, the cultural Hellenistic audience dissolved at the mention of the resurrection. True, some mocked openly, while others laconically suggested an adjournment *sind die,* (indefinite postponement), but a few accepted Paul's message. More important to our discussion, however, is the fact that from Paul's perspective, Greek wisdom, philosophy, and poetry provided hints of truth as to the nature of the only true and living God. Purged of its shortcomings, the wisdom of the day, at least in Paul's mind, provided a starting point for the presentation of the Gospel. John Stott writes, "His precedent gives us warrant to do the same, and indicates that glimmerings of truth, insights from general revelation, may be found in non-Christian authors."[5]

In an effort to express the transcultural message of the good news to his Greek contemporaries, Paul used much of the Hellenistic concepts and jargon of his day. A careful study of Paul's writings reveals a liberal use of phrases, metaphors, and terms used frequently in Hellenistic circles. For example, he uses Greek political terminology (Phil. 1:27; 3:20; Eph. 2:19); alludes to Greek games (Phil. 2:16; 3:14; 1 Cor. 9:24-27; 2 Cor. 4:8-9); employs Greek commercial terms (Phile. 18; Col. 2:14); mentions Greek legal terminology (Gal. 3:15; 4:1-2; Rom. 7:1-3); refers to the Hellenistic slave trade (1 Cor. 7:22; Rom. 7:14); and the Hellenistic celebration of emperor worship (1 Thes. 2:19).

*Other Catalysts of Transformation*
Niebuhr cites Augustine, Calvin, and the influential Anglican theologian F.D. Maurice as examples of Christian leaders who have

attempted to convert and improve the quality of human culture in the name of Christ.

In Augustine's *The City of God,* the theme of human society is an important feature. Basically, he examines history through the analogue of two cities — the city of God and the city of earth. Even though the earthly city represents all that is evil in human history, it is not without redeeming qualities. For example, a nation may seek war, but the good in war is the peace it seeks. Not only does Augustine take the power of sin in human life and its negative effects on all earthly institutions seriously, but he also stresses the potential transformational effects which redemption in Christ could bring to the whole fabric of human life. Furthermore, Augustine stresses that the heavenly city cannot live in this world without being intermingled with the city of earth.

> So also the earthly city, whose life is not based on faith, aims at an earthly peace, and it limits the harmonious agreement of citizens concerning the giving and obeying of orders to the establishment of a kind of compromise between human wills about the things relevant to mortal life. In contrast, the Heavenly City — or rather that part of it which is on pilgrimage in this condition of mortality, and which lives on the basis of faith — must [sic] needs make use of this peace also, until this mortal state, for which this kind of peace is essential, passes away.[6]

Calvin also stressed that humans are creatures of fellowship, who have been created with tendencies that will find fulfillment in two main groupings, namely, church and state. Calvin saw these two institutions differentiated by their different tasks. The church should be concerned primarily with the spiritual realm, whereas the state's principal business should lie in the temporal realm. The transformational theme is demonstrated in Calvin's belief that the church should seek the spiritual welfare of the state, and the state should promote piety among its citizens and apply the law of God to the affairs of civil society.

Niebuhr writes of the Anglican theologian, F.D. Maurice, in the following terms:

> In Maurice, the conversionist idea is more clearly expressed than in any other modern Christian thinker and leader. His

**101**

attitude toward culture is affirmative throughout, because he takes most seriously the conviction that nothing exists without the Word. It is thoroughly conversionist and never accommodating, because he is most sensitive to the perversion of human culture, as well in its religious as in its political and economic aspects. It is never dualistic; because he has cast off all ideas about the corruption of spirit through body, and about the separation of mankind into redeemed and condemned. Furthermore, he is consistent in rejecting negative action against sin; and always calls for positive, confessional, God-oriented practice in church and community.[7]

F.D. Maurice and many others make it clear that in Christ, the radical distinction between the sacred and the secular is overcome. To Maurice, the church is "human society in its normal state; the World that same society, irregular and abnormal. The World is the Church without God; the Church is the World taken back by Him into the state for which he created it."[8]

Furthermore, love of one's neighbor and the obligation to give Caesar his due, requires the followers of Jesus to engage in the world as salt and light. It was this conviction that gave birth to a variety of Christian social movements that reacted to the plight of industrial workers, calling for institutional changes in the political and social order. Association with such activism on behalf of the working class distinguished such figures as the Scottish Presbyterian, Thomas Chalmers, and Anglicans, John Malcolm Ludlow and Charles Kingsley. It was the incarnational theology of the Evangelical-Methodist movement that caused black slavery and the slave trade to be abolished in the British Empire in 1807. To those oppressed victims of economic injustice, the message proclaimed by the Christian socialists of social change and economic justice for the poor, captives, and the oppressed was the best news they had heard for a long time.

However, in the twentieth century, the evangelical movement in the United States, much like its British counterpart, began to change. At one time, it was at the frontlines of struggles for the abolition of slavery, economic injustice, and the establishment of women's rights. However, when America became affluent, many evangelicals compromised the radical message of transformation, which lay at the heart of Christian socialism, and were assimilated into the mainstream of middle-class America. Today, few evangelicals are recognized as transformers of human culture, or as having genuine sympathy for the impoverished hoi polloi of North America. Rather, their bias is more affiliated with the American Dream than the kingdom of God, seen by the emphasis placed on such themes as prosperity (viewing wealth as a sign of divine favor), success, and prestige. Ironically, a movement that once fought to free slaves and support industrial workers, now has a reputation for accommodating racism and for laissez-faire sentiments regarding social justice issues.

## Transformational Ministry to Baby Boomers

We have discovered that the incarnation of Christ into his culture extended beyond mere words, speeches, and promises to that of "action," bridging forever the age-old dilemma between faith and works. With great compassion, Jesus reached deep into those places of loneliness, fear, and need. As the church, theologically speaking, is the extension of the incarnation, in order to be faithful to its master, it must also take its divine mandate seriously to be a transformational agent in the world. This transformation can only occur, however, if the church is willing to break the ghetto mentality that leads to myopic parochialism. To get on with its mission of being "in the world but not of the world" the church must become an agent of transformation, all the while resisting the ever-present dangers of assimilation into the Baby Boomer cultural ethos and thus compromising the transcultural message of the Gospel.

Breaking the "holy huddle syndrome" and becoming truly incarnational involves three things: understanding, communication, and association.

### Understanding

All good missionaries recognize that authentic ministry begins with a reflective comprehension of the culture, myths, and worldview held by those to whom he or she has been called to serve. In my experience as a young Anglican minister, serving the Innuit in the Canadian High Arctic, my first task was to learn to speak fluent Inuktitut. This complex and fascinating language was not easily mastered. Indeed, it took years of daily language study to understand how the intricate pieces of the grammatical puzzle worked together. The whole procedure of acquiring the language seemed at times painfully slow and extremely frustrating. However, in the process of studying the words, I also learned something of the complexities of the Inuk mind. I am convinced that my modest comprehension of the culture made my preaching more relevant and my pastoral counseling more sensitive than if I had chosen the easier route through a translator.

Likewise, ministry to Baby Boomers begins with understanding. Thus, this book begins with a discussion of the historical roots and events that shaped this unique generation. As a subculture they have many distinctive features. They are highly innovative, well-educated, curious, and exceptionally influential. They enjoy particular forms of music and possess exclusive forms of language and dress codes. Their lives are governed by a self-determined set of priorities, and their generation is without parallel in history. Clearly, any attempt to reach out in ministry to them must first begin with identification and understanding.

### Communication
The Innuit are great storytellers and as such, people frequently gather around the local raconteur to hear a good story, which would typically be full of anecdotes, humor, myth, hope, and tragedy. I can recall many such gatherings and feeling thoroughly frustrated at my inability to comprehend much of the content of these sagas. People would laugh whereas I could not see the wit. Others would understand the hidden message, while my comprehension remained quite superficial.

Communication essentially means the sharing of information by means of words whose meaning is understood by the audience. Jesus was a master of communication, as evidenced in his extensive use of parables. Paul was also eager to ensure that his communication was clearly understood by his listeners. Indeed, his extensive use of Greek idioms, buzzwords, common lingo, and the unique contribution that the Greek language played in the spreading of the Christian message cannot be underestimated.

This implies that if the Gospel is to be relevant and our evangelistic pursuits among Baby Boomers successful, we must learn not only to employ the language of the day, but also to address the prevailing issues that exist. I remember as a very young Christian being invited to a series of Bible studies, which I was informed would be "life-transforming." Anxious to grow in my newfound

**104**

faith, having virtually no knowledge of authentic Christianity, except that which I had inadvertently picked up from the so-called Christian cultural environment of Great Britain in the late 1960s, I went along to hear these "life-changing" seminars. Much to my surprise, the discourses turned out to be a series of twenty-five lectures on the significance of Aaron's breastplate! Interesting? Perhaps. Life changing? Hardly!

When was the last time that you heard a sermon addressing such cultural issues as secularism, pragmatism, pluralism, hedonism, or even strategies to help Christians get involved in community service? Are you able to recall seminars in your church which brought to your attention such social issues as feminism, racism, and social justice, or the effects of urbanization on the individual, not to mention global issues such as environmental stewardship, multiculturalism, and human rights? As these are areas of common interest and concern with Boomers, it would seem logical that any attempt to address these issues from a Christian perspective would enable the church to build significant bridges of communication with them.

### Association

Another vital component in the missionary enterprise, coexisting with the acquisition of a new language, is personal involvement in the life of the community. Again, during my experience in the northern extreme of Baffin Island, it soon became apparent that if I was to be accepted into the life of the community, my presence had to be seen to be felt. This involved learning to hunt and dress seal and caribou, build an igloo, make a sled, repair a Ski-Doo engine, and maintain my boat and motor. It also meant being involved in the social life of the community and taking an active role in the various political ramifications of life in a community that had rocketed from the stone age to the modern age in less than fifty years.

Prior to my ministry among the Innuit, I was fortunate to discover the writings of Martin Buber, who influenced my life and understanding of ministry. In his book, *I—Thou,*[9] Buber expressed his conviction that human beings find their deepest intimacy with God when engaged in wholesome associations with others. He distinguished between two kinds of human relationships—the impersonal and the intimate.

**105**

The former, he called the I—IT encounter, which at best are those rather formal and objective relationships, and at worst, those destructive and manipulative encounters. Essentially, the I—IT relationship describes those encounters in which we treat each other as objects or as mere things to be used. I suspect most of us have had some degree of firsthand knowledge of the I—IT relationship, given the fact that we live in an increasingly technological world in which our interpersonal relationships have been seriously undermined. Sadly, these relationships are not found exclusively in our professional lives, but also among our fellowship in the Body of Christ.

In contrast to the I—IT relationships which dominate our society, Buber described those human encounters that spring from the basis of mutual respect, which he called I—Thou. According to Buber, when a human encounter occurs in a true spirit of openness and in the mutuality of dialogue then at that moment we stand also before God. Although Buber did not subscribe to the Christian faith as such, his insights call to mind the incarnation in which God addressed us in the I—Thou relationship in the person of Jesus of Nazareth—and indeed with all those who bear for us the holy presence.

The obvious message that we can take from the insight of this Jewish philosopher is that the love of God is unreal and intangible unless it is crowned with a genuine association and practical love for others. And that love is essential, rooted in a sacred bond of respect for the inexpressible worth and value of other human beings, regardless of creed, color, or social class, recognizing that we are all created in the image of God.

Perhaps one of the greatest stumbling blocks that the Christian community must overcome is the all-pervasive fear that association with the world will inevitably lead to spiritual contamination. Although such a position is correct in emphasizing the constant danger of compromise when entering into dialogue with others who share divergent views, the incarnation of Christ does not permit a faith to separate from a true identification with others. Possibly without the example of the incarnation, the church can take safe refuge in theological reflection, mystic contemplation, and philosophical idealism, matching itself with the ideas of Platonism, Buddhism, and Quietism. However, because of the incarnation, Christianity becomes much more than mere speculative theology; it becomes essentially a faith which seeks to identify with people. In a spirit of humility, it challenges the worldviews of others with the truth of the good news of God in Christ.

The incarnation of Christ, the example of Paul, and the testimony of countless other Christian leaders lead us to believe that within human culture, the *imago Dei* may be discerned. Moreover, because all truth is God's truth, it can be put to use as a handmaiden for communicating the good news of the transcultural Gospel of God. It is to this task of critique, contextualization, and discernment we now turn as we reflect on Baby Boomer culture from a Christian perspective.

# PART THREE

# BRIDGE-BUILDING TODAY: THE TRANSFORMING MESSAGE OF THE GOSPEL

# Chapter 4
# THEOLOGICAL PERSPECTIVES ON BABY BOOMER CULTURE

There are a plurality of bridges that span the world's waterways: there are fixed ones such as the arch, cantilever, and the suspension bridge; also movable bridges such as the swing, bascule, rolling pontoon; or the famous Baily Bridge which can be easily moved, quickly assembled, and is capable of transporting heavy loads. Just as there are many types of bridges, so pluralism asserts that reality in its essence is not to be found in monism, but rather in many different principles and substances.

### Pluralism and the Uniqueness of Christ
Some years ago as a young theological neophyte, I was introduced to a new aspect of religious studies — comparative religion. Given the incredible diversity of the surrounding culture, it was not difficult to see the potential value of such a seminar. After all, North America was built on a kaleidoscope of different traditions, including ethnic groups ranging alphabetically from ABC (aboriginal, British, Chinese) to Z (Zambian). Most people lived in neighborhoods or had close friends of diverse ethnic or racial backgrounds. In any given major city, one heard various mother tongues and experienced a host of ethnic restaurants offering the pallet exoteric delights ranging from burritos to chapatis, dim sum to paella, sauerbraten to haggis! Furthermore, North America was home to

a multitude of Christian denominations as well as members of the Jewish, Muslim, Sikh, Hindu, and Buddhist faiths. This seminar on comparative religion was a course designed to help the student recognize what the world's great religions had in common. If I remember correctly, most of the seminar revolved around the idea that all religions worshiped a transcendent being, all religions led to God in one form or another, and that all shared a common ethical and moral code.

I was never quite convinced by such an expansive claim that all religions shared a common core of belief. The more I read and reflected on this, the more I became aware of the superficiality of this position. In fact, as I began to prod into the faith and worldviews promoted by the great historical religions, I saw just how incompatible they were on basic issues. One only had to contrast the various beliefs on such issues as: the nature of God, the origins and significance of humankind, the meaning of sin, and the way of salvation to see what stark differences existed.

One of the greatest dangers of pluralism within the Christian faith is the challenge it presents to traditional Christian understanding of the uniqueness of Jesus Christ. We will discuss two tenets of the Christian faith which bear witness to the uniqueness of Christ: the incarnation and the crucifixion. These two incredible events are central to the Christian faith and are unparalleled among the world's great faiths. Regardless of the pressures of religious pluralism, these two central features must not be compromised.

As far as ministry to Baby Boomers is concerned, it should be remembered that this generation has been absent from the church for an extensive time. Given the climate of pluralism, combined with biblical illiteracy of basic Christian beliefs, many Boomers have a fuzzy picture of Jesus as being one great religious leader among many. Therefore, the church has the responsibility to point out that although other faiths are to be respected and contain some aspects of truth in agreement with Christianity, the incarnation boldly proclaims that Jesus alone is Lord. John Randolph Taylor writes:

> Christ stands alone in all the history of the world. He holds a place in the faith of Christians which is totally distinct from the place held by the founders of other religions in the minds

**112**

of their followers. He is infinitely more to those who believe in him than Moses is to the Jew, or Sakya Muni is to the Buddhist, or Mohammed is to the Moslem. These men were important, exceedingly so, to the minds of millions, but their importance is primarily historical. They gave the initial impulse to certain movements in history, stamping them somewhat with their own personalities, but . . . it is not so with Christ; he is unique.[1]

Paul describes the message of the cross as "the power of God for salvation to everyone who has faith" (Rom. 1:16, NRSV). It should not surprise us then that the preaching of the cross has always been at the heart of the Christian proclamation. Karl Barth regarded the message of salvation as the heart of the church's dogmatics. Theological truth may be timeless. However, the church in every age must grapple with the task of how to best present the Gospel to its generation in its particular cultural setting. It seems to me that today's message of the cross has a particular bearing in calling people from the culturally encouraged sin of self-fixation. In North America, especially among Baby Boomers, "I" is much more than the ninth letter and the third vowel of the English alphabet. It has become a way of life!

The inherent sin of self-love *(amour de soi)* is twofold. First, excessive self-centeredness effectively dethrones God as center of the universe and consequently places the individual in the place of the divine. This is the original sin or in Augustine's words, "the primal destruction of man." Of course, Augustine is referring to the events of the Fall, where humankind's rightful place in the universe was tested by a simple prohibition, related to the freedom of the knowledge of good and evil. God commanded, "You may freely eat of every tree of the garden; but of the tree of the knowledge of good and evil you shall not eat, for in the day that you eat of it you shall die" (Gen. 2:16-17, RSV). The underlying motive behind the act of disobedience resulted from the human desire to "be like God" (Gen. 3:5).

Secondly, self-love is often a mere step from self-pride *(amour propre)*, which some psychiatrists believe leads to the clinical disorder of narcissism. Theologians, on the other hand, use the term "sin" to describe this state. Interestingly, the moral teaching of the church lists pride first in its itemization of the seven capital sins: pride, covetousness, lust, envy, gluttony, anger, and sloth. When the church makes this judgment, it is of course not referring to a healthy form of self-pride that is necessary for wholesomeness. Rather, it is referring to destructive hubris that leads to arrogance, boasting, and self-exaltation. Scripture considers this form of pride as the very root and essence of sin (Isa. 2:6-22; Zeph. 3:11-13; Ezek. 16:49ff; Amos 6:8; 1 John 2:16) and therefore warns of the dangers of self-serving pride (Mark 7:22; Rom. 2:3; James 3:5-16), and spiritual pride (Luke 18:9-14). Pride accounts for the downfall of powerful nations such as Assyria (Isa. 10:12), Babylon (Jer. 50:29-32), and the Ammonites (Zeph. 2:8–3:20). Presumptive individuals such as Uzziah (2 Chron. 26:16), Nebuchadnezzar (Dan. 5:20) and perhaps Paul's coworker, Demas (2 Tim. 4:10) lost their way as a result of pride. Jesus made it clear that self-denial was a prerequisite for discipleship when he said, "If any want to become my followers, let them deny themselves and take up their cross and follow me. For those who want to save their life will lose it, and those who lose their life for my sake, and for the sake of the gospel, will save it" (Mark 8:34-35, NRSV).

Augustine describes pride as "the start of every kind of sin . . . a longing for a perverse kind of exaltation."[2] Many in this generation have discovered, at great personal cost, that their preoccupation with the pursuit of self has effectively cut them off from God and socially isolated them from friends and associates, leaving them alienated and lonely. It follows then that the preaching of the cross today must address this issue and proclaim Christ as the divine rescuer from the "sin of the first person singular."

We will now consider the history and significance of these two major tenets of our faith, which represent both the uniqueness of Christ and the very heart of Christian theology.

### The Incarnation
The incarnation is an event of unequaled significance in history and a unique feature of Christianity. The church has always fought to preserve its belief in God's self-revelation in the Law and through the Prophets and yet maintain that God is supremely manifest in the person of Jesus Christ (Heb. 1:1-3).

According to the witness of Scripture, God had a specific plan for the world, which began at creation, was activated by the events of the Fall, continued in the election of Israel, and culminated in

**114**

"the fullness of time" when Christ came into the world as one "born of a woman, born under law" (Gal. 4:4; cf. Eph. 1). This great drama of redemption is often referred to by the German word, *heilsgeschichte,* which means "salvation-history." It describes the sacred events of human history in which God takes the initiative to effect salvation for the sin of the world. The incarnation is the supreme consummating act of God to accomplish this plan.

In the Old Testament, the uniqueness of the Christ event is foretold by predictive prophecy, typology, and phraseology, which reappears in the New Testament. The Gospels depict Jesus as an authentic human being, subject to such human weakness as temptation (Luke 4:13), sorrow (John 11:35), anger (Mark 3:5), weariness (John 4:6), thirst (John 19:28), and suffering (Luke 22:15).

At the same time, the New Testament also affirms that Jesus is Lord, and is the Messiah and Son of God (John 1:14; 1 Cor. 8:5-6; Phil. 2:6-11; Col. 1:15-17; 2:9), which was substantiated by the uniqueness of Jesus' ministry. He had authority to heal and forgive sins (Mark 2:1-12), to reinterpret the sacred law of Moses in such a way that his own law transcended the former revelation (Matt. 5:33-47). He presented himself as the final judge of the living and the dead, judging according to obedience to his word (Matt. 25:31-46).

Attempts to comprehend the mystery of the incarnation led to a host of distorted beliefs that threatened to detract from the uniqueness of the incarnational event. Indeed, the first five centuries of the church concentrated its entire theological interest on Christologically related issues. For example, the Adoptionists declared that Christ was merely an inspired man like the prophets. The Docetists claimed that Christ's suffering was not real, and the Ebionites rejected the divinity of Christ as well as the Virgin Birth. Apollinarianism, Monophysitism, and Monothelitism all declared that the incarnation was simply God masquerading as a human being, while Arianism declared that Jesus was an intermediary being, semi-divine and semi-human.

It was these crosscurrents of diverse thought that caused the church to express its understanding of the biblical doctrine of the Person of Christ. The two most important statements made in the language of the day were the Chalcedon definition and the Athanasian Creed. To the Adoptionists, orthodox Christology declared that Christ was "one substance with the Father"; to the Apol-

**115**

linarianists, Christ was "fully human, true humanity"; and to Arianists, He was "truly God and truly man." Wisely, the Chalcedonian fathers saw the need to devise a definition that would rule out all Christological heresies. This denotation was in itself not a full explanation. As a result, it has been more criticized in modern times than any other ancient creed — largely on the inappropriate grounds that it raises too many questions. But the definition was never intended to be a systematic statement on the Person of Christ. It was an attempt to simply rule out heresies. It may be of some interest to note that from time to time, divergent views similar to those held by the previously mentioned groups have reappeared in the Christology of such sects as the Jehovah Witnesses, Christadelphians, Mormons, Moonies, and others. The statement made by the Council of Chalcedon (451) reaffirms the definitions of Nicea (325) and Constantinople (381) by stating:

> Therefore, following the holy Fathers, we all with one accord teach men to acknowledge one and the same Son, our Lord Jesus Christ, at once complete in Godhead and complete in manhood, truly God and truly man, consisting also of a reasonable soul and body; of one substance with the Father as regards his manhood; like us in all respects, apart from sin; as regards his Godhead, begotten of the Father before the ages, but yet as regards his manhood begotten, for us men and for our salvation, of Mary the Virgin, the God-bearer; one and the same Christ, Son, Lord, Only-begotten, recognized IN TWO NATURES, WITHOUT CONFUSION, WITHOUT CHANGE, WITHOUT DIVISION, WITHOUT SEPARATION; the distinction of natures being in no way annulled by the union, but rather the characteristics of each nature being preserved and coming together to form one person and subsistence, not as parted or separated into two persons, but one and the same Son and Only-begotten God the Word, Lord Jesus Christ; even as the prophets from earliest times spoke of him, and our lord Jesus Christ himself taught us, and the creed of the Fathers has handed down to us.[3]

Perhaps the greatest threat to the uniqueness of the Person of Christ in today's society comes from issues associated with religious pluralism. For example, John Hick strongly recommends that contemporary Christians move away from rigid Christocentrism, and he predicts that during the next hundred years most educated Christians will take a pluralistic understanding of the religious life of the world for granted:

> We cannot know how the developing picture will look in a hundred years' time. But if we may take the Western intellectual turmoil of the late nineteenth century as a case study, we see there at work a realistic tendency of the human mind to come to terms with new and initially disturbing knowledge. In the nineteenth century the fresh information concerned the development of life on earth. Looking back, we find that the knowledge disseminated through the debates about evolution has gradually transformed the thinking of the Christian churches. Today the new challenge comes from a flood of information about the wider religious life of humanity. And if the historical analogy provides any indication of what is likely to happen during the next hundred or so years we may expect that in due course most educated Christians will have come to take for granted a pluralistic understanding of the religious life of the world, with Christianity seen as part of that life.[4]

This call for Christians to make the paradigm shift from the traditional understanding of the lordship of Christ leaves Christian mission in a quandary, as it suggests that evangelism is passé. Geoffrey Parrinder reinforces the modern missionary dilemma. He states that in a pluralistic world order, "Christians can only continue to bear witness on the basis of the gospel record; yet as a practical matter they can only expect this witness to find acceptance chiefly among idolaters and illiterates. Theistic Hindus, Buddhists, Jews and Muslims are unlikely to respond."[5] On the other hand, Walter Kasper expresses grave concern over such a position.

> These views are all splendid and ingenious projects. . . . Nevertheless their intrinsic danger must not be overlooked, which consists in transforming the uniqueness of Jesus Christ into something universal and ending with a Christianity which is found anonymously everywhere in mankind, paying for its universality by the loss of its concreteness and uniqueness of meaning.[6]

**117**

Lesslie Newbigin, theologian, author, and missionary of some forty years in India, also expresses caution in the church's quick acceptance of Karl Rahner's position, namely that non-Christians have a salvific role. Reflecting on his missionary experience, he states in a positive way that, "Anyone who has had intimate friendship with a devout Hindu or Muslim would find it impossible to believe that the experience of God of which his friend speaks is simply illusion or fraud."[7] Newbigin's position certainly *seems* logical in that a devout Muslim must be considered closer to the kingdom of God than the cultured Christian, who neither believes nor obeys any of the Gospel injunctions. Against the inclusive view, however, Newbigin states:

> As a human race we are on a journey and we need to know the road. It is not true that all roads lead to the top of the same mountain. There are roads which lead over the precipice. In Christ we have been shown the road. We cannot treat that knowledge as a private matter for ourselves. It concerns the whole human family. We do not presume to limit the might and the mercy of God for the ultimate salvation of all people, but the same costly act of revelation and reconciliation which gives us that assurance also requires us to share with our fellow pilgrims the vision that God has given us the route we must follow and the goal to which we must press forward.[8]

In summarizing his own position Newbigin writes:

> The position which I have outlined is exclusivist in the sense that it affirms the unique truth of the revelation in Jesus Christ, but it is not exclusivist in the sense of denying the possibility of the salvation of the non-Christian. It is inclusivist in the sense that it refuses to limit the saving grace of God to the members of the Christian Church, but it rejects the inclusivism which regards the non-Christian religions as vehicles of salvation. It is pluralist in the sense of acknowledging the gracious work of God in the lives of all human beings, but it rejects a pluralism which denies the uniqueness and decisiveness of what God has done in Jesus Christ.[9]

Stated briefly, it is Christianity's claim that "Jesus is Lord" and that in him alone salvation is to be found. Stephen Neill neatly summarizes the issue in the following way.

> Simply as history the event of Jesus Christ is unique. Christian faith goes a great deal further in its interpretation of that event. It maintains that in Jesus the one thing that needed to happen has happened in such a way that it need never happen again. . . . Making such claims, Christians rebound to affirm that all men need the Gospel. For the human sickness there is one specific remedy, and this is it. There is no other. Therefore the Gospel must be proclaimed to the ends of the earth and to the end of time. The Church cannot compromise on its missionary task without ceasing to be the Church. If it fails to see and to accept this responsibility it is changing the Gospel into something other than itself. . . . Naturally, to the non-Christian hearer this must sound like crazy megalomania, and religious imperialism of the very worst kind. We must recognize the dangers; Christians have on many occasions fallen into both of them. But we are driven back ultimately on the question of truth.[10]

### The Cross

The provocative Scottish theologian, P.T. Forsyth, who wrote extensively about the reconciling work of Christ, stated that "the canon for the incarnation . . . is soteriological. It is the work of Christ that gives us the key to the nature of Christ."[11]

As we look at the Christian doctrine of salvation in contrast to the various paths outlined in other world faiths, we discover yet another unique feature of the Christian faith. In these other religions, humans are found to be in search of God, whereas in Christianity we find the situation reversed: God takes the initiative and comes in search of us. Thus, Paul wrote, "God shows his love for us in that while we were yet sinners, Christ died for us" (Rom. 5:8, RSV). The three parables in Luke 15 illustrate this point further. Each parable is united by the singular theme of looking for lost items—sheep, coin, and son. Significant to our discussion is the fact that it is Jesus as shepherd (15:3-7), housewife (15:8-10), and father (15:11-31), who actively seeks and saves. Not only does this point to the infinite value of the individual to God (Isa. 40:11), but it reveals that humankind is the object of God's relentless search.

**119**

This saving work of Christ is usually expressed in three key words: redemption, justification, and atonement. Let us now consider each of them briefly.

Redemption means emancipation—the liberation of those that are enslaved. In the Old Testament, it was a term used in the context of the divine act of deliverance, such as when Israel was set free from her Egyptian masters (Deut. 7:8). The Apostle Paul used the concept of redemption to express his belief that through Christ, the people of God were delivered from the bondage of sin, demonic powers, and the Law (Eph. 1:7; Col. 1:14; Rom. 3:24-25). A slight paradox exists in that a person set free from one form of slavery becomes a slave of Christ (1 Cor. 6:19-20). However, this one form of slavery is actually liberation, of which the Anglican Prayer Book states, "whose service is perfect freedom."

Justification means acquittal—the passing of a verdict of not guilty. This court of law terminology gives us some insight into Paul's thinking. As a Pharisee, he had a tremendous law-central concept of the Old Testament. We also know from Romans 7 that Paul felt the sharpness of the law's demands and was aware of the difficulty of living up to them. For Paul, becoming a Christian must have been a liberating experience knowing that while he was unable to keep the demands of the law, Christ had met these demands on his behalf.

Atonement fundamentally means the bringing together of those who have been separated in order to seek a peaceful resolution and restoration of the relationship. As we all know, in our human relationships there is a cause and effect phenomena which occurs when we hurt each other. The cause may be a betrayal, a lie, the breaking of a trust, or a serious misunderstanding. The effect of such actions often leads to pain, coolness in the relationship, and possible estrangement. Unless one party (usually the guilty one) actively seeks to restore the relationship, it simply deteriorates and a gulf widens. The Scottish theologian, Donald Baillie, in a marvelous book on the incarnation, offers the following simile:

> We may, I think, find at least a faint analogy of this in the love of a true friend who receives a grave wrong but who generously forgives. If I play my friend false behind his back in a weak moment, basely betraying his confidence, and he discovers it, will he pass over it lightly, without any painful

**120**

explanation and restoration? If he is a shallow soul, and not a very true friend, he may treat the matter in that light way, for the sake of comfortable relations, because he does not care very deeply for me. But he cannot do that if he is a good man and a true friend who loves me deeply. It is not that he will be slow to forgive me; but his forgiveness will not be a good-natured indulgence. It will come out of an inexorable fire of love which I shall shrink from facing. I shall be far more afraid to meet him and look him in the face than I should be if he were a shallow friend. So great a thing is his forgiveness.

But if these things are true, it is also true that in the whole great process of forgiveness it is my friend that has the hardest part to play. It is he that bears the brunt. He suffers more than I. Not because he is the person that has been wronged: nay, it is the shame of what I have done that weighs most on him. He bears my shame as if it were his own, because of his great love for me. He bears more of the agony than I, because he is a better man and loves more deeply. And it is out of all this noble anguish that his forgiveness comes. All that is what lies behind it.

How much more deeply all these things must be true of God, both in His judgment of our sins and in His "atonement" for them![12]

The remarkable contrast between our approach to reconciliation and grace of the Lord is that it is God, the innocent party, who seeks the reconciliation. How God achieved this reconciliation, and what exactly occurred on the cross of Christ, has occupied Christian thinkers for centuries. All are in agreement, however, that on the cross, through Christ, God was reconciling "to himself all things, whether things on earth or things in heaven, by making peace through his blood, shed on the cross" (Col. 1:20; cf. Rom. 5:6-11).

While theories on the atonement vary, the consequences are clearly stated. The New Testament boldly proclaims that through the incarnation, death, and resurrection of Jesus, sin is forgiven (Rom. 5:18-19), and atonement is made (Rom. 8:1-4). This reconciliation brings the opportunity of a new beginning (2 Cor. 5:17), where death is conquered (1 Cor. 15:55). It also allows the individual to again be a partaker of the divine nature of God (2 Peter 1:4) and be progressively refashioned "until Christ is formed in you" (Gal. 4:19). To be "in Christ" is to be incorporated into the body of Christ (1 Cor. 12:12).

## Relativism and the Question of Truth

Jesus said, "the truth will make you free" (John 8:32, NRSV), to which Walter Lippman replied, "We can say the truth will make us free, but that truth is a thousand truths which grow and change." There are two main philosophical systems of thought which deny the possibility of absolute truth—relativism and skepticism.

### Relativism

As previously discussed, relativism maintains that truth is entirely culture-specific and as such has no timeless validity. It argues that in light of the fact that our contemporary intellectual axioms, philosophical categories, and worldviews have significantly changed from those of a previous age, it would be absurd to argue that ancient truth is as true today as it was in the past. Supposedly, the Athenian philosopher, Cratylus, refused to discuss anything and as such only wiggled his finger to indicate that he had heard the information before. It would be pointless to reply, he maintained, since everything was in a constant state of change. Relativists use the analogy of a flowing river to illustrate that one cannot step into the same water twice, as it is constantly moving. Samuel Butler reflected this view when he wrote, "There is no permanent absolute unchangeable truth; what we should pursue is the most convenient arrangement of our ideas."[13]

This is not to say that relativism insults the wisdom of the past, or attempts to detract from the greatness of the intellectual giants of a bygone era. Rather, it seeks to point out that the modern world is irreducibly and unalterably different from the past, and as such, affects our understanding of truth. Obviously, such a view strikes at the very root of the church's view of its history and the theological continuity of its traditional teaching on matters of faith and dogma. Put simply, relativism claims that Holy Scripture and the historic creeds can no longer be considered authoritative.

### Skepticism

Like most young people, I was a curious child and at times it seemed difficult for me to accept a given issue at face value. I

**122**

always felt the need to understand "why" things were the way they were. This constant questioning and probing often exasperated my parents, who on occasion would throw up their hands in frustration and say, "Jim, you are such a skeptic!" To which, of course I in my innocence would reply, "Why?" As I grew more aware of the world, I realized that history had a long list of skeptics—Sextus Empiricus, Montaigne, Bayle, Hume, Santayana, and Camus. Furthermore, I became aware of a philosophical system that was in place to act as a gadfly for the many different "truth claims" over the years.

Generally speaking, skepticism questions whether there is sufficient evidence to support a particular belief and if such evidence can be substantiated in the light of critical analysis. In theology, skeptics raise a variety of tricky epistemological questions about the reliability of Scripture and the literal, allegorical, analogical, and anagogical hermeneutical principals used in biblical interpretation. Extreme skeptics maintain that absolute knowledge may be sought, but it can never be found. Therefore, human beings, especially those who are drawn to dogmatism and fundamentalism, ought to get used to the idea that in this transient life, we can be certain of nothing. To substantiate this rather pessimistic claim, skeptics point to the following three factors: (1) In almost every area of knowledge, there exist insoluble contradictions from theologians, metaphysicians, philosophers, and scientists regarding the nature of reality. (2) Human beings have no adequate norm by which to judge the objectivity of truth. In other words, if truth were to come knocking on our door would we recognize it and bid it welcome? The skeptic thinks not. (3) Skeptics argue that since our senses are finite, corrupt, and defective faculties, they constitute an unreliable receptacle to receive and transmit truth.

The skeptic's position suggests that since it is impossible to prove anything beyond a shadow of a doubt, we can therefore never be certain of the truthfulness of our knowledge. Such a conclusion leaves the inquiring individual with a question: Is there no source of absolute truth where we may put our trust? The Christian answer to that question is found in the doctrine of divine revelation.

### God's Self-Revelation
Revelation means the manifestation of something hidden. In theological terms, general revelation refers to God's self-disclosure in

**123**

the created order, in the moral consciousness of humanity, and in human reason (Rom. 1:18ff; 2:14-16). Special revelation refers to the divine disclosure of certain truths in propositional form about the nature of God, the incarnation, the trinity, and so on. As these truths, necessary for salvation, could not be concluded by human reason alone, God took the initiative to insure that these epiphany events were faithfully recorded in the pages of Holy Scripture. Thus, the Scriptures are not simply the product of mere human ingenuity, but rather the product of divine inspiration. Both Paul and Peter affirm this view when they write:

> All Scripture is God-breathed and is useful for teaching, rebuking, correcting, and training in righteousness (2 Tim. 3:16).

> Above all, you must understand that no prophecy of Scripture came about by the prophet's own interpretation. For prophecy never had its origin in the will of man, but by men spoke from God as they were carried along by the Holy Spirit (2 Peter 1:20-21).

This theme of divine revelation is also echoed in the writings of early Christian theologians such as Clement of Rome who wrote, "You have studied the Holy Scriptures, which are true and inspired by the Holy Spirit."[14] In a similar fashion, Clement of Alexandria wrote, "I could adduce ten thousand Scriptures of which not one tittle shall pass away without being fulfilled; for the mouth of the Lord, the Holy Spirit has spoken these things."[15] Augustine also wrote on this matter in *The Harmony of the Gospels.*

> Therefore, when those disciples [the evangelists] have written matters which He declared and spoke to them, it ought not by any means to be said that He has written nothing Himself; since the truth is, that His members have accomplished only what they became acquainted with by the repeated statements of the Head. For all that He was minded to give for our perusal on the subject of His own doings and sayings, He commanded to be written by those disciples, whom He thus used as if they were His own hands.[16]

In the Old Testament, God's self-revelation is demonstrated in a variety of ways, such as visions, dreams, and especially through

**124**

the prophets. However, it is in relationship to the people of Israel where God's self-disclosure is most evident. In the context of this relationship, God reveals the sacred name, "I am Yahweh" (cf. Ex. 3:6); exercises power through "signs and wonders" (Ex. 7:3), and makes covenant promises (Deut. 7:9). As a result, the people of Israel were able to conceive of a God they could trust, and one who would act as their refuge, Savior, deliverer, and provider. Such a formulation of the character of God would not have been possible without God's self-revelation.

In the New Testament, this self-revelation took a form that was radically new and unsurpassable, that is, in the person of Jesus Christ. With the incarnation of Jesus, a new beginning in the history of God's revelation began.

In the past God spoke to our forefathers through the prophets at many times and in various ways, but in these last days he has spoken to us by his Son, whom he appointed heir of all things, and through whom he made the universe. The Son is the radiance of God's glory and the exact representation of his being, sustaining all things by his powerful word. After he had provided purification for sins he sat down at the right hand of the Majesty in heaven (Heb. 1:1-3).

God's appearance in human flesh was an unexpected event. Who, by reason alone, could imagine that the Creator of the universe would go to such extremes? In the person of Christ, God was revealed in the form of a servant (Phil. 2:6-8) and as such became as a man (Heb. 2:10-18). The sole purpose of this epiphany was a personal manifestion of God's love toward humankind to make salvation possible. Augustine wrote:

Hence [Christ] was pointed out to holy men of old; to the intent that they, through faith in His Passion to come, even as we through faith in that which is past, might be saved. For as man He was Mediator; but as the Word He was not between, because equal to God and God with God, and together with the Holy Spirit one God. How have you loved us, O good Father, who spared not Your only Son, but delivered Him up for us wicked ones! (Rom 8:32). How have You loved us, for whom He, who thought it no robbery to be equal with You, "became obedient unto death, even the death of the cross"

**125**

(Phil. 2:6, 8); He alone "free among the dead," that had power to lay down His life, and power to take it again; for us was He unto You both Victor and Victim, and the Victor as being the Victim; for us was He unto You both Priest and Sacrifice, and Priest as being the Sacrifice; of slaves making us Your sons, by being born of You, and serving us.[17]

The nature and divine origins of Scripture, the apostolic and prophetic preaching incorporating them, and their authoritative quality make it obvious why the Scriptures are the fundamental source of the church teaching magisterium. Without falling into the evangelical sin of bibliolatry by making the Bible into a "paper pope," the fact remains that since the Christian faith stands "on the foundation of the apostles and prophets" (Eph. 2:20), the church has the responsibility to preserve its belief and faithfully transmit its message from one generation to the next (Jude 3; 1 Tim. 4:16; 6:20; 2 Tim. 1:13-14; Titus 2:2).

### The Implications of Divine Revelation
From an applicational point of view, two further points need to be made before leaving our discussion on relativism and truth — the mission of the church and the proclamation of its message.

As Scripture constitutes the theological foundation for mission, and since it provides the answer to the relativist's/skeptic's dilemma regarding the basis for absolute truth, this should constitute a powerful motivation for the church to take its prophetic and transformational role in society seriously. In a culture which has settled for relativism at the expense of truth, Baby Boomers need to hear that truth does exist and is seen most clearly in the face of Jesus Christ. Unfortunately, this is not always the case. Reginald Bibby, commenting on the blatant relativism in the North American religious scene, observes:

> It's not that religious groups never speak out. They are quite welcome to express their views on social and economic issues, and they frequently do. However, most such expressions, regardless of whether they come from a Roman Catholic, United, Anglican or conservative Protestant research base, hardly sound prophetic. Usually they reflect the educational and ideological backgrounds of the people who have prepared them.

**126**

But when a question cannot readily be addressed through social research and collective opinion—for example, a question pertaining to the purpose of life and what lies beyond death—religious leaders, it is clear, have little to say.

Frequently they sound little different from counselors and others in offering what amount to naturalistic interpretations of life and death. . . . Given religion's increasing tendency to abdicate the meaning sphere, it should surprise no one that alternatives are, indeed, being posited and adopted. "Answers" typically take the form of "add-ons," whereby a belief such as reincarnation is added like a foreign food option to one's Protestant or Roman Catholic smorgasbord. People are looking for answers; if conventional religions are silent, the vacuum will be filled by "consumer cults" and non-religious alternatives.[18]

Closely related to truthless forms of religion is the phenomenon of religious consumerism. This occurs when the church says to the culture, "what do you want the Christian faith to be?" Leith Anderson describes the Entrepreneurial Church in the following way.

The Entrepreneurial Church is started by one or a few motivated leaders who welcome the risk and adventure of something new. They are market-sensitive and attempt to take current trends and needs into consideration, using such up-to-date methodology as telemarketing, advertising, and high-tech communications. These churches seek to be highly relational. They plan to be big and offer full services from the start. Some have as many as 300 people, multiple services, and several pastors on the first Sunday. Entrepreneurial Churches are not usually affiliated with a denomination, although many denominations are attempting to start Entrepreneurial Churches.

Part of the attraction is the lack of tradition. There is no one to say, "We've never done it this way before." No creeds, no liturgy, no building, no budget, no history. Everything is new and fresh.[19]

Anderson goes on to describe Robert Schuller's beginning this way: "He [Schuller] . . . polled hundreds of people on what they wanted, and began holding services in the non-threatening context of a drive-in theater." In a similar way, Anderson describes the Willow Creek Community Church as typical of what is to come. The pastor of the church took a similar approach to Schuller by asking people "what they wanted or didn't want in a church."[20] While this model fits well with the mood of the 1990s, Anderson does admit that it has its dangers. He writes: "Lack of tradition, theological training and denominational accountability, increase the potential for doctrinal heresy."[21]

Few church-growth experts doubt that such religious diversity works. The more important question to be asked is why does it work? From a sociological point of view, the popularity of religion "a la carte," is inextricably connected to the cultural developments of the last three decades of North American life. Bibby suggests that if it is true that the Christian faith is a system of meaning that addresses the central issues of life, then perhaps, on some issues, representatives of the church may be accused of "selling the faith out," if the need to be relevant includes dismantling any of the essential ingredients of Christianity and offering it as a piecemeal consumer item to a generation that has grown up in the milieu of relativism.[22]

## Materialism and the Spirit of Generosity

There is a profound truth to the Scripture that says, "The love of money is the root of all evils" (1 Tim. 6:10, RSV). Since 1945, money has been the one commodity that has made it possible for millions of Baby Boomers to live in a way that was once reserved for the rich and famous. The pursuit of "the good life" is made possible by easy credit, generous expense accounts, and the high salaries generated by the growing phenomena of two-income families. Some Baby Boomers have extended beyond the normal desire of want into the sin of avarice.

Hedonism is a very luring philosophy as it puts the quest of personal pleasure above all other pursuits. Generally speaking, three main pursuits mark hedonism: sexual promiscuity, leisure, and eating. However, many Baby Boomers are beginning to discover that the often devastating consequences of the hedonistic ethic far outweigh the pleasure factor. The AIDS virus is killing alarming numbers of people; masses of individuals remain bored after admitting to trying every possible pleasure; and calories and cholesterol are regarded as enemy number one.

Hedonism was a popular philosophy in the ancient world, but it met its match in Christianity which spread like wildfire throughout the known world. This new movement stressed a very different ethical code of self-denial, and it won the allegiance of many pleasure-haggard hedonists. In many ways, history has come full circle in that we now find ourselves, at least in North America, in a similar cultural situation to that of Christianity's birth. Unfortunately, the message that today's church proclaims to our hedonistic generation is best described as schizophrenic. Let us pursue this analogy a little further.

A little over 2 million North American citizens live with the complications which arise from an extremely complex behavioral disorder known as schizophrenia. This sickness is normally characterized by a double orientation problem within the individual's personality. It typically involves such things as perceptional, cognitive, and verbally confusing behavior patterns, where false ideas of reality exist and incoherent or contradictory messages are given.

When it comes to the issue of wealth, the church exhibits its schizophrenia by the double standards seen in the life-styles of its members and the verbally contradictory message it proclaims. To some, wealth is considered as a virtue, a sign of divine blessing, one of the benefits of the inheritance "in Christ," and the normal result of being in relationship with a God who owns "the cattle on a thousand hills" (Ps. 50:10). Subsequently, the message given to the culture is that God desires to bless people with prosperity.

To other Christians, wealth is considered much more of a vice than a virtue. Therefore, the message that ought to be proclaimed is one of self-denial. Those who represent this position maintain that lasting pleasure and true fulfillment cannot be found in the tangible things that money offers, but rather in the cultivation and development of the spiritual life. Happiness and tranquility are not seen as a goal to pursue, but rather as the by-product of a life which finds its fulfillment in seeking intimacy with God. This intimacy inevitably involves withdrawing from the money-making business and all the corresponding hectic schedules, which often lead to burnout and the disintegration of body, mind, and soul. Those in sacramental traditions often represent this form of spirituality. Moderate asceticism is encouraged, and the Lenten disciplines of self-denial and the sacrament of penance are never out of season.

**129**

These radically different approaches to the significance of wealth are seen in the priorities placed on such outward things as church buildings, position, status, and personal life-styles. Those who consider wealth as a blessing from God, tend to construct large and expensive buildings, able to accommodate thousands of people. Large religious empires, possessing a carefully constructed public image, exemplify the visible trappings of success with ministries that are high-profile, slick, and smooth. In this context, one may hear the name Napoleon Hill more frequently than Mother Teresa or St. Francis of Assisi!

The other extreme is represented by such figures as the Trappist monk, Thomas Merton, or Henri Nouwen. Far from seeking status, success, and the fanfare of the crowd, these men chose a more obscure path by living as members of community rather than becoming empire-building figureheads. Historically speaking, this school of thought is represented by such figures as Ignatius of Loyola, who renounced a successful career to live a life of austerity and prayer. His *Spiritual Exercises* which contain a four-week course of study, are designed to lead individuals into a deeper prayer life and meditation. This work is a Christian classic and continues to be widely used in retreat settings.

With such conflicting views as those outlined above, how is a contemporary North American Christian to view wealth in our prosperous society? What is the prophetic word that the church has to offer this present Baby Boomer generation, whose concern about money consumes most of its waking moments and physical energy? How are we to view the claims of the prosperity gospel which declares that God wants us rich? Lest we fall into the cultural relativist's trap of finding answers from the contemporary culture alone, we will look into the pages of Scripture for the answer to these questions.

### Biblical Teaching Regarding Wealth

Scripture actually has an enormous amount of teaching regarding the acquisition and proper use of wealth. Following, we shall attempt to paint the biblical picture in broad strokes, by outlining the most salient points and then by applying these truths to our affluent society.

From the Old Testament, we may deduce the following. First and foremost, all the treasures of this world belong to the Lord

(Lev. 25:23; Ps. 105:44). This implies that whatever wealth nations or individuals acquire, it should be understood as a gift from God. In Deuteronomy 8:17, there is clear teaching that because the Lord has given material blessings to the covenant people, they must not boast, "My power and the strength of my hands have produced this wealth for me." This, of course, flies in the face of the so-called "self-made man" myth so prevalent among North Americans. As with most heresies, some aspects of truth may mingle with error. The prosperity gospel is correct in its teaching that God wants to bless believers with an abundance of good things. However, this does not mean that the apparent lack of material success is a manifestation of God's displeasure (Job 42:1-6), nor that wealth brings a trouble-free life. Indeed, riches very easily lead to perverse ways (Prov. 28:6); give rise to a sense of false security (Ps. 52:7), leaving people feeling that their lives are empty and futile (Prov. 17:1; Ecc. 2:4-11), the result of such anxiety causing sleepless nights (Ecc. 5:12).

Jesus affirms the teaching of the Old Testament in that he neither condemns wealth per se, nor glorifies poverty as the higher good. Rather, wealth is viewed from the perspective of the kingdom of God. Jesus does draw attention to the fact that money possesses an inherent ability to distract people from the kingdom of God, as illustrated by the example of the rich young man mentioned in Matthew 19:16-22. According to Jesus, it is the pursuit of wealth that chokes the seed of the word of God (Luke 8:1-15), making it as hard for the rich individual to enter the kingdom of God as a camel trying to pass through the eye of a needle (Matt. 19:24). The love of money is a clear mark of a worldly way of life (Matt. 6:25-34), which Jesus considers both pointless and dangerous. Pointless because individuals may spend an entire life accumulating luxuries only to have their lives snuffed out in an instant (Luke 12:13-21; cf. James 1:10ff; 4:13-17). Dangerous because money can become a destructive idol. In Jesus' mind, money (mammon) has the ability to exert almost demonic powers over people in that they will make inordinate sacrifices to possess the power and status of wealth (Luke 16:13).

On a more optimistic note, Jesus did endorse generosity in saying that those who gave or even lent money without hope of restoration were on the right track. To that end, he told his would-be followers to "sell your possessions and give to the poor. Pro-

**131**

vide purses for yourselves that will not wear out, a treasure in heaven that will not be exhausted, where no thief comes near and no moth destroys. For where your treasure is, there your heart will be also" (Luke 12:32-34).

However, and contrary to the teaching of the prosperity gospel, the Scriptures do not guarantee that giving ensures a greater return. In fact, one could say that generosity without self-sacrifice is flawed, shabby, and to be viewed with suspicion. Although it is true that Jesus did say, "Give, and it will be given to you. A good measure, pressed down, shaken together and running over, will be poured into your lap. For with the measure you use, it will be measured to you" (Luke 6:38), one cannot conclude from this that greater prosperity inevitably follows. The wider picture of the New Testament does suggest a radical flaw in the bold, "You cannot out give God" slogans of the proponents of the prosperity gospel. As an example, let us consider an incident from the life of the apostolic church. Here, we discover an example of reckless generosity which met everyone's immediate needs. However, such generosity did not lead to material prosperity, but in fact to even harder times as a result of a life-threatening famine.

> All the believers were together and had everything in common. Selling their possessions and goods, they gave to anyone as he had need. Every day they continued to meet together in the temple courts. They broke bread in their homes and ate together with glad and sincere hearts (Acts 2:44-46).

> All the believers were one in heart and mind. No one claimed that any of his possessions was his own, but they shared everything they had. With great power the apostles continued to testify to the resurrection of the Lord Jesus, and much grace was upon them all. There were no needy persons among them. For from time to time those who owned lands or houses sold them, brought the money from the sales and put it at the apostles' feet, and it was distributed to anyone as he had need (Acts 4:32-35).

Paul, hearing of the famine, broached the subject of collecting a gift for the poor and destitute believers in Jerusalem. He wanted the Corinthians to experience the privilege of giving. He raised the matter again and considered their giving as "supplying the needs of God's people" (2 Cor. 9:12-14). Notice that there was not a hint that their generosity guaranteed future prosperity. To the contrary, he suggested that the time would come when they also would need a contribution from the very people they were now assisting (2 Cor. 8:14). This is a far cry from the prosperity gospel that claims "more money in the offering plate guarantees more money in the bank account." While this may be an appealing message to this contemporary generation who have traditionally put health and wealth above everything else, it is nevertheless one which is contrary to the New Testament principle.

### Applications of the Biblical Principles Regarding Wealth

In seeking to critique the accumulation and use of wealth from a biblical perspective, we will address the very issue which lies at the center of other realities connected with life-style. Since lifestyle choices refer to an individual's priorities, varied responses are bound to be expressed. Given the facts of an economic recession, the slowing down of career advancements and the downsizing of corporations and businesses in recent years, the biblical emphasis on generosity will be regarded by some Baby Boomers as unrealistic and threatening. On the other hand, some Baby Boomers are discovering that it is possible to live with less and are beginning to change their life-styles accordingly. In revising priorities and reconsidering values, growing numbers of Boomers are showing a willingness to postpone the exotic holidays, cut back on entertainment, and generally scale down their expectations. Connected with this current interest in values, we find the Baby Boomer horizon expanding beyond personal needs to the needs of others. As this generation matures, it is showing signs of concern for the world around them and for the kind of world they are leaving behind. Thus, we find increasing numbers of Boomers involved as volunteers in the community, engaged in service programs among the poor, the homeless, and the marginalized. One of the most significant aspects of the current change in this "lead generation" is the acknowledgment that they have been given so much and now many are refocusing to give something back. Almost instinctively, they are realizing that "from everyone who has been given much, much will be demanded; and from the one who has been entrusted with much, much more will be asked" (Luke

**133**

12:48). To assist Baby Boomers in the reassessment of their values regarding wealth, let us now consider the following five points:

(1) In a world that is becoming increasingly polarized between the "haves" and the "have-nots," the Christian's responsibility should reflect a bias for the poor. The account of how the church in Jerusalem blessed the Gentiles with the spiritual heritage of the Jews, and reciprocally, how the Jewish Christians received material blessing from the Gentile Christians (Rom. 15:26ff), is significant. Paul called for this reciprocal giving as obedience to the gospel (2 Cor. 8:13-15; 9:12ff; Phil. 4:15-18). Likewise, contemporary partnership in the Gospel should go beyond local concerns to benefit the wider community. The stark facts of world hunger suggest that affluent North American Christians have a responsibility to share their resources. Too often, the Christian community has been content to leave such responsibilities to non-Christian philanthropists.

(2) Compassion for the underprivileged grows through close proximity. From the Gospels, we observe Jesus' compassion for the poor by his interaction with them. By virtue of the incarnation, Jesus identified with the weak, the outcast, and the downtrodden. Even in his hand-to-mouth existence, he still found alms for the poor. Sadly, but all too often, affluent Christians structurally and personally isolate themselves from the poor. Their churches are built in the seclusion of the suburbs far from the sights, sounds, and smells of poverty.

(3) A clearer distinction needs to be made between necessities and luxuries, modesty and vanity. Nowhere is this more obvious than church buildings in most urban cities. Buildings are status symbols of power and wealth, and one has to wonder what message is given to the poor at the sight of the new mega/metachurch edifice, able to seat up to 20,000 and built at enormous expense. To some, the building is considered appropriate and justified from the utilitarian standpoint. To the poor, however, it must appear opulent. This is all the more disturbing considering the fact *The World Almanac* reports that as of 1991, 35.7 million Americans lived in families with incomes below the poverty line.[23]

(4) In ministry among the affluent, there needs to be a clearer understanding of the relationship between salvation and stewardship, poverty and wealth, charity and responsibility. Conversion must include a change in values and priorities. Teaching needs to

**134**

stress that true wealth is found in Christ and his kingdom. The Fall brought deprivation to humankind at every level. Christ's kingdom seeks to come against exploitation, sin, unjust laws, and those things which continue to perpetuate the results of the Fall. This implies that followers of Jesus are called to put their wealth to work for the kingdom of God and to discern those things that have eternal value from those things that are temporary. Teaching should be presented in such a way as to inform Christians on how to live within their means, to control their income and expenditures, live simply, and as much as possible avoid the enslaving cycle of debt.

(5) It is important to remind the Boomer generation, concerned about acquiring assets and tending to overvalue possessions, of a very simple truth, namely that they have been hoodwinked into thinking that wealth produces lasting happiness. The reality is that often the most unhappy people are those who, even though surrounded by every material comfort, lack a sense of personal peace. The Christian message offers a marvelous sense of freedom to those who put their trust in the Lord to meet their needs. To those individuals who are preoccupied with the elusive quest for more, the church's message encourages trust in the "unsearchable riches of Jesus Christ" (Eph. 3:8) to find fullness in self-giving, not in self-serving. Of Christ, the supreme example of such magnanimous living, Paul writes, "For you know the grace of our Lord Jesus Christ, that though he was rich, yet for your sakes he became poor, so that you through his poverty might become rich" (2 Cor. 8:9).

## Individualism and Christian Community

What is in the nature of humanity? What is so special about being human? What does it mean to be a person? How can the individual find wholeness in life? In our previous discussion on individualism, I attempted to show that although the Bible is critical of positioning the individual at the center of the universe, it does nonetheless affirm the significance and uniqueness of men and women.

According to biblical understanding, humanity is created in the image of God (Gen. 1:26; 5:1; 9:6) and as a tripartite being, consisting of body, mind, and soul. This spiritual-intellectual side of humans allows them to ask penetrating ontological questions about the ultimate foundation of finite and infinite realities and to choose

**135**

between obedience and disobedience, good and evil.

People are also viewed as corporal beings, composed of the same material stuff as the inorganic world, as anthropological materialism points out. It is in this material world of time and space that we live out our lives in harmony with the rest of creation, as a creative shaping and transforming force in human culture. Man as male and female is a corporeal entity intended to be a social being, living in the context of the natural biological communities of marriage and family, the corporate community of the tribes or nation, social communities such as clubs or fraternities, and the supernatural community of faith. For example, Jesus was a member of a specific family, which descended from a particular tribe known as Judah. He was a citizen of the Jewish nation, lived within the context of a male-orientated fraternity which included his twelve disciples, and was the founder of a community of faith. Likewise, Paul referred to himself as being "circumcised on the eighth day, of the people of Israel, of the tribe of Benjamin, a Hebrew of Hebrews, in regard to the law, a Pharisee" (Phil. 3:5-6).

It is precisely this lack of community that lies at the root of the tremendous loneliness of our culture. In the short life-cycle of the Baby Boomers, they have witnessed the disintegration of the traditional family unit. Many have encountered the painful experience of divorce or separation, which can result in fear of intimacy, thus making it difficult to commit to any form of long-term relationship. Others have experienced the betrayal of a friend or business associate. In a world that lives by the "do unto others before they do it to you" ethic, many Boomers are simply afraid to trust people. Still others, who have focused on building successful careers have done so at the expense of relationships and are now finding their portentous penthouse apartments very lonely. Due to frequent geographic moves necessary for success in the upwardly mobile circuit, some have simply lost their personal roots.

"Loneliness is such a sad affair," says the singer of a recent pop song. Recognizing this, many Baby Boomers are beginning to search for meaningful relationships in their solitary world. They are asking hard questions. How can I build lasting friendships? Where are such trustworthy friends to be found? For some, this search takes them to malls, nightclubs, bars, fitness clubs, and self-help groups, while others, in increasing numbers, are returning to church in hope of finding authentic community.

### Three Myths about the Nature of Christian Community

Before we consider what the church has to offer Boomers in terms of community, it may be helpful, as Dick Westley proposes, to demythologize this buzzword, "community."[24] Westley suggests that there are three myths about the nature of community.

### Myth 1

"Community is an important creature comfort that can be added to the other creature comforts that grace our lives." This in effect, means that "community is sought as a means to an end, like any other consumer good. It is seen as something that enhances life, making individuals more advantaged than those without it. . . . In our culture, which is largely governed by the law of supply and demand, we often find people shopping for all sorts of things that promise community, eager to pay for the experience." Westley rightly notes that the truth of the matter is that "Christian community is not for sale."

### Myth 2

"Community is a utopia, and . . . we shall forge supportive relationships, which will result in our being brothers and sisters again." In reality, building community is not a simple kind of utopia and is very difficult to achieve this side of heaven. Those who have lived in community will testify that there is always a certain amount of pain involved. There is the pain of not having one's own way. There is pain as a result of the clash of egos, and the realization that the individual's deeply held convictions may not be the measure of reality. Community life reminds us of the reality that there are always people who are implacable enemies or who simply "rub each other the wrong way." Far from being negative features, these tensions are beneficial as it is through this "sandpaper" effect that people learn patience, tolerance, and flexibility.

The truth is there is no authentic community without pain, love, and acceptance. Jean Vanier touches on a more honest view of community, when he writes, "A community is not just a place where people live under the same roof; that is a lodging house or a hotel. Nor is a community a work-team. Even less is it a nest of vipers. It is a place where everyone—or, let us be realistic, the majority—is emerging from the shadows of egocentricity into the light of real love."[25]

*Myth 3*

"We will establish deep and intimate associations with people who are just like ourselves, people who in almost every respect are clones of our interests and desires." This myth reminds us of the age-old principle "like cleaves to like," which to a large extent is encouraged by the "homogeneous unit" theory of the Church Growth School. The underlying idea behind this concept is that the fellowship which binds people together are those things which they have in common. These similarities may be equal social standing, a shared economic status, similar education level, or the same views on religious or philosophical matters. However, the downside of this "like cleaves to like" principle is that it often excludes those who are different. For example, in my own tradition, the Anglican Church has an image of being white Anglo-Saxon, English-speaking, middle-class, and well-educated. It is not unusual to hear subtle, but nonetheless derogatory comments about the poor, black, native, non-Christian, homosexual, or illiterate. By contrast, the New Testament church demonstrated a bias for the poor, and accepted all manner of people — slaves, outcasts, manual laborers, ex-criminals, and soldiers, as well as the privileged. Dietrich Bonhoeffer, in *Life Together,* takes a radically different view from the homogeneous unit theory, when he writes: "Every Christian community must realize that not only do the weak need the strong, but also that the strong cannot exist without the weak. The elimination of the weak is the death of the fellowship."[26]

Furthermore, "like cleaves to like" is contradictory to the revolutionary New Testament teaching of oneness in Christ. Walls, much like the one built in East Germany, are built to keep people apart. Like the recent dismantling of the Berlin Wall, the teaching of the New Testament also proclaims that through the reconciling work of Christ on the cross, the old wall of hostility is demolished (Eph. 2:14). This being the case, Christians, regardless of national, social, or biological status, are to be mutually accepting of one another. Paul, the great champion of Christian unity, wrote, "You are all sons of God through faith in Christ Jesus, for all of you who were baptized into Christ have clothed yourself with Christ. There is neither Jew nor Greek, slave nor free, male nor female, for you are all one in Christ Jesus" (Gal. 3:26-28).

One further passage gives us a glimpse of the multiethnic and

**138**

social diversity of the early church. "Now in the church at Antioch, there were prophets and teachers, Barnabas, Simeon who was called Niger, Lucius of Cyrene, Manaen a member of the court of Herod the tetrarch, and Saul" (Acts 13:1, RSV). What a mixture! Barnabas originated from a Jewish Cypriot family; whereas Simeon was most likely a black from Africa; Lucius, a Cyrenian; Manaen, a Greek; and Saul, a Jew. It was this biblical truth of equal standing "in Christ" and that all human beings deserve to enjoy such basic human rights as dignity, self-worth, and freedom, that inspired such notable social reformers as William Wilberforce and Lord Shaftesbury. In more recent days this fight has been taken up by Archbishop Tutu and others in the ongoing struggle against racial prejudice and apartheid.

Finally, "like cleaves to like" may be a hindrance in ministry to Baby Boomers. Often their sheer numbers obscure their diversity. Not all Baby Boomers are Yuppies. In fact, there exists a very different genre of people who in fact outnumber the Yuppies three to one. The wigs and wags have labeled this group the New-Collar Workers. Unlike the Yuppies, they tend to be less cynical, more loyal to their employers, hardworking, and patriotic. They are the middle-class of the Baby Boomer generation: teachers, dental hygienists, plumbers, electricians, and construction workers, who earn approximately $30,000 a year. Although they tend to be more pragmatic and conservative in consumer habits than their Yuppie counterparts, they nevertheless contribute billions of dollars to the economy. The New-Collar class have the potential of becoming a super class, with the potential of two incomes. The working woman (44 million in America working outside the home) and her husband make a formidable engine of consumption. Although both groups have quite different values, experiences, and expectations, the one thing they have in common is their desire to experience authentic community.

This cultural hunger for solidarity presents the church of Jesus Christ with an opportunity to offer this generation an experience of genuine community where people are accepted without qualification or on the basis of homogeneity. Rather than excluding those who differ by race, class, or sex, Christian community should love unconditionally and respect individual differences. Anything less would be considered a "pseudocommunity" and a pale comparison to the *koinonia* described in the pages of the New Testament.

### The Nature of Christian Community

Returning once again to our bridge theme, medieval bridges were built for two main functions. First they were designed to carry traffic from one side to the other. Second, they were planned in such a way that they could be used as a meeting place. A good example of this was the old London Bridge, which was a crowded thoroughfare of tunnel-like streets, shops, and houses hosting a variety of village fairs and tournaments.

As every first-year theological student is aware, the word *koinonia* is used in the New Testament to denote the concept of fellowship or community. Like the bridge alluded to above, this word also describes a twin function. First and foremost, it refers to a vertical form of fellowship which exists, whereby the believer has a share in the divine nature of Christ (2 Peter 1:4; Jude 3; Titus 1:4; 1 Cor. 1:9; Heb. 3:14), and in the sufferings of Christ (Rom. 6:4-8; 2 Cor. 7:3; Gal. 2:19; Eph. 2:5-6; Col. 2:12-13; 3:1). Secondly, the same apostle who wrote that "our fellowship is with God the Father and his Son, Jesus Christ" (1 John 1:3), also wrote of the horizontal fellowship that Christians share with each other. Thus, the Body of Christ, like the medieval bridge, is a meeting place where Christians "have fellowship with one another" (1 John 1:7). Paul in a similar fashion, described his friends "in Christ" as his *sunergoi* (fellow workers), *sundouloi* (fellow servants), *sunstratiotai* (fellow soldiers), and *sunkleronomoi* (fellow heirs). The whole concept of Christian fellowship on the horizontal level was expressed in love, unity, mutual sympathy, and service. Thus, Paul exhorted all Christians despite their varying backgrounds, to bear one another's burdens (Gal. 6:2), to do good to one another (1 Thes. 5:15), to forgive one another (Eph. 4:32), to serve one another (Gal. 5:13), to edify one another (Rom. 14:19), and to provide a model of coherent community within an increasingly incoherent world (John 17:21).

In tying these two dimensions together, Alan Richardson reminds us that these two relationships are inseparable in the New Testament. He writes, "The vertical is the origin of the horizontal, while the outward expression of the horizontal is at the same time the sign and pledge of the reality of the vertical . . . so Christians are to love one another as Christ has loved them (John 13:34), and to wash one another's feet, because they have partaken in his washing of their feet" (John 13:12ff).[27]

**140**

The first and most obvious aspect of fellowship in the early church was its practical generosity as expressed in the fellowship of giving. The apostolic narrative vividly illustrates accounts of community sharing, and the daily distribution of food to widows (Acts 2:44-46; 4:32–5:11). The Apostle Paul urged Christians to work, not only to provide for their personal needs (1 Thes. 4:11; 2 Thes. 3:12) but to also contribute to those less fortunate (2 Cor. 8:13-15). The origins of the community of pooled goods and generous giving was found in the example of Jesus and his disciples (cf. Mark 10:21) and was encouraged to continue as a Christian duty by the New Testament writers (Rom. 12:13; 1 Tim. 6:18; Heb. 13:16). Paul regarded this generosity as a practical expression of Christian fellowship that transcended cultural boundaries because of a common life in Christ.

The second aspect of their community life together was the liturgical fellowship of worship, which normally took place in the intimacy of a private home setting and included the breaking of bread and prayer (Acts 20:20; 1 Cor. 16:19; Phile. 2). Indeed, the cement that holds Christian community together is that form of Christian living that revolves around the pattern of prayer and study, worship and service, set in the context of caring friendships, common meals, and shared responsibilities. Throughout the subsequent years of the church's history, meeting in small groups in such nonthreatening gatherings as people's homes has accounted for some of the church's best growth and community building. A modern example of this would be the Latin America's *Communidades Eclesiales de Base* (Basic Christian Communities). The alienation of modern life and the Baby Boomers' search for authentic community has prompted many churches to develop small cell group programs. This is an important provision as strangers to the Christian community often find that initial commitment to the larger body of the church forbidding. The cell groups, however, provide a small model of the larger community. Hans Finzel considers the forming of such groups as an essential aspect of evangelism to the Boomers.

In the complex world of the 80s and 90s, boomers need "body life" much more than they did in the 60s and 70s when Ray Stedman first pioneered that movement. The fastest growing churches in America today recognize the essential need for

**141**

small cell groups and place strong emphasis on getting the people off the pew involved in community.[28]

In a community-starved generation like our own, fellowship is a fragrant flower in God's garden. The horizontal aspect of Christian fellowship proclaims that *all* are welcome, regardless of age, sex, race, color, wealth, social status, or ability. All the more so in light of the fact that the nature of Christian fellowship is "love for one another," which reveals itself in material generosity. This not only assists the poor and the underprivileged, but it helps to break the bondage that wealth brings to the rich and privileged.

It has been observed that each generation must face higher expectation, face more daunting challenges and cope with a more complex world than the previous one. This is certainly true for the Baby Boomer generation today. They face a world of economic uncertainty, increasing urban violence, and fragile global peace among nations who are becoming more dependent on the world's depleting resources. Today, more than ever, Baby Boomers need a touchstone, a criterion for judging purpose in their lives, and a living faith that will not fail them. The Christian bridge-builder points not only to a liberating relationship with Christ, but to a faith lived out in the context of Christian community where the believer experiences biblically relevant teaching, transcendent worship, and healing. It is to this paradigm of Christian community that we now focus our discussion.

# PART FOUR

# A MODEL BRIDGE: THE ACTS 2:42-47 PARADIGM

# Chapter 5
# BIBLICALLY RELEVANT TEACHING IN TODAY'S WORLD

When we think of bridges, we usually think in terms of a stable and permanent structure with fixed and secure foundations. However, this is not always the case. Take, for example, the famous London Bridge which extended some 928 feet in length and 63 feet in width. In the early nineteenth century, it was a sight to behold as its strong structure spoke of robustness and permanence. Who would have imagined that such a structure extending over the Thames River in Great Britain could be dismantled and reconstructed in Lake Havasu City, Arizona! So much for permanence.

Baby Boomers are consumers by nature. Consciously or unconsciously, they seek to dictate to the church what they want from Christianity. Although the church must try to be relevant and seek every way possible to bridge the chasm between the biblical and modern worlds, there are some fixed and permanent nonnegotiables. In this chapter, we shall discuss the features of community life as described in the Acts 2:42-47 paradigm. It will be shown that these are not temporary aspects of the church's life, but that they *are* the church's life and I believe the key to a successful ministry to Baby Boomers. From this model of ministry we shall discover the significance of preaching and teaching (chap. 5), the transcendent nature of worship (chap. 6), and the place of healing in the life of the contemporary church (chap. 7).

## The Acts 2 Model of Community Life

In the Acts 2:42-47 passage, Luke endeavored to create a substantial picture of the primitive church in its essence. His goal was to focus on the community of faith that was created through apostolic preaching *(kerygma)*, and was nurtured through apostolic teaching *(didache)*. The structure and content of this passage reflected five chief elements of the early church's religious life: apostles' teaching, fellowship, the breaking of bread, prayer, and signs and wonders.

> They devoted themselves to the apostles' teaching and to the fellowship, to the breaking of bread and to prayer. Everyone was filled with awe, and many wonders and miraculous signs were done by the apostles. All the believers were together and had everything in common. Selling their possessions and goods, they gave to anyone as he had need. Every day they continued to meet together in the temple courts. They broke bread in their homes and ate together with glad and sincere hearts, praising God and enjoying the favor of all the people. And the Lord added to their number daily those who were being saved (Acts 2:42-47).

## The Apostolic Teaching

In the early years of the primitive church in Jerusalem, teaching was exercised mainly by the apostles.[1] They understood themselves to be witnesses of the ministry of Jesus and his resurrection and to be representatives of his person and ongoing ministry. The apostles gave priority to the ministry of teaching after Pentecost as specifically stated in Acts 6. They resisted the temptation of involvement in other forms of service, in order to devote themselves exclusively "to prayer and to the ministry of the word" (v. 4). It was primarily for this purpose that Jesus called them. During his time on earth, Jesus sent the apostles out to preach (Mark 3:14), although temporarily restricting their ministry to "the lost sheep of the house of Israel" (Matt. 10:5-7). After his resurrection, however, he solemnly commissioned them to take the Gospel to the nations (e.g., Matt. 28:19; Luke 24:47). In Acts, Peter and the Jerusalem apostles "spoke the word of God boldly" (4:31), and Paul preached the kingdom of God and taught about the Lord Jesus Christ, undaunted and unhindered (28:31).

How are we to think of this teaching in terms of its content? In this regard, four key words need to be considered: *kerygma* (proclamation), *didache* (instruction), *paraklesis* (exhortation), and *katechesis* (instruction).

### Kerygma

This term normally referred to the content of early Christian preaching. The formative work of the British scholar C.H. Dodd established a substantial basis of agreement between the early sermons of Peter in Acts with that of Paul and the other New Testament writers.[2] Dodd maintained that *kerygma* preaching was the public proclamation of the Christian faith to the non-Christian world. In today's terms, we would call this evangelical preaching, which would include an altar call.

An example of this apostolic *kerygma* is seen in Peter's sermons in Acts 2:14-40; 3:12-26; 5:29-32; 10:34-43. This preaching may be summarized as follows:

(1) The Old Testament promises of salvation were fulfilled (2:16-21, 23; 3:18, 24; 10:43).
(2) This took place through the ministry, death, and resurrection of Jesus (2:22-24; 3:13-15; 10:37-39).
(3) Jesus was exalted as Christ and Lord (2:36).
(4) The Holy Spirit in the church was the sign of Christ's present power and glory (2:33; 5:32).
(5) Salvation would reach its consummation in the return of Christ at which point God would restore everything as he promised (3:21; 10:42).
(6) The apostles were chosen as witnesses of the ministry of Jesus and to proclaim his resurrection (2:32; 3:15; 10:40-41).
(7) This outline was then followed by an appeal for repentance with the promise of the forgiveness of sins and the gift of the Holy Spirit (2:38-39; 3:25-26; 5:31; 10:43).

In short, the preaching of the apostles was a proclamation of the work of salvation made by God in Christ and a call to believe and be saved.

The preaching of Paul did not, as Dodd reminded us, differ from the common preaching as he himself testified (1 Cor. 15:11). In fact, his preaching, as reported in Acts (cf. 13:16-41; 14:15-17; 17:22-31) and the references in his letters, revealed a similar message to that of Peter, with the exception of one feature to his Gentile pagan audience — "faith in the Living God who made the heavens and the earth" (Acts 14:15; 17:24; 1 Thes. 1:9).

The following passage serves as an example of the Pauline *kerygmatic* proclamation.

> Paul, a servant of Christ Jesus, called to be an apostle and set apart for the gospel of God — the gospel he promised beforehand through his prophets in the Holy Scriptures regarding his Son, who as to his human nature was a descendant of David, and who through the Spirit of holiness was declared with power to be the Son of God by his resurrection from the dead: Jesus Christ our Lord. Through him and for his name's sake, we received grace and apostleship to call people from among all the Gentiles to the obedience that comes from faith. And you also are among those who are called to belong to Jesus Christ (Rom. 1:1-6).

We summarized the apostolic *kerygma* by the tidy formula previously mentioned. However, Robert H. Mounce reminds us of the danger of assuming this straitjacketed approach. He suggests that the apostolic *kerygma* was not "a sort of stereotyped six-headed sermon, but a proclamation of the death, resurrection and exhortation of Jesus, that . . . [led] to an evaluation of his person as both Lord and Christ, confronted men with the necessity of repentance, and promised the forgiveness of sin."[3]

### Didache

In contrast to apostolic preaching, which was primarily directed toward non-Christians, the *didache* was considered as catechismal instruction on moral and ethic-related issues. It was directed to the converted and those preparing for baptism into Christ. Dodd believed that much of the Christian *didache* was summarized by the Law of Christ and was an exposition of the two chief commandments, the "Golden Rule" and the "Sayings of Jesus."[4]

Dodd also believed that this form of instruction revealed strong affinities toward the Jewish tradition of *halakha* (regulations for conduct), which grew out of the *haggada* (the exposition of religious truth).[5] This pattern of ethical instruction, which was typical of Jewish catechesis, was adopted by the apostles and early Christian instructors to teach the new converts in the way of Christ.

**148**

Unlike the Jewish instruction on the Law, the Christian believer was encouraged to keep the Law of Christ and the Sayings of Jesus, not through fear of the consequences of breaking them, but because of a passionate desire to conform to the mind of Christ.[6]

In his book, *Gospel and Law,* Dodd identified seven major propositions in the *didache:*

(1) The New Testament Christian was enjoined to reform his or her conduct (Eph. 4:22-24; Rom. 12:1-2; 13:11-14).
(2) These typical virtues of the new way of life were set forth in the New Testament epistles (Gal. 5:22-23; Col. 3:12).
(3) The proper Christian relationship within the family, the primary unit of the Christian community, were reviewed (Eph. 5:22, 25; 6:1; Col. 3:18-21; 1 Peter 3:1-7).
(4) Right relationships within the Christian community were set forth (Rom. 12:9-10; Col. 3:13-16; Phil. 2:1-4).
(5) A pattern of behavior toward pagan neighbors was described (Col. 4:5-6; 1 Peter 2:12, 18).
(6) Correct relationships with constituted authorities were defined (Rom. 13:1-7).
(7) There was a call to be watchful and responsible (1 Peter 5:8; Eph. 6:10-18).

A good example of *didactic* teaching can be seen in the following passage:

Everyone must submit himself to the governing authorities, for there is no authority except that which God has established. The authorities that exist have been established by God. Consequently, he who rebels against the authority is rebelling against what God has instituted, and those who do so will bring judgment on themselves. For rulers hold no terror for those who do right, but for those who do wrong. Do you want to be free from fear of the one in authority? Then do what is right and he will commend you. For he is God's servant to do you good. But if you do wrong, be afraid, for he does not bear the sword for nothing. He is God's servant, an agent of wrath to bring punishment on the wrongdoer. Therefore, it is necessary to submit to the authorities, not only because of possible punishment but also because of conscience.

**149**

This is also why you pay taxes, for the authorities are God's servants, who give their full time to governing. Give everyone what you owe him: If you owe taxes, pay taxes; if revenue, then revenue; if respect, then respect; if honor, then honor (Rom. 13:1-7).

### *Paraklesis*

*Paraklesis* is a beautiful word with a variety of meanings. In the New Testament, two distinct forms of *paraklesis* were at work. First, there was the "word of exhortation," denoting a synagogue homily (Acts 13:5; Heb. 13:22), in which the ancient Christian teachers instructed converts (1 Thes. 4:1; Phil. 4:2; Rom. 12:1). This instruction was not one that originated from the preacher's wisdom or insight, but rather, "by the mercies of God" (Rom. 12:1, NRSV), or "by our Lord Jesus Christ and by the love of the Spirit" (Rom. 15:30), or with "the meekness and gentleness of Christ" (2 Cor. 10:1).

Secondly, given the cost of following Christ for many of the new converts, the ministry of comfort *(parakaleo)* was given to believers in the midst of their tribulations. It gave an opportunity for the apostles to strengthen, console, refresh, relieve those in distress, and encourage those who put their trust in the God of all comfort to keep the faith in the face of their adversity (Isa. 40:1).

Thus, in the following specimen, the Apostle Paul places comfort over and against tribulation and suffering, by identifying his suffering with that of Christ, and at the same time sharing in Christ's comfort.

Praise be to the God and Father of our Lord Jesus Christ, the Father of compassion and the God of all comfort, who comforts us in all our troubles, so that we can comfort those in any trouble with the comfort we ourselves have received from God. For just as the sufferings of Christ flow over into our lives, so also through Christ our comfort overflows. If we are distressed, it is for your comfort and salvation; if we are comforted, it is for your comfort, which produces in you patient endurance of the same sufferings we suffer. And our hope for you is firm, because we know that just as you share in our sufferings, so also you share in our comfort (2 Cor. 1:3-7).

**150**

## Katechesis

The final term, normally associated with the theological education and instruction, was directed to seekers, inquirers, or new converts to the faith (1 Cor. 14:19; Gal. 6:6; Acts 18:25). This training period had a Jewish precedent, as Gentile converts were instructed in preparation for proselyte baptism. By the time 2 Clement was written, *katechesis* was already the normal term in Christian circles for the baptismal instruction given to catechumens. There were several parts of the New Testament which reflected the existence of a rudimentary catechumenate, among them Acts 8:32-37.

> The eunuch was reading this passage of Scripture: "He was led like a sheep to the slaughter, and as a lamb before the shearer is silent, so he did not open his mouth. In his humiliation he was deprived of justice. Who can speak of his descendants? For his life was taken from the earth."
>
> The eunuch asked Philip, "Tell me, please, who is the prophet talking about, himself or someone else?" Then Philip began with that very passage of Scripture and told him the good news about Jesus.
>
> As they traveled along the road, they came to some water and the eunuch said, "Look, here is water. Why shouldn't I be baptized?"

These terms—*kerygma, didache, paraklesis, katechesis* were four ways in which the apostles instructed the early Christian converts "in the way of Christ." Luke, in fact, used many different Greek words to describe the variety and richness of apostolic instruction: heralded, testified, proclaimed, taught, argued, disputed, confounded, proved, reasoned, persuaded, and pleaded—all of which were part of the "teaching of the Apostles." This practice of being instructed in the Word of God continued long after the death of the apostles. In the second century, the Latin father, Tertullian, wrote his *Apology,* in which he described a typical Christian gathering in which the believers assembled "to read . . . [their] sacred writings. . . . With the Sacred words . . . [they] nourished their] faith . . . [they animated their] hope . . . [made their] confidence more steadfast, and no less by inculcations of God's precepts . . . [they made] good habits. In the same place also exhortations . . . [were] made, rebukes and sacred censures . . . [were] administered."[7]

Much of the apostolic instruction was new, in that it was concerned with tracing the history of salvation from the Old Testament to the event of Christ in the present. The concept and pattern of daily Scripture reading and instruction was deeply rooted in the culture of the day. In a typical Jewish home, people motivated by the various injunctions and exhortations of the Old Testament read and meditated continually in God's Law (Deut. 17:19; Josh. 1:8; Pss. 1:2; 119:97) and consequently taught the Law to their children (Gen. 18:19; Deut. 6:7; 11:19; 32:46; Ps. 78:4-7).

Likewise, Luke reminds us that the early Christians also gathered in homes for instruction. References were made to an "upper room" (Acts 1:13, RSV; probably the same room in which Christ appeared on Easter Sunday while the disciples were at their meal), and Solomon's Porch (Acts 5:12; cf. 3:11). In addition to private home settings, the early Christians gathered in the temple and local synagogues. Although the synagogue ministry is a subject in itself,[8] the chief element in the worship of the synagogue included the reading and exposition of the Hebrew Scriptures, the Aramaic paraphrases *(Targums),* and the recitation of the *Shema* or *Tephillah.* Only when the cleavage between Judaism and Christianity became complete and Christians were forbidden access to the temple and synagogue, did the early Christians develop their own individual services and unique features.

One of these features was the deliberate distinction the early Christians made in their selection of Sunday for their main gathering time (Acts 20:7; cf. Rev. 1:10). It was on this day that the community gathered to celebrate the resurrection of Christ, to partake of the Lord's Supper, and to hear the Word of God. It was in this context that the early Christian teachers taught the new converts from the Hebrew Bible, not in a rabbinical method of detailing legal instructions, but by wrestling with the Old Testament text in a way that would throw light on the meaning of Christ's death and resurrection. Like their Master (whose teaching was authoritative), the content of their teaching also powerfully penetrated their hearts, encouraging and strengthening them in their faith.

Interestingly, the New Testament gives little evidence of strife over this change of day. Furthermore, as Christianity spread to the Greeks, Sabbath Day worship was never made binding for the believers. Here was another example of how the early church made it easy for new converts to become members of the household of God.

## Contemporary Implications from Apostolic Teaching

### Study: A Prerequisite for Christian Teachers

In the summer of 1992, the world was once again invited to watch the Olympic Games in Barcelona, Spain. No other sports spectacle has a background so historic or thrilling. At the opening ceremony, flags fluttered and the crowd cheered as the swift runner carried a blazing torch into the arena to light the Olympic flame. The light was brought many miles by runners in cross-country relays (and by planes) carrying it from Greece to the stadium of the hosting nation.

When one considers the noble call of preaching the Gospel and teaching the message of the kingdom of God, we are reminded of that great cloud of witnesses called to run with perseverance the race that is set before them (Heb. 12:1-3). The Apostle Paul saw himself as a runner in the Gospel race (2 Tim. 4:7) with the responsibility of passing the entrusted message to others (2 Tim. 1:12-14). As we look back in time, those witnesses to the faith include such great Gospel orators as Tertullian, Chrysostom, Augustine, Luther, Latimer, Whitefield, Edwards, and in our own day Billy Graham.

As a runner must train diligently to qualify to participate in the Olympic Games, so must preachers learn the discipline of regular study (2 Tim. 2:15) in order that their preaching is truly a word in season (2 Tim. 4:2). The necessity for the scholarly study of Scripture in the preacher's life is illustrated in the following story from the life of the Scottish theologian, James Denny. As a professor in the Free Church College in Glasgow, Denny, along with his students, were addressed by a well-known evangelist in a homiletics seminar. In the course of the afternoon, the speaker suggested that on occasions the preacher should go into the pulpit, find a text on the spur of the moment and preach, trusting in the Holy Spirit to give the inspiration for the sermon. On hearing this, Denny rose from his chair, his face red with outrage, turned to the speaker, wagged his finger, and said, "We, here in this college, set aside by the church, tell these men that there is no preparation too sacred or solemn for the ministry of Jesus Christ, and you come now and try to undo our work with these students. I think, sir, you confuse inspiration with desperation!"

### The Importance of Relevance

Pastor Leith Anderson offers the following observation on today's church and culture.

> The church has a responsibility to understand people and the culture in which they live. This means that the Bible must be made relevant in today's culture in order to benefit today's people. Life is difficult and disappointing, and typical church goers are struggling to survive. They came to church over-flowing with needs—family, marriage, job, money, health, re-lationships—and looking for answers. They need hope and meaning and have turned to the church because they can't find it elsewhere. Frankly, evangelical Christianity has done well on revelation (the Bible) but poorly on relevance (the culture). This phenomenon may be partially explained by the static nature of the Scripture and the dynamic nature of soci-ety—that is, the Bible doesn't change but culture does. This has been markedly evident over the past fifty years.[9]

Anderson is obviously concerned with bridging the historical/cultural gap between the ancient Near East and modern culture. This is important because an individual's outlook is the result of a particular philosophy of life. Philosophy is a perennial discipline which forms patterns of thoughts and creates a worldview, which in turn forms a grid through which individuals interpret and make sense of their world. As we discovered, Baby Boomers possess a pluralistic/relativistic worldview which controls not only their un-derstanding but also their response to life situations. Obviously, ministry to Boomers must challenge their philosophy if it is to produce conversion and the transformation of the mind (Rom. 12:2). The primary task, therefore, of the Christian instructor is to speak to the void of the hearts and minds of this generation. It is not necessary to produce a "new theology," but rather to reintro-duce classic theological truth within the sociological structure of the day and in a language that is understood.

In most Christian traditions, instruction at the local church level takes place in three distinct levels: pulpit preaching, Bible study in small groups, and adult catechumenate/discipleship classes. Those

**154**

responsible for these specific areas of ministry and who are concerned about maintaining an equilibrium which reflects a faithfulness to Scripture, a respect for tradition, and relevance to the secular humanistic cultural ethos of the Baby Boomer generation should consider the following three points:

(1) In the noble quest to be relevant, it must be remembered that the Christian faith carries a specific traditional content which has been formulated over the centuries on the basis of the biblical revelation. Christian teachers must recognize that they stand in a long theological tradition which cannot be ignored, regardless of the pressures of pluralism or the lure of religious consumerism. Karl Barth, battling the liberalism of his day, warned that the dangers of trying to formulate a "reasonable" faith molded by mere human preconceptions is threefold: intellectual, ethical, and soteriological. He maintained that the herald of the Gospel must always be faithful to proclaim the genuine meaning of the biblical text, even if it presents a hard pill for the listener to swallow. No matter how strong the temptation may be to minister to the obvious social needs of the Baby Boomers, the battle for truth must take precedence. To engage in less than this conflagration may justifiably bring the accusation that the church is, in Kierkegaard's words, merely caught up in the "twiddle twaddle patter of mediocrity."

(2) The contiguity between *kerygma* and *didache,* those characteristic elements of early church instruction, should be maintained at every level of the community's teaching ministry. In actual fact, the New Testament does not neatly compartmentalize, as Dodd suggests, *kerygma* for unbelievers and *didache* for believers as two successive activities. We read that Jesus taught in the synagogues and preached the Gospel of the kingdom (Matt. 4:23; 9:35; 11:1), and we see the Great Commission employing a similar juxtaposition (Matt. 28:19-20). In Acts 5:42, the apostles "did not cease to teach and proclaim Jesus as the Messiah"(NRSV). In the more organized and established communities of a somewhat later period, the *presbyteroi* (elders) and the *episkopoi* (overseers), were, among other things, responsible to both edify the believers and address apologetically all metaphysical and ethical doctrines incongruous with apostolic belief.

(3) There are a staggering number of contemporary issues pleading for a Christian response: social issues such as racism, human

rights, crosscultural prejudice, as well as poverty and homelessness; sexual issues such as the changing roles between the sexes, homosexuality, and pornography; personal issues such as physician-assisted suicide, abortion, euthanasia, and capital punishment; global issues such as pollution, population growth, and environmental stewardship.

The critical dimension of ethics needs to be explored from the Christian perspective. This area is particularly acute in light of the advancement of medical science which offers an enigmatic contribution to society. While the advantages and advances are incontestable, the other side of progress is also revealing. Science and technology not only solve problems, they also create new ones and run the risk of leading us perilously astray. The science that helps cure the child also makes it possible to drop the bomb. Too frequently, "can" supersedes "should", "ability" supersedes "obligation," and "no problem" supersedes "love."

Innovative scientific research in the area of medical technology is taking us into new places and, as it does, it creates new ethical problems for our society. Perhaps one of the most current and controversial fields of research is genetic engineering. At one time, this area moved at a snail's pace, but in recent years it has accelerated into the great unknown. Some scientists are presently engaged in projects mapping every gene in the human body and investigating ways in which to alter human cells — with positive and negative results. The potential consequences of this research are revolutionary, for good or evil. The ability to correct genetic deficiencies and cure genetically transmitted diseases may result, but the science of eugenics in producing designer babies according to a consumeristic society may also occur.

This example reveals one of the fundamental problems with the application of science and technology — namely, that its evolution excels the rate that human beings evolve in a social sense. This results in a tension wherein we find ourselves at odds with our technological capacity and scientific potential. The consequences of such genetic research may result in positive ways in the healing of bodies, but it may also cater to our vanities as demonstrated in the indulgence of cosmetic surgery. The underlying question that screams out to us as a society is not whether we *can* do all that science has to offer, but rather whether we *should* do all that is possible.

## Three Areas of Teaching in the Local Church

### Proclamation: Teaching from the Pulpit

Although the method of Bible study and instruction varies considerably from church to church, the sermon remains of primary importance. It is not, as it has sometimes been in church history, a moral essay or an emotional appeal. Neither is it a purely intellectual exercise, nor a dry lecture on theology. It is an essential aspect of the overall experience of worship. The sermon's traditional elements (liturgical, expository, and prophetic) combine the varying strands of worship with the goal of challenging the congregation. It is here that teaching, preaching, evangelism, and education merge to edify the Body of Christ.

However, it should be noted that laypeople notoriously complain that sermons contain too many ideas and are frequently too formal, impersonal, and propositional. Furthermore, preachers tend to be pedantic, assuming too much theological understanding from their listeners; their sermons often reach a dead end, giving little guidance for commitment or action. In order to address these concerns, the modern preacher may want to consider employing a variety of creative tools to assist in making communication more effective.

*Drama.* Historically speaking, Christians have expressed mixed feelings regarding the value of drama as a method of conveying theological truth. For example, Tertullian, the Puritans, as well as some modern evangelical groups, have condemned drama as a worldly intrusion into the life of the sacred. Other Christians, however, believe that drama is a powerful vehicle in which to present religious truth, as it has the ability to touch people at the depths of their imagination. Thus, the stories of such biblical characters as Cain, Abraham, Jacob and Esau, King Saul, Esther, and Jesus Christ, as well as such biblical events as the Fall, the Exile, the Captivity, and the Crucifixion, have been retold in dramatic form with considerable success. For example, since 1663, the eight-hour Passion Play, performed by 1,200 local actors in the Bavarian village of Oberammergau, continues to draw thousands of people by its dramatic re-creation of the events of the Crucifixion.

At a less elaborate level, I have found it useful to employ dramatic stage presentations and musicals during the high seasons of the Christian year—Christmas, Palm Sunday, Easter, as well as once or twice through the year. My musician/composer wife has co-written three musical dramas based on various aspects of Scripture: "When the Cock Crows," "These Are the Words of Jesus," and "The Kingdom." These musicals were designed to draw upon the talents of a typical congregation, to incorporate the full age span of all members, and to combine unlikely groups of people who would not normally interact with one another. Musical and acting experience was not the major requirement to become involved, as many congregational members used their skills on costumes, sets, props, programs, and hospitality for rehearsals. Without exception, the six weeks of rehearsal proved to be a powerful community-building experience. Finally, each musical was presented to the congregation in two packed performances with an atmosphere as exciting as any Broadway musical. In the final analysis, those on stage were as instructed in their faith and knit together in a close bond of fellowship, as those in the audience. The resulting effect of such an effort was evident by the new-found friendships, by the sense of oneness in sharing a memorable experience, and in the revelation of many hidden talents.[10]

Given the fact that the Scriptures contain such a wide range of subjects, it is not difficult to see why the preacher would want to use drama in support to the theme of the sermon. In addition, there is the educational value of the research, rehearsal, and presentation of a particular dramatic enterprise. In one sense, the weekly liturgy of the church is a form of drama. This is particularly evident in the death and resurrection themes of the baptism and eucharistic liturgy.

*Dance.* Dance has a significant role to play in the worship life of many religious traditions. In the Judeo-Christian tradition, dance was used in the expression of joy because of liberation from the physical slavery of political bondage (Ex. 15:20-21) and as an outward expression of spontaneous praise (Ps. 150:4). Since World War II, liturgical dance has gained wide acceptance in many Christian communities, largely due to the efforts of the Sacred Dance Guild and the Christian Dance Fellowship.

Like drama, I have found liturgical dance to ba a particularly useful form of teaching during the festive seasons of the Christian year—Palm Sunday, Easter, and Thanksgiving, as well as baptism and wedding services. Far from being a frivolous intrusion into the worship experience of the community, a carefully choreographed liturgical dance can be a great blessing to many.

There are many valuable aspects of liturgical dance that recommend it to the life of the worshiping community. It reinforces worship as our active response to God's love. In the well-known story of the Prodigal Son (Luke 15:11-32), Luke informs us that when the wayward son eventually found his way home, his father celebrated the homecoming with music and dance (v. 25). Likewise, liturgical dance is a Christian response in celebration of our Heavenly Father's love for us and in our homecoming to God's redeeming grace.

It is unfortunate that for many Baby Boomers the church has been traditionally viewed as having a damper on such outward manifestations of joy and celebration (cf. Luke 15:28). Nonetheless, it has been my experience that liturgical dance, offered with sensitivity and care, can be a deeply moving experience that enriches and enhances corporate worship.

In the natural order we see how the wind blows, the clouds move, and the grass, flowers and trees sway in motion. Likewise, when the Spirit of God blows through our congregational worship, movement among the people of God can be expected by such physical expressions as hand clapping, lifting of holy hands in praise, and the physical movement of dance.

In a world weary of words, interpretive dance has the ability to penetrate the depths of the heart in noncognitive ways by communicating the love of God to a hurting world. Dance recognizes the integral relationship between mind and body and acknowledges that there are many occasions when words alone cannot fully communicate the deep and mysterious ways of God. Dance can be a meaningful avenue to express theological truth when it takes the form of storytelling, accompanies a Scripture reading, or illustrates a biblical theme, all supplementing the sermon.

*Lectionary Preaching.* Over the years of my ministry, I have been privileged with many opportunities to preach and teach in a wide variety of denominational settings. I have been truly blessed by such occasions and value the diversity of the Body of Christ as a result. However, in preparing for such times, it always struck me a little odd to discover that the text choice for a particular Sunday was my choice. While I appreciated the freedom and trust given to me, I was usually in a quandary in trying to decide what passages might be applicable and appropriate. Trying not to approach Scripture in a haphazard fashion, I would invariably settle on the familiar, not knowing when the text was last expounded on, nor when it might be used again in the future.

For better or worse, in my own tradition such freedom to choose at random is not encouraged. Rather, the preacher is invited to deal with the Scripture text in a systematic way in the context of the church's calendar year. Frequently, these passages cause me to chart a course into the unfamiliar and wrestle with the more obscure aspects of the biblical message. The idea behind the lectionary approach is the attempt to expose the people of God to "grasp how wide and long and high and deep is the love of Christ, and to know this love that surpasses knowledge" in order that the Body of Christ "may be filled to the measure of all the fullness of God" (Eph. 3: 18-19). For this reason I urge my fellow pastors and teachers, regardless of denominational affiliation, to consider using the lectionary for the following reasons:

(1) It provides an opportunity for the Word of God to be read publicly, systematically, and thematically through the daily and weekly set texts, which includes an Old Testament, Psalm, Epistle, and Gospel reading. As discussed earlier, the public reading of Scripture was part of Christian worship from the very beginning. Furthermore, the formulating of worship around Scripture was a Christian inheritance from the Jewish synagogue. The lectionary is helpful in that it prevents the practice of the favorite-and-familiar-passage syndrome of either the preacher or visiting guest speakers.

(2) The lectionary exercises a theological control of the sermon by exposing the congregation to the "whole counsel of God," rather than a consumer sampling provided by random texts.

(3) The lectionary connects preaching with the church's calendar of Advent, Christmas, Easter, Pentecost, and Trinity. This ensures that proper weight be devoted to each person of the Trinity.

(4) The lectionary guarantees the status of the Old Testament in the spectrum of divine revelation.

A short-term preaching series, carefully planned and deliberately advertised in advance of the event, also has value. As most congregations consist of needy individuals looking for answers to problems of family, marriage, job, money, health, and relationships, the preacher may find it occasionally beneficial to teach on the more immediate domestic issues.[11]

*Teaching: The Small Groups Context*
When it comes to teaching in small groups, the form of instruction changes from monologue to dialogue. From individual persuasion to the community perspective. The inductive approach to Bible study is one of the most helpful in bridging the gap between the ancient text and modern culture.[12] The major advantage of this approach is that it produces a sense of individual self-discovery through the process of reading the actual text in its proper context and then applying its meaning through a series of questions. The stages involved in the process of inductive Bible study are threefold:

(1) Observation of the Actual Text
   ● Who/when/where/what happens list
   ● Identification of key words and ideas
   ● Note of figures of speech
   ● General observations

(2) Interpretation of the Text
   ● Categorizing observations
   ● Why/how
   ● Cultural background
   ● Meaning of key words
   ● Literary links
   ● Thought flow

(3) Application of the text
   ● First-century application
      — to people in the story
      — to those who read it
   ● Twentieth-century application
      — to our culture
      — to our communities
      — to us personally

**161**

One of the most challenging aspects of this process is the preparation of the questions which provoke the interactive process. In forming these questions, one must keep in mind the following types:

Fact Questions
- Focus observation
- Facilitate self-discovery
- Key words: who, where, when

Meaning Questions
- Analyze/ Interpret
- Use assembled facts
- Open-ended
- Key words: why, what, how

Application Questions
- Link passage to experience
- Resonance
- Open-ended

Other Questions
- History giving
- Interaction
- Generalizing
- Personalizing
- Clarifying

Basic Guidelines on Question Preparation
- More open than closed
- One question at a time
- Specific not general
- Answerable
- Too compressive?
- Too easy, too hard?

*Instruction: Adult Catechumenate/Discipleship Classes*
As the church grew and spread into the Roman Empire, it became necessary to instruct new converts on how to live their new Christian lives in the midst of a pagan society. This instruction took the

form of a catechism, which laid the groundwork for such formulas as the Nicene and Apostles' Creeds and the Chalcedonian formula. Likewise, similar instruction should be provided for those inquiring about the nature of the Christian faith, as well as those seeking baptism, confirmation, and/or membership into the church. In some traditions, interested parties are presented with a threefold mnemonical introduction to the Christian faith: the Lord's Prayer, the Apostles' Creed, and the Ten Commandments. There can be little doubt that teachings on these three subjects are very useful as they contain a significant amount of doctrinal, traditional, and devotional material. However, to some extent they reflect a bygone age, when it was assumed that individuals possessed a foundational knowledge of Christianity. Times have changed. It is therefore incumbent upon those who teach adult catechumenate classes in a post-Christian society, to cover elementary aspects of the faith.[13]

## Other Opportunities for Theological Formation

Ours is an expeditious age and as such many individuals who are living at breakneck speed neither have the time nor the energy to think deeper than the latest emotive newspaper headline or sensational TV news broadcast. As a result, they find it difficult to penetrate further than their unexamined prejudices. Furthermore, their evaluations of issues often reflect the opinions of the last person they spoke to or the last book they read. In view of these circumstances, the church should take advantage of every opportunity for expanding the mind.

### Retreats

Countless people today testify to the barrenness that the busy life can bring and the devastating effects of multitudinism. In an attempt to create balance in their lives and find time for reflection, many individuals are rediscovering the value of a retreat. Examples of such times of temporary disengagement are modeled in our Lord's journey into the wilderness, St. Paul's withdrawal into the Arabian desert, and in the lives of many of the great saints.

Retreats usually include rest and recreation as part of the spiritual formation process. It is a particularly significant event for Baby Boomers, who are generally overcommitted and caught up in the fast lane of the modern world. However, life at breakneck speed exacts a hefty tariff. One has only to consider the toll that busyness renders to the creative side of human beings. Having precious little time or energy for recreation, much less for study or specialization, people can become nothing more than mere replicas of their heroes. Plagiarism, once frowned upon as a form of intellectual larceny, becomes a way of life. Less people are willing to be risk-taking innovators of change, as more are content to remain clones of tradition and prisoners of the status quo.

"Know thyself," said the ancient philosopher. Perhaps the most tragic consequence of life in the fast lane is that it often causes polarization in human personality, disconnecting people from their true selves. This lack of self-awareness causes individuals to become what others judge them to be. In other words, they know themselves chiefly by hearsay. Christian leaders are certainly not immune from such forms of self-neglect. Indeed one of the hazards of parish ministry is the "borrowed identity syndrome," which a leader may be tempted to adopt in order to fulfill a pre-described role. The sad reality is that from a leadership standpoint, it is doubtful whether anyone can make a significant innovative contribution to the life of the institution, ecclesiastical or secular, while hiding behind the mask of a borrowed identity. The retreat allows people the opportunity to turn away from the hectic rat race to examine who they truly are and whether their lives are going forward, backward, or in repetitive self-destructive cycles.

A retreat also focuses on developing personal faith and fellowship within the church. The teaching component should be related to some field of theology, pastoral care, biblical studies, or spiritual formation.

*Quiet Days*
Solitude is an indispensable part of the Christian life (Ps. 46:10). Without deliberate withdrawal from the busy world, individuals are particularly susceptible to the buffeting pressures. Such stress and tension frequently drain the individual's emotional and spiritual reservoir. A quiet day or two in solitude often goes a long way in the replenishment of that precious limited supply of vitality. A quiet day resembles a retreat in many ways, only shorter in time. It offers an opportunity for busy people to relax, read, pray, and receive spiritual direction. Again, this is a relevant form of ministry to a generation who find that life is passing them by.

**164**

## Personal Development Seminars

General studies on Baby Boomers reveal that many are interested in strengthening the family. To harness this interest, seminars can be offered that deal specifically with family/parenting issues from a Christian perspective.

Studies also reveal that large numbers of Baby Boomers have experienced the trauma of at least one divorce and several subsequent unhappy relationships. This suggests that divorce-recovery workshops and interpersonal relationship-oriented seminars may meet a deep need.

Many sociological studies affirm the fact that technological gains in our society cause the loss of human dignity. Christianity asserts that humankind has value and that human dignity can be found in a loving relationship with God. In these dehumanizing times, this Christian message has great significance to Boomers, having now discovered that dignity cannot be discovered in a plastic world.

Furthermore, stress is a very serious phenomena within our contemporary culture due to increasing fears of job security and the intense competition that exists for advancement. Topics that assist individuals in dealing with stress may prove to be valuable and relevant.

## Theater

Along with the guild of sacred music, some congregations and Christian organizations are rediscovering the guild of sacred drama. Take, for example, the Rosebud School of the Arts which is located in a small rural community in Alberta, Canada. As a Christian organization, its central mandate is the promotion and advancement of the Gospel through the medium of theater. Its ministry is geared to serving both the church and the world. A guest at the theater is first treated to a country banquet-style meal, while being serenaded by guild members. Supper is then followed by a quality, live theater production, whereby a Christian perspective on a particular subject is presented in the form of drama. An example of such a performance would be *Valjean: La Condame,* a revised version of "The Bishop's Candlesticks" from Victor Hugo's classic novel *Les Miserables.* This creative and nonthreatening approach to presenting the Gospel has been so successful that advance booking is essential. The theater is presently attracting some 16,000 Christian and non-Christian people annually.

**165**

### Cultural Awareness Instruction

Historically, the Christian community has been divided in its attitude toward the arts. Broadly speaking, those who adhere to the Christ-against-culture position, generally doubt the didactic value of the arts for the Christian community. As a result of this defensive position, new converts are subtly or overtly encouraged to listen exclusively to Christian music, to read only Christian books; to avoid dances, movies, and theaters; and to attend exclusively Christian institutions of learning. It is not that the arts are forbidden, but rather that aesthetically acceptable art tends to be that which can be easily recognized as being "Christian." Consequently, many Christian homes and institutions are decorated with stereotypical paintings, plaques, and posters of suitable art.

Others, who adhere to the Christ-the-transformer-of-culture position, are less cautious in their approach. While careful to reject those aspects of the culture that are incompatible with Christian belief, they recognize the value of the arts for the following three reasons:

### God the Artist

Theologically speaking, a Christian may argue that the ultimate foundation and basis for aesthetics is derived from the biblical doctrine of Creation. This doctrine declares that the complexity and awe-inspiring beauty of our world is the supreme masterpiece of a creative God. It also implies that since God is the source of all creative energy and that nothing exists except by providence, then God's handiwork may be found in the rich variety of expressions created by individuals formed in the image of God.

In the medieval period of the church's history, scholars quested after truth by probing into a wide variety of sources and disciplines. This search is expressed in the well-known scholastic formula, *fides quaerens intellectum* (faith seeking understanding). Recognizing the principle that all truth is God's truth, they believed that theology was the ultimate tutor of all knowledge. Having this foundation, they were open to being informed by, and contributing to, the ongoing exploration after knowledge, known then as *trivium* (grammar, rhetoric, and dialectic) and *quadrivium* (music, art, geometry, and astronomy).

The scriptural injunction to "glory in God's handiwork" (Ps. 19:1, RSV) should give Christians courage and perhaps even permission to inquire after truth and beauty wherever it may be found. This search for truth naturally involves a lifelong study of the Scriptures, which inevitably leads into the area of epistemology, while the search for beauty leads into the so-called secular world of aesthetics. Whenever truth and beauty are found, they may be understood as creative contributions by individuals formed in the image of God and therefore to be used in the service of God.

## Enrich the Community of Faith

The arts have played a significant role in the edification of the Christian community. Consider the contribution that drama has made to the liturgical life of the church. Music, as diverse as Mozart's *Coronation Mass* to Amy Grant's praise songs, has also played a significant part in the enrichment of the worship life of the church. Music offers the Christian community an opportunity to formulate faith in ways that cannot be adequately accomplished by traditional methods. It also facilitates a valid emotional experience and guards against the tendency to be overly left-brained and cognitive in theological education.

Furthermore, the art of Michelangelo, Raphael, Rembrandt, and such modern artists as Grunewald, remain tremendous sources of inspiration for the Christian community, not to mention the didactic value of the beautifully illuminated texts of the Middle Ages and the graphic presentation of biblical stories retold in the form of stained-glass windows. The poetry of John Donne, George Herbert, and T.S. Eliot also contribute to deepening the faith of the Christian community.

## Inform the Community of Faith

The arts also inform the Christian community of the state of the world it has been called to serve. If the church truly desires to get its finger on the pulse of the surrounding culture, it only has to look to the influential world of film. Movies are not made in a vacuum, but rather are a carefully marketed product which reflect the good, the bad, and the ugly of our society and as such offer a mirror image of the cultural realities of our day. This medium has more than its fair share of crass, pornographic, violent, and occult-related productions to be avoided. However, we must be careful not to throw the baby out with the bathwater, as there is a growing trend among some producers to develop movies of substance

**167**

which project an obvious message of concern regarding the destructive and dehumanizing aspects of our society.

My point may be further illustrated by three recent films which not only informed but challenged me to reconsider my previously held prejudices against some aspects of liberation theology. The first movie, *Romero,* chronicles the true story of an apolitical academic Roman Catholic priest who served the peasants in El Salvador. Much to his surprise, Romero was elected Archbishop and in his new role was confronted with the option of either maintaining the status quo or taking a stand against the social injustice and oppression. This compelling and deeply moving story details the Archbishop's choice to swim against the tide by speaking out on behalf of the oppressed and underprivileged masses under his care. The movie concluded with his 1980 cold-blooded assassination while celebrating the eucharist.

A similar theme is portrayed in *The Mission,* which narrates the story of two very different Jesuit priests, who unite to shield a South American tribe from brutal subjugation by the invading eighteenth-century colonial empires. The movie revolves around the question of whether or not the priests should take a passive role and pray for God's intervention, or take an active role by taking up arms to defend the tribe from pending exploitation by greedy European interlopers.

The third movie, *Cry Freedom,* deals with the contemporary issue of apartheid by documenting the true story of Stephen Biko's fight for equality and justice in South Africa and that of a liberal white editor, who risks his life to take Biko's message of nonviolence to the world. This riveting story offers the viewer a stirring account of humanity at its most evil and most heroic form.

To a generation raised on television and videos, an opportunity to view and discuss the philosophical worldviews imbedded in such popular movies may have significant value to the ongoing theological education of Baby Boomers in particular as well as the Christian community.

The arts can also inform the church of its blind spots and shortcomings. This may be illustrated by drawing an analogy from the world of psychiatry. The Johari Window is represented by four windows of perception in aiding the individual to understand oneself from a broad perspective. The public window denotes the insight individuals have of themselves; the private window reveals that perception which is known to self, but hidden from others; the unknown window indicates the lack of individual and collective cognition, and the blind window describes that which is unknown to self, but known to others.

In applying this analogy to the corporate life of the church, it can be enlightening for a congregation to discover how its self-perception can be quite different from the perspective of new members and visitors. A recent incident in my own experience demonstrates this well. A few years ago, I was the senior pastor (rector) of a large urban church known for being "in renewal." The church perceived itself as being inclusive, welcoming, and as a loving Christian family. Few could doubt that our Sunday morning worship was a wonderful celebration of our "new life in the Spirit," and a great effort was exerted toward building a sense of community. One day I received a very moving letter from a Baby Boomer couple who had attended our church for some time but had decided to move on. The content of their letter added a wider perspective, revealing that we were in danger of becoming a spiritual club for the spiritually elite. The letter mentioned that while they appreciated our worship services, they found themselves isolated during the after-worship coffee hour, unable to penetrate the invisible "club status" wall. Their perception revealed that while we prided ourselves in inclusiveness in worship, we had neglected to see that we had become exclusive in fellowship. In ministry to Baby Boomers it is vital to keep in mind such blind spots. Unnecessary rules, secondary doctrinal matters, anachronistic language, and clubism all create unnecessary roadblocks in their spiritual journey.

It was the Scottish poet Robert Burns who wrote, "Oh wad some power the giftie gie us to see ourselves as others see us." On a lighthearted vein, the English author and TV host Adrian Plass helped the Christian community to laugh at itself in the humorous accounts of the *The Sacred Diary of Adrian Plass* and *The Horizontal Epistles of Andromeda Vear.* On a somewhat more satirical and sophisticated level, the Roman Catholic novelist Flannery O'Connor made use of her surroundings in the rural south to express her view that while Christianity is a revealed faith it is also a mystery. Through a series of unforseen circumstances, her oddball characters (who typically are the know-it-all type) suddenly experience new insights into the nature of reality.

**169**

The point made throughout most of her writings is the ever-present danger of myopic focus which invariably obscures the wider perspective. Her stories particularly address the don't-confuse-me-with-the-truth types among us.

## The Challenge Before Us

By way of summary, biblically relevant teaching should be viewed as a life-long process whose ultimate goal is focused toward the transformation and the renewing of the mind (cf. Rom. 12:2). It is also a life-oriented process which attempts to enable the believer to discern "the spirit of the age" (cf. Eph. 4:13-14; cf. Col. 2:8). Given that one-sided forms of specialization in any field invariably produces a narrow and distorted view of reality, it is imperative that the content of Christian education be as all-embracing and germane to the contemporary scene as possible. One of the most significant events that has occurred in our day is the growing quest among physicists to develop a comprehensive picture of the nature of reality. In constructing such a worldview, scientists have been forced to move beyond scientific empiricism and rationalism to include metaphysics. Likewise, theological education must move beyond the narrow confines of "in house" issues that all to often dominate the Christian adult education programs. In seeking to relate theological education to the contemporary scene, a staggering amount of issues evoke theological reflection:

- What are distinctively Christian values?
- What does it mean to follow Christ in a pluralistic society?
- How does technology affect our faith?
- What is the meaning of money, credit, and financial power from the Christian perspective?
- How should the Christian define success, wealth, and the abundant life?
- How much should believers contribute to "the common good"?

Since the Christian faith is a "living faith," we must now move beyond those matters which refer to the cognitive apprehension of theological and doctrinal matters to those which relate to our encounter with the "living God," through the gift of worship. Once again, we can refer to Buber's categories by saying that in moving from matters of the *head* to matters of the *heart,* we make the shift from the I–It encounter with God to the I–Thou experience.

# Chapter 6
# TRANSCENDENT WORSHIP

There are many different types of bridges. However, regardless of their obvious diversity, bridges serve one major purpose—to shorten the distance separating people and to remove obstacles that would make commuting difficult. For example, the erection of the 3,540 foot suspension bridge across the Bosporus at Istanbul, became the first permanent highway to link Europeans with Asians.

The major obstacle between God and creation was that of human sin, pride, and rebellion. This barrier was so extreme that close fellowship became impossible, and time and distance only further complicated matters. The dilemma itself was clearly visible. However, the resolution as to how to overcome this great distance was not. As we discovered, God overcame this stumbling block through the death and resurrection of Christ, who once and for all became our divine Pontifex (Latin: bridge maker).

Likewise, the church's ministry of worship is intended to act as a bridge in which worshipers find a pathway to the presence of God. At such times of intimate communion, we often discover that the endless concerns of career, finances, security, and interpersonal relationships lose their stranglehold, giving way to a perception of the divine which is often lost in the busyness of modern life. The way that our awareness of a transcendent reality can alter our perspective of our earthly reality is illustrated by an incident that occurred to a college friend of mine. As a newly ordained pastor, he was sent by his bishop to a small rural community. Anxious to make a good impression on his first Sunday, he prepared the liturgy with care and his sermon with sensitivity. However, he was terribly discouraged to discover a mere handful of people gathered for the Eucharist. Feeling obliged to continue the service, he began to read the liturgy. When he arrived at the familiar words "with Angels and Archangels, and with all the company of heaven, we laud and magnify Thy glorious name," his disheartenment suddenly lifted. For above and beyond the empty church he was able to see the wider perspective of the unseen world.

## Worship and Social Responsibility

It is important to state at the outset of our discussion that Christian worship is never meant to be an end in itself, nor does it exist to simply meet our personal and selfish needs. Rather, it has to do with the purpose of life as a whole and should have a profound impact on the individual's personal ethics and social responsibilities. Frequently, the term "numinous" (probably coined by Martin Buber) is used to describe the wide range of responses that worship can evoke. This term denotes emotions such as awe, fear, excitement, and tranquility. However, it should be noted that Scripture never gives the impression that the sacred is completely divorced from the secular. Let us briefly consider the experience of Isaiah, Peter, and John, the writer of the Apocalypse, to illustrate this point.

When Isaiah suddenly found himself in the presence of God, his first response was not "hallelujah!" or "praise the Lord!" rather fear and remorse. His reply to this remarkable encounter was, "Woe is me! For I am lost; for I am a man of unclean lips" (Isa. 6:5, rsv). As the story unfolds, the Lord asks an open-ended question, "Who shall I send, and who will go for us?" To which Isaiah responded, "Here am I! Send me" (Isa. 6:8, rsv). The task that followed was not an easy one as it involved the prophet delivering a word of judgment to his people.

Peter's divine encounter occurred on a mountaintop. His reaction, however, was quite different from that of Isaiah. He seemed to bask in the heavenly presence stating, "Lord, it is well that we are here." On descending the mountain, however, Peter was im-

**172**

mediately faced with the harsh realities of life. In this instance, the bubble of divine serenity burst when he was confronted by a desperate epileptic seeking healing, the shortcomings of the disciples' faith, and a sharp rebuke from Christ (Matt. 17:1-21).

John had the fascinating experience of being in the Spirit on the Lord's day. This encounter led him to an extraordinary vision of the risen Christ, of whom we are told that "His face was like the sun shining in full strength" (Rev. 1:16, RSV). John's response was that of trepidation, which caused him to fall at the feet of the glorified Lord "as though dead" (Rev. 1:17). Once again, we discover that this was not the end of the story. John was commissioned to communicate a personal message from Christ to the leaders of the churches in Ephesus, Smyrna, Pergamum, Thyatira, Sardis, Philadelphia, and Laodicea.

From these three examples we learn that Christian worship has a bearing on our relationship with others. It carries the social responsibility of bringing the sacred into the secular and vice versa. At the local church level, this may be achieved by ensuring that in preparing for worship, the prayers, music, and the sermon should in some significant way address the pertinent issues of the day. These would include such national issues as racial tension, homelessness, victims of child and drug abuse, and gang violence, not to mention such global concerns as apartheid, mass destitution, population explosion, and environmental issues. Certainly there is a time and place for prayer, personal concerns, and songs that express such sentiments as, "I love you, Lord, and I lift my voice to worship you." However, this should be balanced by intercession for others less fortunate. Songs like Graham Kendrick's, "O Lord, the Clouds Are Gathering," takes the words from Isaiah 58:6-9 and Amos 5:24 as a starting point in requesting that the church be forgiven, restored, and revived. It also mentions such germane issues as lawlessness, war, hunger, and street violence, crying out to God for justice in the nation.

## Maintaining the Integrity of Worship in a Consumeristic Society

The church, in seeking to express its worship life in Christ, draws its form of expression from two sources: the Christian past (Scripture and tradition) and the culture of the surrounding community. Here, balance is the key in making this merger a happy one. It

**173**

should be noted that some authors and church leaders dismiss the significance of Christian traditions or treat these time-honored cultures "lightly" in an attempt to reach the unchurched Baby Boomers. Considering the fact that Boomers are notorious destroyers of tradition, this is a very tenuous position. Throughout their lives, Boomers consistently challenged and changed conventions to suit their consumeristic needs. The phrase, "we came, we saw, and we conquered" is particularly apt in describing this generation. With this in mind, this book has argued against change for change sake, as it is my conviction that it is dangerous to the health of the church for ministry to be practiced without solid foundations in Scripture, tradition, reason, and experience. Far from holding tradition "lightly," it may be more prudent to hold tradition "tightly." New forms of worship may not be as expedient as the reintroduction of classical forms of worship, paralleled with corresponding education on the profound historical meaning behind the church's ritual and symbolism.

In some ways, the Roman Catholic Church, since Vatican II, led the way in this area with its policy of *aggiornamento,* that is the adaptation of worship to the temperament, tradition, and culture of people. Competent scholarship in this process of adaptation is essential to insure that changes in worship are based on solid biblical, historical, theological, and pastoral principles. Otherwise, as previously mentioned, such changes are subject to the personal whims of a consumeristic society or other factors irrelevant to the Gospel.

## Traditional Worship and Contemporary Reform

The author of the *Book of Common Prayer* (1549/1552), Archbishop Thomas Cranmer, used a fourfold set of guiding principles when making his sweeping liturgical reforms in the worship life of the newly formed Church of England. These four principles continue to provide a solid foundation for discussing the form and nature of Christian worship.

### Doctrine and Worship

Cranmer suggested that worship should be biblical in familiarizing worshipers with the context of Scripture and that it draw on the imagery of the Bible.

Considering the fact that Baby Boomers have been absent from

**174**

the church most of their adult lives and are biblically uninstructed, Cranmer's recommendation is helpful for two reasons. First, in a society so permeated with relativism, this is a timely reminder that the words and actions used in worship reflect the beliefs and theological values of the worshiping community. After all, God can hardly be glorified by saying wrong and careless things about Him. Second, if the language of worship is permeated with Scripture, it provides Boomers an opportunity to learn more about the "unsearchable riches of Christ" (Eph. 3:8) and safeguards worship from simply being an emotional experience, void of a sound theological framework.

Cranmer's suggestion that worship be biblical is not a novel idea. In the Old Testament, extensive teaching informed worshipers how to approach a holy God. For example, in Exodus, Leviticus, Numbers, and Deuteronomy, careful descriptions were given about the tabernacle, the altar, the show bread, the candles, the incense, and the movements of the priest on the Day of Atonement. This suggested that the words and actions used in the context of worship were of considerable significance to God. In the New Testament, similar instructions governing the basic principles for worshiping God "in Spirit and truth" are given. They outline such aspects as God-centered worship (1 Peter 4:11); the congregational nature of worship (1 Cor. 14:26); prayer and worship (1 Tim. 2:1-3); the intelligibility of worship (1 Cor. 14); and patterns for worship (Acts 2:42-44).

### Worship and Language
Cranmer suggested that worship should be adaptable to the language, customs, and circumstances of the worshipers.

When the early missionaries translated the New Testament into Inuktitut (Eskimo), they were immediately faced with some very knotty problems. For example, how were they to translate such well-loved biblical terms as "salvation," "redemption," or "regeneration" to a people who had no word for "guilt" in their language? How were they to explain such terms as "shepherd" or Jesus as the "Lamb" of God to a people who had never seen a herd of sheep roaming the tundra of the high Arctic? What did it mean to the Inuk ear to hear the opening words of the eucharistic prayer, "Lift up your hearts"?

Believing that the Scriptures were above having to be adaptive

**175**

to the receiving culture, the texts were translated as written in hopes that somehow the cultural gap could be bridged. Those involved in a subsequent revision of the Inuktitut Bible some fifty years later, took a radically different approach by searching for culturally dynamic equivalents to foreign biblical concepts. An example of this approach would most likely translate Jesus as the "Seal of God," who, like God's sacrificial Lamb, laid down His life sacrificially by shedding His life-giving blood for the health and nourishment of the community.

Language, whether in native community or a sophisticated city in North America, is never stationary but grows and develops. Unfortunately in this present generation, much of the language seems to be decaying. Although new words have been added from many parts of the earth and from the world of technology, there has been a corresponding decline in the ability of expressing feelings or abstract thought. This creates a generation far less adept in the creative understanding of symbols and metaphors.

Cranmer wrote in a language clearly understood by the common people, thus his choice of Tudor English over Latin. However, his true genius was found in his ability to produce a *Book of Common Prayer* that was biblical, dignified, attractive, and yet contemporary. In recent years, liturgical traditions in many parts of the world have been introduced to a variety of alternative service books of worship. The liturgical scholars responsible for these books recognize that however quaint the language of the sixteenth century, its continued usage implies a preservation of a historical artifact, as meanings once significant to a people of an earlier time are no longer expressive of modern community. These liturgical scholars attempt to maintain the theological content of Cranmer, update the pre-Industrial Revolution language of thee's and thou's with a language of today, and be sensitive to exclusive and sexist language that may be offensive to others.

Cranmer's observation that the church should be "adaptable" applies significantly in reference to the Baby Boomers who make up such a large segment of the North American post-Christian society. Frankly, too much Christian jargon is used with the underlying assumption that the terminology is widely understood at the congregational level. In reality, much of this ecclesiastical language is as bewildering to the uninitiated as Latin was to the pre-Vatican II Catholics living in America.

**176**

## Charismatic, Evangelical, and Catholic
## Dimensions of Worship

Cranmer believed that worship should continue the traditions of the ancient church.

The tension between charismatic, evangelical, and Catholic approaches to worship has existed since New Testament times. Those in the charismatic camp have tended to be highly suspicious of prayer books and liturgical services. Believing that worship should be under the direct guidance of the Holy Spirit, individuals are encouraged to "wait upon the Lord" and to be open to whatever spontaneous work the Spirit may desire. This may include such things as prophecy, speaking in tongues, and healing. Within the context of worship, believers are invited to manifest their praise in demonstrative ways by such expressions as clapping, raising of hands, dancing in the Spirit, or singing in the Spirit. A scriptural example of such extemporaneous worship can be found in the Acts of the Apostles, where the Holy Spirit suddenly announced to the Antiochian congregation that Paul and Barnabas were to be set apart for the enormous task of carrying the Gospel to Europe (Acts 13:2-3).

Evangelicals, while more formal in their worship services, also tend to avoid liturgical services, acquiescing only for such occasions as weddings or funerals. Whereas charismatics emphasize spontaneity, evangelicals emphasize the primacy of preaching as the crux of the worship event. Believers are exhorted to seek opportunities in their daily lives to bring Christ to those who are broken, bruised, or suffer poverty of body, mind, or spirit. Once again, Scripture has much to say about the importance of preaching the Gospel (Matt. 28:19-20). There can be no doubt that many evangelical churches are numerically growing, while other denominations are diminishing. They have discovered the simple truth that the church that lives to itself will die by itself.

Those in the liturgical traditions unashamedly use prayer books at all main services of worship. As traditionalists they are quick to point out that the church has a past that extends beyond the sixteenth century and like all living organisms has an ancestry which includes the saints of a bygone age as well as a long and rich heritage. The importance given to the church's history is seen in the incorporation of the contributions of these past saints in the form of the creeds, confessions of faith, litanies, and prayers. Tra-

**177**

ditionalists believe that to exclude this historic legacy from the worship life of the community, or to judge liturgy as merely an archaic relic of the past, is tantamount in denying the church's spiritual legacy.

One of the most significant developments in bridge-building history was the decision to tether the single fallen tree trunk to others, thus providing a crossing that was not only stronger but also wider, allowing more people to cross over and to furthermore permit them to journey together. In a similar manner, if the church were willing to cord together the charismatic, evangelical, and Catholic dimensions of worship, it could also provide a wider, more balanced and secure bridge to connect the Baby Boomers with the living God.

The binding of these three legitimate expressions represents a holistic approach to worship. Indeed, the whole question of how human personality types and worship preferences fit together is a fascinating area to be explored. Suffice to say that such a connection does exist. Generally speaking, extroverts being more gregarious and vociferous are more likely to be drawn to charismatic worship, whereas the more analytical types will be drawn to the denominations where preaching is central and where the emotional level is subtly monitored and controlled. Introverts on the other hand, being more reflective and reserved, are more likely to be involved with those traditions where symbolism, sacrament, and liturgy are emphasized.

A healthy balance between these three strands would provide a means of ministering to the needs of the whole person. Human beings are emotional creatures, and the church should encourage this emotional dimension which charismatic worship can provide. However, any form of worship, exuberant and rapturous as it may be, which invites individuals to leave their critical faculties outside in the church parking lot, is not beneficial to the process of spiritual formation. Along with a heart to feel, human beings have also been gifted with a mind to think. This means that our faith must be reasonable, intelligent, and communicable. The church that diminishes its teaching and prophetic role does so to its own peril. To this extent the evangelical emphasis on good, solid biblical preaching is both justifiable and necessary.

While we must avoid the dangers of an inflexible and fixed liturgy which leaves no room for the freedom of the Holy Spirit, we must also avoid that position that allows traditional patterns of worship to fall into a "Babylonian captivity" because of their previous misuse. There can be little doubt that ritualism, formalism, and the slavish use of the liturgy can produce a predictable and mechanical form of worship, but they also offer many positive aspects; and there is surely a place for the formal dimension to worship that liturgy offers. Consider the following:

• There is the value of having "heard it all before," in that the words and ideas become internalized — and therefore an intrinsic part of the individual.

• A balanced liturgy, which allows room for individual extemporaneous contributions, gives both objectivity and subjectivity to a worship service.

• The use of a form of service insures that worship does not become overly dependent on the worship leader. Liturgical services normally include significant responsive participation for members of the congregation.

• Worship books provide a balanced diet of praise, penitence, prayer, and confession to services.

• Service books are thoroughly punctuated by the language and ideas of Scripture rather than the personal views of a particular individual denomination.

• A carefully written service of worship ensures that the community has a rich theological content to its worship.

It is sometimes common to hear Christians speak of the "Third Wave." This term is used to describe the acceptance of the charismatic dimension into a particular denomination's tradition. For example, if a Baptist church were influenced by the Third Wave, it would not abandon its tradition to become a charismatic church, but rather allow its tradition to be transformed and invigorated by the power of the Holy Spirit. It is difficult to tell whether or not the Third Wave will prove to be a widely influential and lasting movement in effectively changing the mainline churches. However, there are indications to suggest that there is interest among growing numbers of evangelicals to explore the liturgical and sacramental dimension of worship. Several Episcopal bishops have informed me that many nonconformist pastors wish to be received into Episcopal ministry. In my pastoral experience, the last two congregations I served were largely comprised of a mixture of Pentecostals, Alliance, and Baptists, who valued liturgical worship, especially the frequent celebration of the Eucharist. If we put these movements together we discover that there is a growing groundswell of Christians who desire to grow in all the dimensions of the charismatic, evangelical, and Catholic traditions.[1]

### Prayer, Christian Festivals, and the Breaking of Bread

Thomas Cranmer believed that worship should continue the customs of the ancient church. At first glance, Cranmer's position may appear as one more indication that the church is an anachronistic institution from a former age, incongruous with the concrete realities of modern life. Prayer, seasons of celebration, worship, and the sacramental breaking of bread may be fine for monks secluded in monastic cloisters, worlds apart from the hum of the inner city, but irrelevant for the vast majority of Baby Boomers who are unavoidably caught up in the pressures of modern life. Those who advocate the importance of the spiritual are perceived as ghostly voices from the past, completely out of tune to the present state of affairs in the "real world."

While not denying that we live in a material world, Christianity maintains there is more to a person than mere matter, that people are more than human computers; rather, human beings are essentially spiritual beings with an innate capacity to be cultivated through the historical spiritual disciplines recommended by Cranmer. These ancient traditions deserve our attention because they have endured the passing of time. Generations have found them to be of value in the quest toward human holiness, and there is no reason why Baby Boomers would be any different.

Christian communities, as distinctive as the Greek Orthodox to South American Pentecostals, the Egyptian Coptics to Southern Baptists, and the Presbyterians to Roman Catholics, express their worship in many diverse ways. To the casual onlooker, these multifarious expressions of worship appear as incongruous and unrelated. However, there exists a pandemic form to Christian worship, which the church inherits from Christ. These features imprint a Gospel shape on church communities around the world and contribute to a distinctive tradition of Christian spirituality. Let us briefly consider three of these facets: prayer, festivals of celebration, and the breaking of bread.

**180**

*Prayer*

In the Christian tradition, prayer is the response to a belief in a living and personal God. This belief in God is more than the assent we give to such facts as the sun being 93 million miles away or that William the Conqueror landed in England in 1066. When the creed of the church states, "I believe in God," the term used is a verb, implying an active response. Thus, prayer is a conscious focus toward God as creature to Creator with the expressed goal of unification with God. Or as the Spanish Carmelite nun Teresa of Avila was fond of stressing, prayer is both a conversation with God and an exchange of friendship with God.

Jesus practiced the spiritual discipline of prayer. At all focal points in his ministry it was important for him to pray (Luke 3:21; 5:16; 6:12; 9:28; 10:21; 11:1). His prayers not only related to those times when praise and thanksgiving were in order (Matt. 11:25-27), but also in those times of great sorrow and anxiety when he faced excruciatingly difficult choices (Mark 14:32-36; cf. Heb. 5:7-8). As a spiritual director par exellence, Jesus gave guidance to his disciples on how to best formulate their prayers (Luke 11:1-13) by simplifying the structure and suggesting the removal of "empty phrases" (Matt. 6: 5-8, RSV). He also introduced a new sense of intimacy in prayer by the use of the Aramaic word, *Abba* (Mark 14: 36). Finally, Jesus taught his disciples to pray in his name (John 14:13; 15:16; 16:23ff).

We know from the Book of Acts that the apostles rooted their lives in the habit of prayer. As a community of faith they frequently gathered for prayer, whether in the Upper Room (1:12-14, 23-26; cf. 2:42; 4:23-31; 12:5), at the Temple (2:46; 3:1; cf. 22:17), or in the simple setting of a home (2:42, 47). When divine guidance was required, their first response was to address God in prayer (1:24-25; 6:6; 13:2-3; 14:23; 20:32). When a healing was needed, they called out to God in prayer (9:40; 28:8). Prayer was also offered in times of great insecurity (4:23-31), and it was during the act of prayer that the Holy Spirit descended, filling the apostles with a new and intoxicating spiritual wine that left them reeling with a holy joy and a new boldness to proclaim the Gospel (2:1-4; cf. 4:31).

Since prayer has the uncanny ability to lift individuals beyond their immediate pragmatic needs and invites them to put their faith in the providential goodness of God, its cultivation should

**181**

provide a significant relief for Baby Boomers. It was Kierkegaard who suggested that the efficiency of prayer lies in the inner transformation of the one who prays. As this generation is stressed as a result of the bind of narcissistic self-interest, the practice of prayer and the frequent worship of God can only assist individuals in breaking free as it focuses trust beyond themselves into the greater reality of the existence and presence of Almighty God. Essentially, Christian prayer is rooted in the existential question of trust. It focuses toward a God who cares (Ps. 68:5; Matt. 6:26, 32; Luke 12:30), who protects those who call upon God's name, and who is unconditionally trustworthy (Ps. 89). Take, for example, the Lord's Prayer (Matt. 6:9-13). The first half of the prayer is devoted to God alone: God's name, kingdom, and will. The second half is concerned with human needs of bread, forgiveness, guidance, and protection. Learning to practice the prayer of supplication bestows a peace that transcends all understanding (Phil. 4:7), but does not imply that "what you ask is what you get." Rather, it often results in clarifying the difference. St. Augustine recognized this when he wrote, "Good is the God who often does not give us what we want so that he may give us what we should want."

As previously mentioned, Baby Boomers are discovering the importance of spirituality and in doing so are realizing that while science explains many mysteries in life, it does not dispel all mystery—one being spirituality and another, the mystery of prayer. Mystery and transcendence are essential aspects of human life, without which we would become mere thinking machines with no interest beyond the rational and the pragmatic. The spiritual nature of humankind is evident by the millions of believers throughout the world and from every walk of life who take time to regularly cultivate their religious life and times of prayer.

During the Renaissance, there were also those who challenged science as omniscient—one being the brilliant mathematician and Christian philosopher, Blaise Pascal. This French prodigy contributed much to the world of science in discovering the principles of the barometer and hydraulics and by devising a calculator. Nonetheless, he feared that the worship of science threatened spiritual values. He also felt that science's claim to contain the only truth and certainty for which assent should be given, had overextended itself. Although Pascal did not deny the value and power of rational thought, he also upheld the importance of faith in the pursuit of truth. He maintained that we know truth not only by reason, but also by the heart. He noted that the heart had its reasons, but reason knew nothing.[2]

A contemporary indictment of modern science comes from the pen of Bryan Appleyard. He believes that science has done appalling spiritual damage to humankind. Science, he maintains, rules the day but offers no truth, no guiding light, and no sure path. According to Appleyard, this crisis began in 1609 when Galileo peered through his telescope inventing the concept of experiment and observation as the ultimate bastion of knowledge. This new perspective which eschewed value and meaning eventually found its philosophy in Cartesian dualism and ultimately in its final expression in Darwinism. Appleyard maintains that there is a conspiracy at work in modern science in that it frequently poses its own questions, insisting that these are the only ones which exist. Science, ignoring that which it cannot understand, suggests such a conspiracy is at work — one being those subjective experiences indicating that human beings possess not only self-consciousness but also a soul, a category that modern science does not take seriously.[3]

*Christian Festivals*

During the era of the Reformation, a reaction occurred against seasons of prayer and celebration. This reaction was particularly strong in the Reformed and Anabaptist wings of the movement. In extreme cases, it led to the total rejection of all Christian festivals and prayer customs not explicitly sanctioned in the Bible.

This response has cast a long shadow on the history of the church's worship. However, in recent years another revolution is taking place in the worship life of the Christian church. These changes include such things as the widespread adoption of the ecumenical lectionary and the creative use of drama, mime, and dance in festivals of praise.

Human beings have a natural desire to celebrate important events and turning points in life. They celebrate victories in war, national events of significance, birthdays, wedding anniversaries, graduations, and the winners of sports events. Given the fact that individuals establish routines, customs, and habits to govern their lives, it seems logical that the people of God cultivate routines of worship. The church calendar helps establish these routines by providing liturgical forms for events worthy of human celebration. The following will provide some examples of liturgical celebration that may be used to draw people together in a worshipful way.

*Classic Christian festivals*

| Christmas | Harvest | Ash Wednesday |
| Easter | Lent | Good Friday |
| Pentecost | Advent | Remembrance |
| Trinity | Palm Sunday | Thanksgiving |

*Relational liturgies*

| Marriages | Baptisms | Mother's/Father's Day |
| Confirmation | Anniversaries | |

Renewal of Marriage and Baptismal vows

In order to restore the rhythmic nature of the liturgy back into the life of the church, several significant changes need to take place. One would include dethroning the evangelistic sermon from being the chief focus of worship to simply a part of the overall service. In many traditions this change would include a major paradigm shift regarding the nature of the church's existence, as the present predominant view sees it existing primarily to win lost souls for Christ. James F. White calls this one of the greatest apostasies of evangelical worship, as it gives "the unscriptural notion of the church as merely an instrument for gaining citizens for the future kingdom, rather than involved as an essential part of life in the kingdom itself."[4] According to White, this reversed priority is seen in the prevalent order of worship concocted by revivalism: preliminaries, a sermon, and a harvest. White concludes that this basic threefold order is worship as a means of changing humans rather than offering praise and glory to God. A more biblical position is one that places the adoration and praise of God at the center of the church's worship life.

This balance between word and worship, sermon and song, is vital in light of the fact that spirituality is becoming a topic of great interest to Baby Boomers. Contemporary spirituality attempts to see faith from a holistic perspective which includes the rational with the emotion. Baby Boomer interest in this holistic approach is demonstrated by the number of books on matters of spirituality — works from such Christian classics as Thomas à Kempis' *The*

*Imitation of Christ,* Ignatius of Loyola's *Spiritual Exercises,* to that of T'aichi, plus a host of spiritual psychologies that perceive spiritual/religious practice as a form of mind training. Retreat centers offering workshops on spirituality are also popular. Spiritual directors, involved in guiding others on prayer, meditation, and other matters of the soul are becoming as sought after among Boomers as psychological technicians and therapists.

Therefore, apart from being a good theology of worship, it is important that Christian spirituality be a broad form of spirituality that not only engages the head but also the heart. The ultimate goal of every worship service is not to solely present the Christian faith in a rational way, but to lift the whole person into the presence of God. Like the experience of the two disciples on the road to Emmaus, we should desire that Baby Boomers leave a worship service saying, "Were not our hearts burning within us while he . . . opened the Scriptures to us?" (Luke 24: 32)

### The Breaking of Bread

Fellowship meals, as mentioned in the Acts 2 passage, reflected the empirical crisis in Jerusalem, that is, a famine which threatened starvation to impoverished members of the community. *Koinonia,* as table fellowship, gave expression in this context as one of the essential elements of the newly created community life. Closely connected to this table fellowship (which St. Ignatius called the *agapa*) was the sacramental meal called the "breaking of bread," a technical term for the whole meal *pars pro toto.*[5]

Again, the cultural context is important. There is plenty of evidence in the New Testament to support the importance of meals in the life of the Jewish people. To the Jewish mind, a common meal tended to symbolize a common faith. The fellowship, which Jesus practiced at the meal table, had both a *kerymatic* and *didache* significance. He shared in the meals of friends, officials, poor people, and the rich. However, in each instance, he did not come with empty hands, but with a revelation of the kingdom of God (John 2:1-11; Matt. 9:10-13; Luke 5:29; 7:36-50).

Perhaps the greatest example of this is found in the event of the Last Supper which Jesus shared with his disciples. After offering the familiar prayers of thanksgiving and praise, Jesus took bread and said: "Take it; this is my body." Then he took the cup, gave thanks and offered it to them, and they all drank from it. "This is

**185**

my blood of the covenant, which is poured out for many" (Mark 14:22-24).

At the same time, Jesus saw his sacrificial death in the light of the final coming of the kingdom of God: "I tell you the truth, I will not drink again of the fruit of the vine until that day when I drink it anew in the kingdom of God" (Mark 14:25). Interestingly, after the resurrection, when Jesus appeared to his disciples during their fellowship meals, it was in the breaking of bread that they recognized him (Luke 24:13-43; John 21:1-14).

The early Christians continued the tradition of meeting in homes for fellowship meals, which among other things, included the "breaking of bread," a fellowship meal held in remembrance of their Lord (Acts 2:42; 20:7, 11; 27:35; 1 Cor. 10:16; 11:23; cf. Luke 24:35). Originally, the phrase, breaking of bread *(tei klasei tou artou)*, was a technical expression for the action of tearing the bread apart and pronouncing the blessing over the food at the beginning of the meal.[6] Eventually it referred to the informal supper of shared food, during which they formally celebrated the Lord's Supper in anticipation of the heavenly marriage feast that lay ahead at the end of the age (Acts 2:46; cf. Rev. 19:9). Whether or not the Acts 2:42 passage can be properly described as sacramental is outside the scope of this discussion. However, the passage does provide a picture of the simplicity of the event. At the gathering, the believers simply and reverently passed the bread and the cup from hand to hand, reflecting on what it cost Christ to allow his body to be broken and his blood to be shed for them.

So prominent was the place of preaching, teaching, and Eucharistic fellowship that it is not surprising to find the same emphasis among the early church fathers. In the following quote from Justin's *First Apology*, prominence was given to both word and sacrament.

And on the day called Sunday, all who lived in cities or in the country gathered together to one place, and the memoirs of the apostles or the writings of the prophets . . . [were] read, as long as time permitted; then, when the reader . . . [had] ceased, the president verbally instructed, and exhorted to the imitation of these good things. Then we all . . . [rose] together and prayed, and as we before said, when our prayer . . . [was] ended, bread and wine and water . . . [were] brought,

and the president in like manner offered prayers and thanks-
givings, according to his ability, and the people assented,
saying Amen.[7]

Another development of the sweeping renewal in today's worship is the rediscovery of the significance of the Eucharist as the
sine qua non of Christian worship since the first century. Although, White suggests that *some* American Protestant denominations prefer to approach the sacraments in the spirit of eighteenth-
century rationalism, that is, not viewing the sacraments as a
divinely appointed means of grace, characteristic of Luther, Calvin,
and Cranmer, but rather relegating them to the margin of church
life by making them pious memory exercises of humans.

> The legacy of the Enlightenment among American evangeli-
> cals led to infrequent celebration of the Lord's Supper and
> then in a most perfunctory fashion. Instead, preaching tended
> to make worship more cerebral as if there were no need for
> God's love to be made visible in sacraments. Indeed, the term
> "ordinance" was often substituted for "sacrament" and tend-
> ed to foster a legalistic attitude. Christ commanded baptism
> (Matt. 28:19) and said "Do this" of the Lord's Supper (1 Cor.
> 11:24-25). The legalistic term "ordinance" hardly touches the
> sense of mystery in God's self-giving that sacrament implies.[8]

Hans Küng summarizes the central importance of this meal for
the church in this way.

> So much is clear: The Lord's Supper is the center of the
> Church and of its various acts of worship. Here the Church is
> truly itself, because it is wholly with its Lord; here the
> Church of Christ is gathered for its most intimate fellowship,
> as sharers in a meal. In this fellowship they draw strength for
> their service in the world. Because this meal is a meal of
> recollection and thanksgiving, the Church is essentially a
> community which remembers and thanks. And because this
> meal is a meal of covenant and fellowship, the Church is
> essentially a community, which loves without ceasing. And
> because finally this meal is an anticipation of the eschatologi-
> cal meal, the Church is essentially a community which looks
> to the future with confidence. Essentially, therefore, the
> Church must be a meal-fellowship, a *koinonia* or *communio;*

it must be a fellowship with Christ and with Christians, or it is not the Church of Christ. In the Lord's Supper it is stated with inccmparable clarity that the Church is the ecclesia, the congregation, the community of God.[9]

Interestingly enough, the return to a richer sacramental life of worship may help the church meet the Baby Boomer quest for transcendence and, at the same time, develop a deeper sense of community. Take, for example, the service of the *agapa* meal. This word, *agapa* (love), is a New Testament term which denotes a gathering of believers around a common table for an informal time of fellowship and worship. Such occasions are specifically referred to in Acts 2:42, 46; 6:1-2, as well as other Christian literature dating back as early as the middle of the second century. From these references and with a little imagination, we are able to construct a fairly accurate picture of these festive and joyful "love feasts." The evening would consist of food, conversation on spiritual matters, prayers of thanksgiving and petition, and a message of encouragement. It was probably on such occasions when the believers would exercise spiritual gifts (1 Cor. 12 and 14), as well as sing psalms, hymns, and spiritual songs (Col. 3:6-17; cf. Eph. 5:19-20).

The appropriateness of this meal is obvious. Unlike the formal, liturgically ordered Eucharist, the agapa meal resonates with the basic human ritual of eating and drinking around the kitchen table. It is in this context where individuals gather to share a meal, to experience a feeling of companionship and family while providing an opportunity to discuss matters of common concern.

In its distinctively Christian context, the *agapa* meal with its horizontal and vertical emphasis provides an excellent opportunity for Christians to experience what it means to be the family of God and to take an active part in the affairs of the household of faith. For many traditions, Maundy Thursday liturgy provides an opportunity to experiment with such a meal, but for nonliturgical readers the *agapa* meal can quite easily be celebrated in small group settings, at retreat weekends, and other special occasions at any time throughout the Christian year. To ease the concern of adequate preparation of food, tickets may be provided. If the meal is a success, plans may be made to incorporate the *agapa* meal into the regular life of the parish. Below is a suggested pattern for the meal I have used on many occasions.

**188**

Opening hymn
Confession and Absolution
Soup or fruit juice
Ministry of the Word
Main course
Teaching
Intercessions
Sweet Course
Prayer of Humble Access
Consecration and Distribution
Closing Hymn
Dismissal

## Worship and the Role of Music

Cranmer suggested that worship be orderly, reverent, and a corporate activity which includes the whole people of God. When we consider the question of orderly and reverent worship, we inevitably think of the role of music. While few would doubt the intrinsic value of music in the enhancement of corporate worship, the contention usually revolves around the style and content of the music used. Some denominations seem to have an eclectic preference, which ranges from the Gregorian chant and the elaborate choral anthems of Bach to the grandiose organ music of Mozart, Mendelssohn, and Tallis, while others favor simple guitar-based choruses and folk masses, or the congregational hymn singing of the Moody/Sankey era, black gospel, pop, country, rock, and even Christian heavy-metal music.

### Music Ministry and Baby Boomers

Baby Boomers, rebelling against the secularism of today's society, are questing after transcendence. This presents a challenge for the church to provide a meaningful corporate worship experience that enables this generation to encounter the living God. One way of encouraging the intimate presence of God is in the proper use of music. In this context, it should be kept in mind that this generation grew up with television and is accustomed to being entertained. But in the noble quest to be relevant to the Baby Boomers, the church must be careful that its choice of music serves a greater purpose than simply drawing a crowd.

Some authors suggest that Baby Boomers require a form of

worship that is lively and relevant, thus causing them to be attracted to those churches which cater to their musical tastes.[10] This view unashamedly promotes the use of bluegrass, rap, jazz, and rock/pop styles of music in the sanctuary to win the hearts and minds of Baby Boomers for Christ. However, as every church leader well knows, introducing new forms of music is a tricky business that needs to be handled with care — especially for the elderly whose traditional music is full of sentiment and security. The following points should be kept in mind in seeking to offer this generation a form of music that communicates theological values and integrity:

(1) The Bible views music as an intrinsic part of life and as such has validity in the worship life of the community of faith. David, a talented singer, composer, and musician, is credited with organizing professionally trained groups of musicians. These instrumentalists and singers utilized a wide range of musical instruments which enriched and ameliorated worship expressed in the temple of the Lord (2 Chron. 5:12-14; 7:6).

(2) The type of music used in the corporate worship of Almighty God should be didactic in nature and aesthetically tasteful. Music that smacks of sentimentalism, theatricalism, and virtuosity should be avoided.

(3) The lyrics of sacred songs should act as a handmaiden of theological truth in being God-centered and God-directed. The singing of scriptural passages has always been a strong element in the tradition of Christian worship, as it provides a wonderful way for the worshiper to internalize the Word of God. However, a comparison between some forms of contemporary Christian music with the sacred music of an earlier time will reveal an almost narcissistic self-interest and entertainment approach today. Certainly we can applaud the intimacy with God that many of the contemporary songs provoke, focusing more on the immanent rather than the transcendent presence of God. However, care must be taken to insure that a healthy balance is maintained between the personal and possessive pronouns "I," "me," and "my" with the "we," "us," and "ours" of the great hymns of the nineteenth century. Furthermore, the music director must always keep in mind that the goal of the music offered in worship is not simply to help people "feel good," but rather to lead them into the *mysterium tremendum* of God's holy presence.

(4) The innovators of contemporary sacred music need to value its past and keep in mind the fact that Christian worship has deep and historic roots. To deprive the Baby Boomers of the hymns of William Cowper, George Herbert and music by Thomas Tallis, Orlando Gibbons, and Ralph Vaughan Williams would be a crime. Furthermore, it is simply uncouth to suggest that such master-pieces as Handel's *Messiah* or Beethoven's *Missa Solemnis* have no place in the modern church.

(5) The traditionalists need to bear in mind that not all contemporary Christian music is shallow. Much of today's music is outstanding in terms of music style and theological content. Recent years have seen great improvements in the quality of choruses and praise songs from the previous decades.

(6) As much as possible, a church should seek to balance the old with the new. Scripture recommends such a balance when it speaks of the threefold order of "psalms [traditional], hymns, and spiritual songs [contemporary]" (Eph. 5:19; Col. 3:16). This communicates the message to the congregation that the Christian community values its past and at the same time embraces the future in terms of worship styles and musical flavors. In the prevailing pluralistic ethos of the day, such diversity poses few difficulties even to Baby Boomers.

(7) Either contemporary or traditional music, if performed well and dedicated to the glory of God, is a powerful ministry. The greatest danger in music ministry is not the date of a particular composition, but rather "mediocrity." Unimaginative arrangements and fifth-rate compositions, regardless of the instrument, do little to enhance the atmosphere of worship.

(8) Churches seeking to reach the Boomer generation are wise to develop a mission statement that communicates the values of the church regarding the purpose and role of music in worship.

The following is an example of such a statement developed by the music ministry of a Baby Boomer congregation in Eastside Foursquare Church in Kirkland, Washington:

● We believe music—scores, as opposed to lyrics—is amoral (neither moral nor immoral).
● We believe music is a communicative tool and device for evangelism and outreach.
● We believe music is one of the clearest and most profound

forms of worship expressions our human spirit can offer to God, who deserves the best, not mediocrity.

● We believe every human being was created to worship God and hungers to do so. Truly heartfelt worship is in itself not only an expression of evangelism, but also of healing to our human spirit.

● We believe music is a viable tool to instruct and to allow our human spirit an opportunity to experience God's divine touch.

● We believe music in church should be of a quality and style comparable to that of the culture-at-large.

● We believe music in church shouldn't be very much different from the music that fills our everyday lives in order for it to communicate effectively.

● We believe music should be the balance of a vertical, God-related focus and a horizontal ministry of comfort, exhortation and evangelism. This balance must be maintained seriously if the worship, through musical experience, is to be fruitful.[11]

## Worship: Continuity in a Contemporary Environment

Christian worship is a multifaceted and precious jewel. It is through worship that the believer finds a vehicle in which to express those deep-rooted emotions of love and praise, joy and gratitude, pain and anguish to the living and immanent God. Since worship plays such an important role in the spiritual formation of the believer, it is vital that pastors and church leaders exercise considerable discernment when setting the tone of the church's worship life.

It goes without saying that the church "militant here on earth" in contrast to the church "invisible of the faithfully departed," exists in time. Therefore, we should expect the worship life of the church to evolve with each succeeding generation. As history unfolds and human culture develops the church carefully appraises, appropriates, and refines those aspects of life—cultural, aesthetic, social, and intellectual—within its worship life. Given the fact that the church does not exist in isolation from its context, such discerning appropriation is to be encouraged and indeed celebrated. However, while saying that the church exists within the flux of human history is not to deny the fact of its own historical root which spans the centuries returning to Christ himself. From its past, the church has inherited a distinctive Gospel imprint that defines the very nature of Christian worship. In our day, when religious consumerism is widely practiced and people go to churches with a shopping list of personal wants and needs, it is imperative that we understand the indispensable aspects of the church's worship life. True, creativity is a hallmark of the Spirit of God. To change is to grow, and to grow is a sign of health. But creativity does not demand the abolishment of the distinctive aspects of Christian worship, nor for that matter is it necessary to "invent" novel ways of expressing worship in order to be relevant. Rather, it is the church leaders' task in every generation to reinterpret and contextualize the traditional forms of Christian worship in a meaningful way. To proclaim the good news, to celebrate the great drama of redemption in song and sacrament, to pray for peace and unity in the world, and to live our lives in a doxological way, is at the heart of the Christian worship. It is not up for sale.

In referring to our Acts 2 model which has guided our discussion thus far, Luke informs us that in addition to the fellowship, teaching and worship of the community, "many wonders and miraculous signs were done by the apostles" (v. 43). It is to these miraculous signs that we now turn as we discuss the concept of healing.

# Chapter 7
# HEALING IN THE CONTEMPORARY CHURCH

A major breakthrough in the history of bridge building occurred when the ancient Romans developed the arch bridge. This structure consisted of massive concrete blocks, carefully cut and fitted to form a semicircular arch. When the bridge came under duress, the pressure was first diverted to the keystone situated at the top of the arch, then transferred outward and downward to the rest of the structure. The *Ponte Sant' Angelo* bridge in Rome, built during the reign of Hadrian in A.D. 136, is a testimony of the durability of this design.

Likewise, we can think of Christ as the keystone in the bridge leading people to health and wholesomeness. Considering the amount of pain in a fallen world, the church's healing ministry can become overwhelmed by the heavy loads exerted upon its structure. To survive such duress the church must first direct its prayer of intercession to Christ who mediates his grace outward and downward to the community.

In this chapter we shall explore the topic of healing by drawing from the familiar analogy of a hospital. In hospitals we typically find physicians, patients, and medicine, as well as holistic therapy programs which have been developed to speed up the recovery process. In our discussion we shall think of Jesus in terms of the Divine Physician, the Christian community as a hospital, and the sacraments/rituals of the church as the medicine which aids recovery. Before we proceed, however, we must say a brief word about miracles.

## Miracles: Past and Present

Miracles have played an important part in the history of the Christian church. The biblical records, from their very outset, presented a view of the world in which the miraculous or supernatural element was a natural and significant part. It is difficult to read about Jesus' ministry in the Gospel accounts, without a strong awareness of the great number and versatility of the miraculous deeds. Take, for example, the Gospel of Mark. About one third of the Markan material is devoted to miracles, and the range of these recorded miracles is staggering: eight healing miracles, four exorcisms, four nature miracles, and one account of resuscitation.

It is interesting that in the Acts of the Apostles, almost every type of miraculous phenomenon was duplicated to those attributed to the historic Jesus. Thus, we find various accounts of physical healings (Acts 3:1-10), exorcisms (16:16-18), and even two accounts of the raising of the dead (9:36-41; 20:9-12). See also Acts 9:17-19, 32-35; 14:8-11; 28:8. Reading further in the New Testament, we discover that the ability to perform such "signs and wonders" was attributed to the miraculous gifts of the Holy Spirit. These gifts included such supernatural phenomenon as prophecy, speaking in tongues, the interpretation of tongues, healing, and the working of miracles. Today, these gifts are often called charisma, charismata, charismatic gifts, or the gifts of the Spirit. (See Rom. 12:6-8; 1 Cor. 12-14; Eph. 4:11.)

The main purpose of miracles in the life of the early church seemed connected to attesting to the truth of the apostolic proclamation, in particular, its witness to the resurrection of Christ. Luke wrote that, "with great power the apostles gave their testimony to the resurrection of the Lord Jesus" (Acts 4:33, NRSV). In the first century of the church's history belief in miracles was considered a foundational aspect of Christian apologetics and the healings and exorcisms that continued in Jesus' name were viewed as confirming the promises made during his ministry (John 14:12). So extensive were these miracles of healing that some of the early Christian writers began to employ medical terminology in their christological and soteriological teaching, and it was not unusual to

**196**

hear of Jesus described as "the Great Physician."[1]

In classical Christian theology God is seen as the author of miracles by virtue of the attributes of supernatural existence and omnipotence. Since miracles are difficult events to prove conclusively if natural science could give a complete explanation of a miracle this would negate by definition what a miracle is, there have been many thinkers, scientists, and philosophers who oppose the possibility of the miraculous interruption or suspension of the natural process of things.[2]

Theologians also have wrestled with these matters to such an extent, that no clear consensus exists within the Christian community.[3] Many of the more liberally minded, Protestant critics tend to dismiss the New Testament miracle stories as mere distortions of history and regard the authors of such texts as incredulous. The more conservative wing of Protestantism tends to adhere to a "cessation theory" that maintains that miracles were intended only to empower the original proclamation of the Gospel in the Roman world. On the other hand, members of the Roman Catholic and Orthodox traditions, as well as other Protestant groups, Pentecostals, charismatics, and those under the "Third Wave" banner are swift to point out that miracles, far from dying with the passing of the apostolic age, are attested to in such texts as the New Testament Apocrypha, the writings of Patristic Fathers, and in the countless miracles stories recorded and associated with the lives of the saints in the medieval period.[4]

Those who seek to demythologize miracle stories tend to assume that the people of the prescientific age were unable to distinguish between supernatural phenomena and that of the natural order. Unquestionably, there were many such gullible and naive people, but there were also many sophisticated thinkers who believed in supernatural interventionism. Less we think of this latter group as confined to the untutored, it should be pointed out that some of the greatest scholars of the Christian faith have believed in the possibility of miracles—Ignatius, Irenaeus, Tertullian, Augustine, Bede, Aquinas, Abelard, and Anselm of Canterbury, to name but a few.

At this point, I should make my position clear. My spiritual formation began within a tradition where the cessation view was maintained. However, as I began to think more independently, I recognized that there was no clear evidence in the Scriptures nor in tradition to validate the cessation theory. My growing persuasion was further confirmed by a personal healing. This occurred while serving as a pastor in the High Arctic. Apparently I contracted an encephalitis virus, which caused severe headaches, nausea, disorientation, amnesia, and eventually paralysis. As there were no hospitals or doctors in my community, considerable time passed before an airplane transported me to a hospital in a major community. Upon arrival, the prognosis was not favorable. Concerned friends at home were informed by my doctor to expect the worst so as not to be too optimistic. While in a coma, my congregation organized a prayer vigil. Much to my doctor's bewilderment, I was soon up and around and shortly thereafter discharged. Reflecting back on this experience, I thank God for the doctors who cared for me and acknowledge the power of the prayer of faith made on my behalf. This experience did more to convince me of the efficacy of prayer and the power of God to heal than a library of theological treatises on miracles.

## The Divine Physician: Jesus

Although miraculous events were recorded regularly throughout most of Scripture, there seemed to be an intensification of supernatural activity around the great focal points of salvation history. One of these axis points was certainly the advent of Christ and the period of the birth and growth of the early Christian church in Jerusalem, as described in the Book of Acts. From the early church emerges a picture in which the believers took part in the fellowship and worship of the community, where the signs and wonders occurred. A study of these signs and wonders *(semeia kai terata)* reveal that the same power *(dunamis)* which enabled Christ to effect supernatural healing, was also at work in the apostolic community. Thus, we find various accounts of physical healing (Acts 3:1-10; 9:17-19; 9:32-35; 14:8-10; 28:8), exorcisms (16:16-18), and even two accounts of the raising of the dead (9:36-41; 20:9-12).

In the Gospels, Jesus manifested himself as a healer of the sick. Indeed, the designation "the Great Physician" was a favorite title of the early Christians and remains popular today in some Christian circles. From the beginning of his ministry, Jesus performed healing miracles (Mark 1:29-32, 40-45). These miracles were essentially meant to be "signs" that the new age of God's activity, as

**198**

mentioned by the Prophet Isaiah (61:1-2), had now dawned in the person of Jesus Christ (Matt. 1:5; Luke 4:18-19; 5:17; 7:22). While a detailed study of the healing ministry of Jesus is outside the scope of our discussion, the following general observations will be made regarding Christ's healing ministry.

## Extensive

Morton Kelsey comments that "nearly one-fifth of the entire gospels is devoted to Jesus' healing ministry and the discussion occasioned by it."[5] Jesus healed many individuals and unspecified numbers of sick people in groups. His ministry also included the healing of a wide variety of diseases, including physical disease, such as blindness and lameness, chronic disorders, such as paralysis, as well as those suffering from a variety of emotional illnesses. In him, the promise of the Prophet Isaiah was fulfilled. "Then will the eyes of the blind be opened and the ears of the deaf be unstopped. Then will the lame leap like a deer, and the mute tongue shout for joy" (Isa. 35:5-6; cf. Luke 7:22).

## Didactic

Frequently, Jesus performed healings more for theological purposes than altruistic. His wondrous deeds were not meant to be merely spectacular events in themselves, but rather as signs of the presence of the kingdom of God. They were performed primarily to reveal to Israel that he was the Messiah, whom their Scriptures had foretold (Matt. 11:4-5; cf. Isa. 29:18-19). The writer of the fourth Gospel makes the same point by referring to acts of healing as signs of who Jesus was (John 3:2; 20:30-31). For example, the healing of the blind man and the raising of Lazarus reinforce Jesus' claims to be the light of the world (9:5) and the resurrection and the life (11:25). These healings were outward and visible signs to reveal that in Jesus "the kindness and the love of God our Savior had appeared" (Titus 3:4).

Likewise, the main purpose of miracles in the life of the early church was to attest to the truth of the apostolic proclamation and serve as a means to accredit Jesus to the Jews. In particular, the miracles were a witness to the fact of the resurrection. They were the convincing proof that Jesus was alive, which Luke referred to in his introduction to Acts (1:3). "With great power the apostles gave their testimony to the resurrection of the Lord Jesus" (Acts

**199**

4:33, NRSV). Thus, miracles were a demonstration of the continued presence of Jesus with his people through his Spirit. They confirmed the promises he made during his ministry (John 14:12).

### Not Dependant on Faith

It is often a very disappointing experience for those individuals who, after seeking restoration from their sickness, are not healed. At such times, it is difficult to deal with the question of why the healing is denied. In the need to resolve this question, answers, even blame, have been cruelly directed toward the lack of faith by the sick patient, or the lack of faith by those involved in healing prayer ministry. In point of fact, faith is not always a necessary condition for healing. It is true that Jesus sometimes required faith before a healing would occur as "he did not do many miracles there because of their lack of faith" (Matt. 13:58; Mark 5:34-36), but this was not invariably the case. Clearly in the example of the blind man of John 9, the cripple of John 5, and the demoniac of Mark 5, Jesus healed them without being asked, and in return, demanded no conditional faith from them (see also Matt. 9:1-8; 12:9-13).

## The Church: A Hospital for the Sick

One of the most remarkable developments in American evangelicalism over the last decade is the new phenomenon known as the "Signs and Wonders Movement." Those reading the literature of this movement, or "Third Wave," may get the impression that the practice of healing is a relatively new phenomenon. This is not so. Throughout its history, the Christian church has accepted its God-given responsibility for the care and the healing of the sick. This responsibility was discharged in two ways. First, the church consistently provided hospitals, infirmaries, and similar institutions where the sick were housed as inpatients or treated as outpatients. The establishment of religious orders with the *hospitia* attached was another important factor in the spread of hospitals and the growth of nursing care. Second, in addition to providing such havens of hope for the sick, the church also ministered to them by means of anointing with oil, the laying on of hands, and prayer. In the annals of the history of the church past and present, there are many well-documented cases of miraculous healing.[6]

To see the church as a healing community is particularly significant in light of the sociological realities of our day. North American affluence has taken care of basic human needs, leaving people with considerably more time to dwell on personal issues of well-being. The fragmentation of family life has caused an explosion in the number of rootless and hurting people. The dehumanization of society has fostered an acute sense of alienation. And the stress of modern living has caused an increase in such illnesses as: colitis, hypertension, migraine headaches, obesity, insomnia, and peptic ulcers. In many ways, the Christian community may be the only hope Baby Boomers have left in their quest of health and wholesomeness. Furthermore, as healing is rarely an instantaneous event, individuals need the love and encouragement that community life has to offer in their journey from sickness to health. Not only does a loving community provide an atmosphere of hope to those seeking healing, but it also provides a community of support for those to whom healing has been delayed or denied.

## Medicine for the Indisposed: The Sacraments

The church acts as a therapeutic and healing community by its time-honored use of the prayer of faith, laying on of hands, and anointing with oil. There is also a strong Christian tradition suggesting that these liturgical acts on behalf of the sick should take place in the context of the Eucharist. Considering that the altar is associated with those special times of commitment, transaction, and rites of passage in our lives (the Eucharist, weddings, baptisms, funerals, confirmation, and ordination), it should also provide a very natural setting for us when we seek healing.

Centering it in this context of the community at worship not only gives healing its rightful place, as one facet of the church's ministry, but it also removes any danger of it being considered a "fringe activity" practiced only by virtuoso healers. It ensures that ongoing pastoral care will be given. There is a constant danger with this particular ministry, in that the actual healing segment may be elevated to the neglect of the necessary after-care which is so vital to insuring lasting success. To some involved in the healing ministry, the lengthy process of rebuilding the emotional and spiritual life of the individual pales in comparison with the more spectacular aspects of praying for the sick. However, if the ministry of healing addresses only the "symptoms" of the sickness and not the "cause," the risk is high that the patient may return to the former way of life and, with due irony, the last state may be worse than the first. The after-care process inevitably involves such things as pastoral care, personal counseling, elementary discipleship, and assimilation into the worship and sacramental life of the community.

Introducing anything new into the life of most congregations takes sensitivity, careful teaching, and a great deal of patience. With so many potential misconceptions and superstitions surrounding healing, church leaders are wise to write a philosophy of healing before launching out into this highly controversial and potentially divisive area. Such a statement of belief in the healing ministry is more likely to be supported by the congregation if it is written in a way that reflects the liturgical tradition of the denomination. Regardless of the particular theological tradition of the church, the healing ministry ensued inevitably includes the two liturgical gestures of laying on of hands and anointing with oil.

### The Laying on of Hands

In the Scriptures the imposition of hands was used for various purposes. It was practiced when conveying a blessing upon another person. In the Old Testament, we read of the custom of a father, aware of his imminent death, laying hands upon his oldest son in order to bless him. The blessing was given in the hope that his heir would continue the family name and the remaining family would prosper in every way (Gen. 27:1-40; 48:17-18).

In the early church, the imposition of hands was a frequent practice (Heb. 6:2). It was used in the commissioning of individuals (Acts 6:6; 13:2-3; 1 Tim. 5:22), to confer the power of the Holy Spirit (Acts 8:14-17; 19:6) as well as the gifts of the Spirit (1 Tim. 4:14; 2 Tim. 1:6). It was used by Jesus and his apostles in their healing ministry to the sick (Mark 6:5; 16:18; Acts 28:8). The laying on of hands is particularly significant in this regard, as it not only represents an outward and visible sign of the inward and invisible faith which one person shares with another, but it also serves as a means of conveying sympathy, affirmation, compassion, and identification with those whose health has failed them.

### Anointing with Oil

Oil has been used as a sacramental means of healing grace since New Testament times. When Jesus sent the Twelve on mission, we read these words: "They drove out many demons and anointed many sick people with oil and healed them" (Mark 6:13). Likewise the elders of the church were instructed to pray over the sick and anoint them with oil:

> Is any one of you sick? He should call the elders of the church to pray over him and anoint him with oil in the name of the Lord. And the prayer offered in faith will make the sick person well; the Lord will raise him up. If he has sinned, he will be forgiven. Therefore confess your sins to each other and pray for each other so that you may be healed (James 5:14-17).

The oil itself was not considered to be the agent of healing, but rather an outward and visible sign of an inward anointing of healing power of the Spirit. Oil is also regarded as a biblical metaphor for the Holy Spirit and when mixed with balsam, it is regarded as a symbol of the gifts of the Holy Spirit and the fragrance of Christian virtue.

## First Rate Therapy: A Holistic Approach to Healing

The modern division of human personality into physical and mental is a foreign concept to the biblical understanding of humankind. It was this philosophical view of people, as suggested by Descartes and others, which led modern science to view the human body as a complex aggregation of atoms, which reacted to physical laws like any other organization of matter.

Today, however, the tide of opinion has fundamentally changed from the strictly somatist view. It is now almost universally recognized that human beings are interdependent psychosomatic entities. This indicates that a person's emotional health (or more accurately, lack of emotional health) directly affects the body's immune system and vice versa. This recognition of the psychosomatic nature of people broadens the previous definition of health from being simply "soundness of body" to "soundness of body and mind," to which we may add "spirit" or "soul." While this contemporary development in our understanding of the nature of humans may be considered an advancement, in actual fact it is really a return to a position which was already understood by the Hebrews of a by-gone age.

Jesus viewed the individual as essentially a physical, psychologi-

**203**

cal, and spiritual being. The salvation and healing which He made available touched the whole person. Indeed the verb used to describe healing, *sozo* (Mark 5:23; Luke 8:36), can also be translated to describe the act of salvation. Let us now consider how the church might adapt a holistic approach to its healing ministry to insure that the ministry offered meets the total needs of the whole person in body, mind, and spirit.

### Physical Healing

Whatever the root cause, a chronic debilitating physical sickness permanently alters the course of an individual's life. In some instances, healing may occur by a natural process of recovery. In the Judeo-Christian tradition, this is normally understood as an expression of God's ongoing creation and as a token of the divine desire to restore humankind to what it ought to be. When physical sickness persists, it is normal Christian practice to pray for healing by intercessory prayer and the laying on of hands.

In this regard, most churches have to struggle with the mystery of why some are healed and some are not. Much confusion arises when some are apparently healed of lesser ills such as aches, nausea, and general malaise, while those with chronic organic-based sicknesses remain unhealed, even after persistent prayer and fasting. This very tension exists within the pages of the New Testament where many were healed in response to the prayer of faith, while others such as Trophimus (2 Tim. 4:20), Epaphroditus (Phil. 2:25-30), Timothy (1 Tim. 5:23), and Paul (2 Cor. 12:7-9) lived with their sicknesses and were sustained by God's grace.

### Emotional Healing

A healthy body is relatively easy to describe compared to that of a healthy mind. Good mental health cannot simply mean freedom from anxiety. Human life is a series of forked-road situations, and as such few people escape the anxiety which choice inevitably brings. Which of us, when pausing to reflect upon life experiences, cannot recount numerous instances of crisis that temporarily rendered us impotent in action? But with proper insight and perspective, these very crises became the spawning ground for a mature, purposeful response which led to further development in our growth toward wholeness.

A healthy mind cannot mean freedom from guilt. In fact, the

**204**

guilt emotion is a sign of mental health, as it is the psychopathic person who feels no guilt. Guilt feelings are a normal psychological experience and are inherent to most healthy people. Indeed, for many, guilt was the "painful blessing" which started the journey to salvation, as demonstrated by the pre-converted lives of such noted individuals as Paul, Augustine, Luther, John Newton, and John Wesley.

Likewise, a healthy mind cannot mean freedom from failure. To be human is to err, and at some point in our lives we all make mistakes. Perhaps the healthy mind is more apt to make mistakes due to the willingness of the creative mind to take risks and bold enterprises. As we are neither infallible nor omnipotent, failure is inevitable. These mistakes may be regretted, but for a healthy mind, past failures teach important lessons for the future. Sound mental health does not guarantee freedom from doubt. Human beings are not omniscient. We learn from our questioning about the nature of things, and from uncertainty and incertitude faith can grow. This was the experience of Thomas, whose doubts about the resurrection led him to eventually proclaim, "My Lord and my God" (John 20:28).

Anxiety, grief, guilt, and doubt are normal healthy emotions and if used wisely, constructively, and prayerfully can be important vehicles to lead us on the pathway to wholeness. Even suffering can be a tremendous agent of growth if embraced, rather than feared, avoided, or resented. Such experiences in our lives can become an opportunity for growth, reform, and renewal, without which our lives would become shallow, flabby, and futile.

An unhealthy mind manifests itself in such things as excessive forms of self-love which leads to narcissism and by the desire to dominate people or situations, through manipulation, deception, and other forms of egocentric behavior. An unhealthy mind produces such ambitious strivings for power, prestige, and status that all-consuming preoccupations develop, causing a breakdown in the equilibrium necessary for a healthy, balanced life. The unhealthy mind also produces individuals who are either excessively dependant, extremely passive, emotionally apathetic, or prone to self-delusions and self-deception.

Such destructive habits and actions, which we can call sin, produce a form of moral sickness which in turn affects an individual's health. From a Christian perspective, this moral sickness can be substantially healed by the act of repentance. Theologians, as well as psychiatrists and psychoanalysts, such as Freud, Jung, and Fromm, agree that such destructive tendencies as those mentioned above can be healed through confession (honesty), repentance (a change of behavior patterns), and the giving and receiving of forgiveness. As conversion is a critically important step to the recovery of the individual's health and the reorganizing of life's priorities, it is therefore important to keep the relationship between sin and sickness, repentance and health at the fore of the church's preaching and ministry of pastoral care. This is not to assume that healing is guaranteed on the basis of Christ's atonement. It does suggest, however, that the experience of regeneration can permeate the whole personality and initiate such a healing influence on the mind, that it precipitates the journey toward wholeness.

An unhealthy mind may also be the result of painful hurts in the distant past, rather than the personal choices one makes as an adult. These deep hurts, usually from painful experiences in early childhood, are often repressed and left unresolved. These repressed hurts frequently express themselves in irrational behavior, such as depression, compulsive tendencies, or persistent anxieties. The church can bring healing to such individuals by the use of the Healing of Memories. This ministry has been defined as:

> The prayerful process whereby the presence of Jesus Christ is symbolically introduced into a person's painful memory by one who functions as the intervener. The counselee is encouraged to relive the painful memory or set of memories in as much vivid detail as is possible, in order that the particular memory may be reconstructed in a positive way.[7]

The ministry of inner healing applies to all generations who have experienced pain and trauma. However, it should be noted that since Baby Boomers are one of the most indulged generations in human history, such egocentrism has exacted a high emotional toll. For many, the cost of success has been high, both psychologically and spiritually. When counseling Baby Boomers, I am repeatedly astonished by the recurring themes which arise during these sessions. Either in reflection of past events in childhood, or more frequently as a consequence of a narcissistic, sybarite life-style which sometimes has led to a series of unhappy relationships,

I frequently hear such expressions as, "I feel so guilty," "I'm so ashamed," "I've been so selfish" or, "If only I could control my impulsiveness."

In such situations, I usually refer to the biblical view of the interrelatedness of the whole person—body, mind, and spirit. I then try to explain how episodic memories are recorded and stored in our permanent memories in much the same way that a video tape records and stores information. From time to time, certain situations trigger the replay switch, causing those past painful memories to be retrieved from our permanent memory to our conscious experience and also causing the feelings of guilt and shame to surface. If these memories are not erased they will likely be manifested in some form of emotional sickness, which can ultimately express itself in highly destructive behavior. I then explain that through prayer and confession, whatever dark shadows lie deep within the ego, superego, or id, the light of Christ can reach down and dispel the repressed hurts with healing grace, or in other words, erase the tape.

## Spiritual Healing

While the notion of spiritual health is the most difficult to elucidate, we can say that a healthy spirit is always in a state of growth and changes toward maturity (Eph. 4:13). It also sustains the individual in the face of pain, grief, failure, or even boredom. Basic to a healthy spiritual life is its yearning for daily communion with God, its reaching upward in devotion to God, and its willingness to live each day in obedience to the will of God. In Christian theology, sickness of spirit is thought to be a result of unconfessed sin which exposes the individual to evil, eventually leading to destructive and compulsive behavior. Or, it is thought to be the result of willful dabbling in the occult through such avenues as astrology or as a result of intergenerational sin.

In connecting spiritual sickness with evil in this way, I am aware of the many theologically controversial and pastorally sensitive issues associated with the notion of the existence of a supernatural being operating at an ontological level. The cosmic "principalities and powers" that flowed across the pages of Paul's writings have been disregarded as mere anachronisms since the Enlightenment and the birth of the scientific age.

The extent to which belief in the existence of supernatural powers has declined can be readily seen by examining the content of scholarly works in theology written during this period. As a result of the prevalent disbelief in the objective reality of these powers, we find, for the most part, that these works make the barest of references to supernatural powers, benevolent or menacing.

However, there are signs that this phenomena, once consigned to the limbo of superseded myths, is being reconsidered. Growing numbers of scholars are wrestling with such biblical themes as principalities and powers, the discernment of spirits, and the nature of diabolical evil.[8] Perhaps underlying this resurgence of interest is the quest to understand why, in our post-Enlightenment world, such an abysmal degree of viciousness, truculence, and bestiality continues to flourish among humankind. Events at home and abroad force the thinking person to wonder if there is a radical wickedness endemic in the very structure of our individual and corporate life. As we become aware of the horrendous abuses that occur in the area of basic human rights, we ask if there are no limits to which even civilized nations will stoop when driven by an insensate madness for power and control. Not wanting to diminish human responsibility in any way, it would seem however, not unrealistic to consider that perhaps behind such odious social injustices and senseless inner-city violence may indeed be malevolent forces at work.

In returning to the New Testament text to reexamine the nature of supernatural phenomena, we discover a fallen archangel portrayed as the antithesis to the will and the purpose of God. As the leader of spiritual forces, this angel known as Satan, wages war against God by hindering the growth of the kingdom of God and conversely advancing the cause of evil. Satan is described as the prince of demons (Mark 3:20ff; cf. Eph. 2:2), the father of lies (John 8:44), and as one who is dedicated to embitter and obstruct believers in their spiritual journey. Demons are described as possessing vulnerable people, causing illness (Luke 13:11, 16; cf. Acts 10:38; 2 Cor. 12:7), and forcing people to act in highly self-destructive ways (Mark 5:5ff).

In the Gospels, a significant part of the ministry of the historical Jesus was given to the liberation of those trapped in this form of spiritual bondage. For example, the Gospel of Mark describes the life and work of Jesus as a battle with Satan (Mark 1:23-28; 32-34, 39; 3:22-30). Reflecting on this aspect of this ministry of Jesus,

**208**

1 John 3:8 states that, "the reason the Son of God appeared was to destroy the devil's works." The Pauline epistles offer additional insight into how Satan works to thwart the purposes of God. Paul describes Satan as one who can appear as an "angel of light" (2 Cor. 11:14) to tempt believers to forfeit their self-control (1 Cor. 7:5) and to deceive those seeking spiritual insight (2 Cor. 4:4). Therefore Paul urges Christians to give no opportunity to the devil (Eph. 4:27), to stand firm against satanic wiles (Eph. 6:11), and to recognize their struggle is not simply against human agencies but "against the cosmic powers of this present darkness, against the spiritual forces of evil in the heavenly places" (Eph. 6:12, NRSV).

Considering that Jesus deliberately gave power and authority over all demons to his disciples (Luke 9:1), it can been assumed that he meant for the practice of deliverance and exorcism to continue in the ongoing ministry of the church. Consequently, there is no shortage of historical records showing how this vital ministry to the spiritually afflicted has continued to be widely practiced in both liturgical and nonliturgical traditions since apostolic times.

Not only are there theological ambiguities connected to this form of ministry, but there are also pastoral ones. Since this kind of phenomenon, by its very nature, eludes human empirical observation and normal intellectual categories, pastors often find themselves with the complex task of making a valid diagnosis regarding the kind of ministry required.[9] Peter Mullen reminds us that many of the symptoms and manifestation often associated with this form of ministry can be duplicated in the form of pseudopossession, psychotic reactions, and cinematic neurosis.

> A Freudian psychiatrist faced with similar clinical manifestations might prefer a vocabulary which includes words like "neurosis," "repression," and "hysteria." A Jungian would want to talk about "the archetype of the shadow." A Behaviorist might try to reduce the subject's anxiety by a careful measured programme of "operant conditioning." And so on.[10]

In order to maintain a high level of rectitude in this somewhat complex type of ministry, some denominational groups, such as the Anglican Church and others, have developed the following guidelines for their clergy and laypeople to follow.

(1) It should be done in collaboration with the resources of medicine.

(2) It should be done in the context of prayer and sacrament.

(3) It should be done with the minimum of publicity.

(4) It should be done by experienced persons authorized by a diocesan bishop.

(5) It should be followed up by continuing pastoral care.[11]

In reference to Baby Boomers, it is important to recognize that their religious journey has been diverse and unconventional. Many of them have been involved with Eastern mysticism or have experimented with various forms of New Age spirituality. Others have explored the supernatural, probed the dark world of the occult, or used drugs to produce religious experiences. Consequently, some Boomers approach Christianity under the direct power of evil and various forms of spiritual bondage. The remedy for this sickness is found in the prayer of deliverance, or in more extreme cases, the ministry of exorcism.

## Incorrect Diagnosis: Popular Misconceptions about Healing

### *Divine Healing Supersedes the Need for Medicine*

Divine healing does not negate God's use of physical or natural means to bring about health. The author of the apocryphal book of Ecclesiasticus understood that no unnecessary antagonism need exist between medicine and the belief in God's power to heal. Such a belief enabled him to celebrate the efforts of the physician and retain his belief in the supernatural intervention of God. In the *Jerusalem Bible,* the passage under discussion (38:1-8) is translated thus.

Honour the doctor with the honour that is his due
  in return for his services;
    for he too has been created by the Lord.
Healing itself comes from the Most High,
  like a gift from a king.
The doctor's learning keeps his head high,
  he is regarded with awe by potentates.
The Lord has brought medicines into existence from the
  earth,

**210**

and the sensible man will not despise them.
Did not a piece of wood once sweeten the water,
  thus giving proof of its virtue?
He has also given men learning
  so that they may glory in his mighty works.
He uses them to heal and to relieve pain,
  the chemist makes up a mixture from them.
Thus there is no end to his activities,
  and through him health extends across the world.

Whenever possible, multidisciplinary approaches should be encouraged, and the sick should make full use of both prayer and the wisdom of surgeons, doctors, physiotherapists, and psychiatrists. Jesus was not against a natural means of healing. In his public healing ministry, he occasionally used recognized forms of natural methods of healing, such as the medical use of oil, wine, clay, and spittle. These were popular remedies of the time, similar to our cultural use of medicine (cf. Mark 7:32-35; 8:23; John 9:6; 1 Tim. 5:23). In the Parable of the Good Samaritan, Jesus mentions that the "mugged" individual's wounds were soothed by the application of oil and wine (Luke 10:34).

## Sickness: The Result of Sin

While it is true that there is often a connection between sin and the sickness of a person, it is not true that those who "sin" will necessarily become sick. Jesus deals with this issue head-on in John 9. The disciples inquired regarding the source of the man's blindness, "Rabbi, who sinned, this man or his parents, that he was born blind?" Jesus' reply was unconventional. "Neither this man or his parents sinned, but this happened so that the work of God might be displayed in his life" (John 9:2-3; cf. Luke 13:1-5). Today, one hears this view of sickness being the result of divine retribution reiterated as judgments on those who suffer from emotional difficulties such as manic depression or physical sickness such as AIDS. These conclusions give the impression that God loves only healthy and holy people, which is clearly not the case. Scripture sees sickness as a sign of a world that is disturbed by sin, but it refuses to see sickness as an immediate punishment for personal guilt. Rather, God is seen as one who wills life. In the Gospels, Jesus is depicted as a great opponent and vanquisher of

**211**

sickness (Matt. 4:24; Acts 10:38), who identifies with the sick (Matt. 25:36, 43; Isa. 53:4) and commissions his disciples to care for them (Matt. 10:8).

### Healing: Performed Only by the Specially Gifted

Recently I observed a televised healing service that was conducted by a well-known evangelist. The events of that evening left me not only embarrassed by the antics of the evangelist, but outraged by the incredible claims of healing. The lack of pastoral sensitivity displayed toward those seeking restored health was upsetting. As the evening progressed, I saw some disturbing parallels between the ministry I was viewing and that of my Arctic knowledge of shamanism. Consider the following observations:

(1) The word "shaman" means, "he who knows." On this occasion, the evangelist claimed to have such supernatural insight that he could discern the nature of people's sickness. Furthermore, as a result of these "words of knowledge," he supposedly pinpointed areas of difficulty in interpersonal relationships. I found myself wondering if he could also tell that I had oatmeal for breakfast!

(2) The shaman is known as a charismatic figure with a supernatural ability to heal the sick. There was no question that our speaker was oozing with charisma. He was articulate, aggressive, and persuasive. In Scotland they would say that he could "charm a duck out of water." The audience was duly informed that he had a supernatural ability to heal the sick.

(3) A shaman is not typically a member of the community, as he prefers to work independent of others. Similarly, our speaker claimed no denominational loyalties except that of his own particular organization, which incidentally, God was using in "a mighty way."

(4) The shaman normally develops his own methods and techniques to effect healing in people's lives. The TV evangelist exhibited none of the classical methods of healing used by Christ and subsequently employed by the church throughout the centuries (i.e., the anointing with oil, prayer, and the laying on of hands by community members). What I did observe, however, was shouting, screaming, and the strange peculiarity of thumping people on the forehead prior to announcing them healed, a ritual that I must have missed somewhere in my theological and liturgical training!

(5) The shaman is exclusively supported by the community. It

came as no surprise that the congregation was also given the opportunity to give generously in support of their speaker's ministry.

The fact of the matter is that healing belongs first and foremost to the church. Those who have been entrusted with such gifts are not soothsayers who can magically manipulate the power of God, as Simon the sorcerer was to discover (Acts 8:9-19). Rather, healing is a Christ-centered activity, mediated in the context of the worshiping community. Independent healing evangelists, whose ministry is not connected to the life of the local church, should not be encouraged. It is a sad fact that there has been so much fakery in the use of this God-given gift, discrediting it to the extent that many observers regard healing as nothing more than charlatanism. As a result, the conventional wisdom of many church bodies recommends that the Christian community be the context of the healing ministry as it provides the necessary accountability for those who are so gifted. This, in turn, gives a significant amount of credibility to the ministry.

From the biblical perspective, the concept of healing is embodied by the word "salvation," also implying the idea of health and well-being. Healing has both vertical and horizontal implications in that it extends beyond our need for personal healing to include reconciliation with God. From this broad perspective, healing involves the whole person—body, mind, and spirit. In other words, in taking the message of salvation to the Baby Boomer generation we are inviting them to embark upon a journey toward wholeness, whereby they can break the self-destructive cycles of behavior. These life-styles which frequently lead to pain and trauma need to be reevaluated from the overall perspective of the kingdom of God.

As Baby Boomers come of age they also exhibit a greater sense of wisdom and maturity. I have noticed in my pastoral involvement with Boomers that many are now recognizing that the life-style that affords them a certain degree of autonomy, also contributes to their "dis-ease." As a pastor, I have had the privilege of seeing many Boomers healed psychologically, emotionally, relationally, and spiritually as a result of intercessary prayer, the laying on of hands, anointing with oil, and the sacramental medicine of the soul. Christian healing is not a mere consumer item to be peddled as "health for health's sake," but rather, it is a by-product of a new way of life initiated by the death and resurrection of Christ and nurtured by the fellowship, teaching, worship, and healing ministry of the community of faith.

# A FINAL WORD

In July 1992, many North Americans watched in horror the fifty-four hour rampage of Hurricane Andrew, as its dangerous winds caused thirty-three deaths, destroyed 63,000 homes, and left 180,000 people without shelter and 600,000 without power in Florida, Louisiana, and the Bahamas. Government officials stated that this was the most expensive national disaster in its history with estimated costs of damage in the area of 15–20 billion dollars. News telecasts of Miami left one with the impression that the city looked more like Kuwait after the Gulf War than a national holiday resort, as the wind tossed boats from their moorings, washed away waterfront homes, and cleared entire blocks of trees.

Using a similar parallel, this book has attempted to establish that since 1945 the stormy winds of change have swept through North American culture, troubling the water, leaving an entire generation of Baby Boomers stranded on one side and the church on the other. As a result of this gulf, each has preconceived notions of the other. However, as is the case with most storms, the winds eventually die down, giving way to a period of relative calm which marks a time for rebuilding.

There is a sense in which we can legitimately think of the nature of the church by such images as an "island" which provides shelter from the storms of life's uncertainties, or as a "safe haven" for those whose lives have been shipwrecked by the unrelenting waves of the modern world. The psalmist writes, "He will cover you with his pinions, and under his wings you will find refuge; his faithfulness is a shield and buckler" (Ps. 91:4, RSV). Furthermore, for those increasing numbers of individuals who feel frazzled and weary due to the hectic pace of modern life, the image of "sanctuary" is one to which they can readily relate. Psalm 61:4 states, "Let me abide in your tent forever, find refuge under the shelter of your wings" (NRSV). These ideas are beautifully summed up in Psalm 57:1 where the psalmist writes, "Be merciful to me, O God, be merciful to me, for in you my soul takes refuge; in the shadow of your wings I will take refuge; until the destroying storms pass by" (NRSV).

While there is something comforting in the image of the church

215

as a provider of shelter in what often seems like a pugnacious and hostile world, faithfulness to Scripture requires that we must also combine this "passive" imagery with the more comprehensive biblical perspective of the Christian community as a dynamic and transforming agent in the world. The church has not been raised up by God simply to be, but also to do—to fulfill a mission within the context of salvation history. A mission that must take place not apart from the world, but in the world!

By way of summary, let me reiterate four reasons why the church must actively seek to build bridges of hope and reconciliation with the Baby Boomer generation.

## The Example of Christ

I have attempted to show how God, through Christ, provided a bridge that traversed the parameters that once separated the Lord from the human race. We discovered that the Lord Jesus Christ did not, at his incarnation, introduce an alien culture, nor impose a language that had little bearing or association with those to whom it was directed. Nor did he show an unwillingness to use the Jewish concepts deeply embedded within the receiving culture of his day. Although he was always prudent enough to reject those cultural aspects that were incongruent with the essential message of the kingdom of God, He viewed many aspects of the receiving culture as providing an important *praepartio evangelica* (preparation for evangelism) in which to build bridges into the hearts of his audience.

The church in its proclamation must also do likewise as it seeks to call this generation to faith in Christ. Taking the incarnation of Christ as the primary model for the church to emulate, we may assert that the church in any age—first or twentieth century—can never be acultural or asocial if it is to be incarnational. Simply stated, the biblical doctrine of the incarnation does not allow an unbridgeable gulf to exist between God and the world. I have tried to show that the Gospel can never exist in isolation, but rather it must speak in a relevant way to the particular concrete historical setting in which it finds itself. This is what Archbishop William Temple meant when he stated, "The Gospel is true always and everywhere, or it is not a Gospel at all, or true at all." As far as ministry to Baby Boomers is concerned, bridge building involves a number of factors:

(1) A willingness to grapple with the dialectical issue of understanding and evaluating both the prevailing issues of pluralism, relativism, individualism, and hedonism, as well as the careful study of Scripture to ascertain how Christian teaching impacts the culture both positively and negatively. This delicate work of exegeting the virtues and vices of these cultural realities is vital for the Christian pastors, evangelists, and others involved in the proclamation of the Gospel, as it is only through this critique that the necessary clues will be found in enabling them to communicate the Good News with lucidity and applicability.

(2) A willingness on behalf of the church to reexamine its particular modus operandi, to insure that its ministry will present as few obstacles as possible to the effective conversion, assimilation, and spiritual formation of this generation. While such a reevaluation will inevitably bring about change, I have also argued that care must be taken to insure that such changes do not conflict with the essential characteristics of our faith, or the long-standing and valid Christian traditions that express our uniqueness. To compromise these aspects of the church's life would amount to nothing less than selling out our spiritual birthright in the ideological department store of today's consumeristic society. Transformation is our goal, not assimilation or conformity.

## The Priestly Nature of the Church

In the celebrated text from Exodus 19:16, those chosen by divine election are called a "kingdom of priests." From the teaching of the Old Testament, we can deduce that a priest had primarily responsibilities in areas of teaching and worship. He was expected to teach justice and the Law of God (Jer. 18:18; Ezek. 7:26) as well as offer sacrifices on the altar of God (Deut. 26:1-11).

In 1 Peter 2:4-9, Peter transfers both the title and function of the Old Testament priesthood and applies it to followers of Christ, whom he describes as those who "have tasted the kindness of the Lord" and have "come to him, to that living stone, rejected by men but in God's sight chosen and precious" (vv. 3-4, RSV). In this passage, Peter first of all points out that the priestly ministry of the church is exercised "through Jesus Christ" and is in no way independent of him (vv. 4-5). He then goes on to define the nature of the church's priesthood in terms familiar to the Old Testament twofold formula by making mention to both priesthood and proclamation: "But you are a chosen race, a royal priesthood, a holy nation, God's own people, that you may declare the wonderful deeds of him who called you out of darkness into his marvelous light. Once you were not people but now you are God's people; once you had not received mercy but now you have received mercy" (1 Peter 2:9-10, RSV).

In this book I have tried to show that these two primary functions of "word and worship" have one specific thing in common, that is to "mediate" the grace of God, or as I preferred to call it, to "bridge build." The church is priestly in its preaching when it is facing toward humanity on behalf of God and calling them into relationship with God through Christ. As I have pointed out, this proclamation includes ideas commonly associated with *kerygma* (that is to awaken faith and point to the necessity of conversion and decision-making), *didache* (the moral implications of faith), and *katechesis* (a detailed form of theological instruction in doctrinal matters). The church is priestly in its worship when it faces toward God on behalf of humanity as offering of a form of worship that is both spiritual in nature (Rom. 12:1; cf. Phil. 4:18) and practical in its expression (James 1:27). It is in this sense of the interrelationship between faith and action that the influential German theologian Schleiermacher was correct in his sentiment that it is only in active experience that any talk about God can be truly meaningful.

## Baby Boomer Receptiveness

Midlife transition for many individuals is a painful experience of disorientation, reevaluation, and reworking of a life-style philosophy that apparently proves inadequate in the first half of life. There is abundant evidence to suggest that Baby Boomers, en masse, are entering such a time of reassessment, and like Peggy Lee's lament, are questioning, "Is that all there is?" More profoundly, some are experiencing the nagging loneliness that St. Augustine expressed as "restless until we rest in Thee."

In an effort to creatively cope with this perplexing time, many Boomers, who once sought solutions from the latest pop-psychology paperbacks or self-help gurus, are now looking to the church to provide them with a deep and meaningful form of spirituality that will help them to survive the demands of modern life. Essentially, many are discovering that life lived on the individual or material level alone eventually breaks down. While it is rarely fruitful to give people answers to questions they are not yet asking, Baby Boomers have reached the point in their lives when they are asking significant questions about the nature of ultimate reality and their place within the grand scheme of things. I believe that the church must take advantage of this unique opportunity, by being sensitive to these distinctive intellectual, spiritual, and emotional needs and by proclaiming our faith in such a way that it will give hope as well as purpose to their broken and often confused lives.

## The Uniqueness of the Gospel

While the world keeps changing, people's needs remain the same. We have discovered that many Boomers are experiencing a sense of loneliness, rootlessness, and alienation. There is a yearning for meaning, purpose, and transcendence. The Gospel message that we proclaim is unique in that it is able to address intellectual, social, emotional, and spiritual needs, thus providing a way of salvation for the whole person. I have tried to show that the unique attributes of the Acts 2:42-47 paradigm of community life continues to provide an excellent model of Christian community that will not only insure the ongoing renewal of the local church, but also provide helpful strategies for the conversion and spiritual formation of the Baby Boomer generation. Issues of loneliness and rootlessness are addressed by the provision of authentic community where Boomers can find fellowship, love, acceptance, and friendship. As in the first century, where new converts met in small groups for nurture, worship, and teaching and were strengthened in the Christian life, likewise, these very features are effective in the conversion, assimilation, and spiritual formation of the Baby Boomer. It is these very features of Christian community life that lift "life in Christ" far above the great variety of bridges which span the troubled water of modern life.

# APPENDIX 1

## One-Year Preaching Plan

The first objective of the church's teaching ministry is to address the prevailing issues of its day. Too often the Christian community spends a great deal of its energy answering questions that nobody is asking. The following topics are an attempt to define some of the pertinent questions our secular world is posing. To address these types of issues will enable the body of Christ to exercise right judgment in all things (cf. 1 Cor. 2:15).

*Advent* is the season which anticipates the birth of Christ and is celebrated at Christmas. However, its primary focus is the yearly reminder of the anticipated return of Christ. It traditionally deals with the New Testament texts foretelling Jesus' coming and lends an opportunity to teach on the person of Jesus Christ.

| | |
|---|---|
| Advent 1 | Jesus, Son of Man |
| Advent 2 | Jesus, Son of God |
| Advent 3 | Jesus, Lord and Savior |
| Advent 4 | Jesus, Prince of Peace |

*Christmas* is the theological backdrop to the incarnation. This permits the preacher to grapple with the uniqueness of the person of Jesus Christ in a world of religious pluralism. The publication of the book, *The Myth of God Incarnate,*[1] demonstrates that this topic needs examining even within the walls of the Christian community. The theme of the incarnation also hints at the problems of the homeless, the powerless, refugees, poverty, and social justice-related issues.

| | |
|---|---|
| Christmas Eve | God in Christ |
| Christmas Day | Christ in His World |
| Christmas 1 | The Christian and the World |
| | (Implication of the Incarnation) |

*Epiphany* is a Greek word whose basic meaning lies in the idea of showing forth, manifesting, or revealing something by "going public." This season avails itself to sermons on divine revelation, eschatology, and the new contemporary movements which have been birthed by the Holy Spirit in recent years.

Theme: The Scriptures
    Epiphany 1    God's Book (Divine Revelation)

**221**

Epiphany 2      The Church's Book (The Place of Tradition)
Epiphany 3      Our Book (A Book to Be Read and Applied)

Theme: Miracles
Epiphany 4      Signs and Wonders in a Scientific Age
Epiphany 5      Healing
Epiphany 6      Exorcism

Theme: Renewal Movements in the Church
Epiphany 7      The Charismatic Movement
Epiphany 8      The Ecumenical Movement
Epiphany 9      The Liturgical Movement
Epiphany 10     The Third Wave of the Spirit

*Lent* is a forty-day period of fasting and preparation commonly associated with the forty days that Jesus spent in the wilderness. The traditional disciplines akin to this season (fasting, giving, self-reflection, and self-denial) are highly relevant in today's culture. The four weeks of Lent provide the preacher an opportunity to teach on the following subjects:

Lent 1      What Is Worldliness?
Lent 2      Materialism
Lent 3      Sexuality and Spirituality
Lent 4      The Cult of Self-Worship
Lent 5      Lenten Cure for Worldliness

*Easter* celebrates the great doctrines of death and resurrection, atonement and justification as summarized in Paul's words, Christ "was delivered over to death for our sins and was raised for our justification" (Rom. 4:25; 1 Cor. 15:3). This "feast of feasts" offers an opportunity for the preacher to address many of the cultural presuppositional mythologies associated with Easter (a renewal rite of springtime with all the fertility cult symbols of eggs and rabbits) and to examine some of the core issues of Christian doctrine regarding forgiveness, salvation, redemption, and immortality.

Easter 1      The Death and Resurrection of Christ
Easter 2      Forgiveness (Guilt Is Lifted)
Easter 3      Reconciliation (Separation Is Overcome)
Easter 4      Redemption (Set Free from Self)
Easter 5      Salvation (Complete Healing)
Easter 6      Justification (A New Beginning)
Easter 7      Immortality (Living Forever)

*Pentecost* celebrates the coming of the Holy Spirit to the disciples in Jerusalem, where they were filled with a sense of purpose and power to continue the ministry of Christ by proclaiming the kingdom of God to the ends of the earth. The obvious theme of this season is that of Christian mission. This long season (which continues until the First Sunday in Advent) lends itself to themes such as the person and work of the Holy Spirit, the church, and Christian witness in a modern world. The following examples are set in short-series form.

Theme: The Holy Spirit
    Pentecost 1    Who Is the Holy Spirit?
    Pentecost 2    Gifts of the Holy Spirit to the Church
    Pentecost 3    Fruit from the Holy Spirit to the Individual

Theme: The Church
    Pentecost 4    Worship: Rediscovering the Missing Jewel
    Pentecost 5    Worship: Teach Us to Pray
    Pentecost 6    Fellowship: Bind Us Together, Lord
    Pentecost 7    Witness: Salt, Light, and Protest

Theme: The World: Global Issues
    Pentecost 8    A Christian and Environmental Stewardship
    Pentecost 9    Well-fed Christians in a Hungry World
    Pentecost 10    Indulged Christians in a Poor World
    Pentecost 11    Vocal Christians for a Voiceless People
    Pentecost 12    Peacemaking Christians in a Violent World

Theme: The World: National Issues
    Pentecost 13    The Importance of Cultural Awareness
    Pentecost 14    Secularism
    Pentecost 15    Pragmatism
    Pentecost 16    Pluralism
    Pentecost 17    Positivism
    Pentecost 18    Hedonism

Theme: Engaging Culture with the Gospel
    Pentecost 19    Christian Values in the Home
    Pentecost 20    Christian Ethics in the Marketplace
    Pentecost 21    Dual Citizenship
    Pentecost 22    Speaking Up for Christ

1. John Hick et al. *The Myth of God Incarnate* (London: SCM, 1977).

# APPENDIX 2

## Suggested Outlines for Small Group Study

The following are ideas for Bible studies, relevant to the intellectual and spiritual formation of Baby Boomers.

Outline 1: *Worldviews*

It was Socrates who said that "the unexamined life is not worth living." To examine one's life is to evaluate; to evaluate requires examining values and value systems. The following outline challenges Baby Boomers to examine their worldview in the light of Christian truth.

1. The Importance of Cultural Awareness
2. Secularism
3. Existentialism
4. Humanism
5. Pragmatism
6. Positivism
7. Pluralism and Relativism
8. Hedonism

Outline 2: *The Christian in Society*

It is difficult for any church to avoid politics entirely, unless it retreats from society. The outline below suggests that the church's contribution to society is unique and that the proclamation of Christian ethics and the values related to the justice of God be considered in the light of the cultural milieu.

1. World Economics
2. Christianity and Science
3. Christianity and Government
4. Christianity and Social Justice
5. Peace, Just Wars, and Pacifism
6. Racism
7. Feminism
8. Ethics and Human Rights

Outline 3: *Global Issues Bible Studies*[1]

This series on global issues, presented in attractive self-contained workbooks, focuses on global issues and relates how Scripture speaks to our world. The approach taken in this Bible study is inductive. There are six studies to each booklet, complete with questions and additional material for the group leader. Titles include the following:

*Basic Human Needs*
*Economic Justice*
*Environmental Stewardship*
*Fundamental Religion*
*Healing for Broken People*
*Multi-Ethnicity*
*People and Technology*
*Sanctity of Life*
*Spiritual Conflict*
*Urbanization*

Outline 4: *Life Recovery Guides*[2]

Designed to assist the individual to discover what the Bible says about different aspects of recovery, this study series is similar to the *Global Issues Series* in that it contains six self-contained study booklets. The phenomenon of addiction in our culture, especially among Baby Boomers, makes this series highly relevant. Titles include the following:

*Recovery from Addictions*
*Recovery from Family Dysfunctions*
*Recovery from Distorted Images of God*
*Recovery from Shame*
*Recovery from Bitterness*
*Recovery from Abuse*
*Recovery from Loss*
*Recovery from Co-dependency*

Outline 5: *GroupBuilder Studies*[3]

GroupBuilder Studies are geared for Baby Boomers and specifically designed to help small group members share what is happening in their lives as a basis for relationship building and searching out scriptural truth. In addition to providing opportunities to practice truth, each of these studies includes a personal enrichment section and a leader's guide. Small group studies available from GroupBuilder Resources:

*Let's Get Together*
*No Strangers to God*
*Open to Closeness*
*Defeating Those Dragons*
*The Gift of Gender*
*Getting the Job Done Right*

*Don't Look Back*
*Dare to Risk*
*Confronting a World Gone Wrong*
*When the Walls Are Closing In*

Outline 6: *Lifestyle Small Group Series*[4]

This series of group Bible studies applies Scripture to the stresses and strains of everyday living. The topics included in this series are designed with Baby Boomers in mind.

*Lifestyles*
*Singles*
*Stressed-Out*
*Success*
*Transitions*
*Career*
*Family*
*Money*
*Wholeness*

Outline 7: *The Critical Concern Series*[5] (Book Series)

*Abortion: Toward an Evangelical Consensus*
*Beyond Hunger: A Biblical Mandate for Social Responsibility*
*Birthright! Christian, Do You Know Who You Are?*
*The Christian, the Arts, and Truth: Regaining the Vision of Greatness*
*The Christian Mindset in a Secular Society: Promoting Evangelical*
  *Renewal and National Righteousness*
*Christians in the Wake of the Sexual Revolution: Recovering Our*
  *Sexual Sanity*
*Christian Countermoves in a Decadent Culture*
*The Controversy: Roots of the Creation-Evolution Conflict*
*Depression: Finding Hope and Meaning in Life's Darkest Shadow*
*Euthanasia: Spiritual, Medical, and Legal Issues in Terminal Health Care*
*A Just Defense: The Use of Force, Nuclear Weapons and Our Conscience*
*Life-Style Evangelism*
*The Majesty of Man: The Dignity of Being Human*
*The Trauma of Transparency: A Biblical Approach to Inter-personal*
  *Communication*
*Worship: Rediscovering the Missing Jewel*

1. Stephen Hayner and Gordon Aeschliman, eds. (Downers Grove, Ill.: InterVarsity Press, 1990).

2. Dale and Juanita Ryan (Downers Grove, Ill.: InterVarsity, 1990).
3. Julie Gorman, gen. ed. (Wheaton, Ill.: Victor Books, 1991–1993).
4. Peter Menconi, Richard Peace, and Lyman Coleman (Colorado Springs: NavPress, 1988).
5. Distributed by Questar/Multnomah.

# APPENDIX 3

## Adult Discipleship/Catechumenate Classes

The following outlines suggest different approaches. The time factor required to teach these courses may seem intimidating. However, the object of the class is to enable catechumens to give an intelligent account of the faith they are seeking to embrace. In some ways, our age parallels the post-apostolic period, in that we are making disciples among people with little background knowledge of the faith. In the early church catechistic training for initiation was lengthy and detailed (up to three years before baptism was administered). Likewise, Christian instructors need not apologize for making similar demands on interested inquirers and new converts.

These outlines are fairly exhaustive and may be adapted easily for alternative uses.

*Outline 1: Basic Christian Beliefs*

This series is based on the three classic Christian creeds: Apostles', Nicene, and Athanasian. As creeds are a concise, formal, and authorized statement of important points of Christian doctrine, the following may be divided into four tidy sections.

God the Creator
- The Challenge of Materialism
- Science and Religion
- Natural Law
- Design and Purpose in Nature
- Process Philosophy
- God's Freedom to Act
- The Fatherhood of God
- Estrangement from God

God the Son
- The Virgin Birth
- The Deity of Christ
- The Arian Heresy
- Theories of the Atonement
- The Resurrection of Christ
- The Return of Christ

God the Holy Spirit
- The Nature of the Holy Spirit
- The Work of the Holy Spirit

229

- The Guidance of the Holy Spirit
- The Paraclete Sayings of Jesus

The Christian Community
- The Catholicity of the Church
- The Apostolicity of the Church
- The Ministry of the Church
- The Ongoing Renewal of the Church

*Outline 2: The Bible*

This course introduces the catechumen to the Scriptures, by looking at how the Bible was written, how it bears the testimony of the original eyewitnesses, and what is meant by such terms as the "inspiration" and "authority" of the Bible.

(1) The Bible As a Human Witness
(2) The Bible As a Divine Witness
(3) "General Revelation" (Is there revelation of God to be found outside the biblical tradition?)
(4) "Special Revelation": God's Revelation of Himself
(5) The Formation of the Canon of Scripture
(6) The Old Testament
- Creation and the Fall
- From Egypt to Canaan
- Kings and Prophets
- Post-Exilic Judaism
- An exposition series on the Book of Amos
(7) The New Testament
- The growth of the new community based on Acts
- The church goes to the Gentiles
- An exposition series on Ephesians or 1 John
(8) The Life of Christ
- A series on the plain fact of the life of Christ in the synoptic Gospels or the Gospel of John

*Outline 3: The Church in History*

(1) The Impact of Hellenism on the Eastern Church
- Character study: Clement of Alexandria or Origen
(2) The Imperial Church of the West
- Character study: St. Augustine
(3) Medieval Christendom
- Character study: Charlemagne or Thomas Aquinas
(4) The Reformation
- Character study: John Calvin or Henry VIII

(5) The Dawn of Modernity
- Character study: Jonathan Edwards or Benjamin Franklin
(6) The Contemporary Scene
- Character study: Dietrich Bonhoeffer or Gustavo Gutiérrez

*Outline 4: Discipleship*[1]

(1) Live a New Life
- How can I know?
- How can I grow?
- How can I show?
- How can I overcome?
(2) Christian Foundations
   a. What can we know about God?
   - Who is Jesus Christ?
   - Who is the Holy Spirit?
   - Is the Bible the Word of God?
   b. Why the Cross?
   - Prayer
   - Is there life after death?
   - The church
(3) Christian Living
   a. Helping others find God
   - Common questions
   - Giving
   - Guidance
   b. Faith
   - Suffering
   - Forgiveness
   - Love
(4) Spiritual Renewal
- Worship
- The Gifts of the Spirit
- Being Filled with the Spirit
- Spiritual Warfare

1. I am indebted for this outline to David Watson, *Discipleship* (London: Hodder and Stoughton, 1981), Appendix B.

# NOTES

## Chapter 1: Troubled Water: The Baby Boomer Milieu

1. Daniel Yankelovich, *New Rules: Searching for Self-Fulfillment in a World Turned Upside Down* (New York: Random House, 1981), 188–89.
2. For further details relating to the Vietnam War, see Stanley Karnow, *Vietnam, a History* (New York: Viking, 1983), 2–48; and *The New Encyclopedia Britannica*, 15th ed., s.v. "Vietnam War."
3. Landon Jones, *Great Expectations: America and the Baby Boom Generation* (New York: Ballantine Books, 1980), 103.
4. The modern counterpart of this frame of mind was the Moral Majority Movement, whose fundamentalist views on Scripture have harvested right-wing conservative views in politics and morality. Those involved in the movement crusaded vigorously in opposition to abortion, homosexual rights, and the Equal Rights Amendment, and in support of school prayer, increased defense spending, and a strong anti-Communist foreign policy. Jerry Falwall, the leader of the group, consistently called for the peoples of the United States to return to their former glory by preaching his fundamentalist "old time religion" and right-wing political stands.
5. *U.S. News & World Report,* 16 May 1960.
6. David Sheff, "Portrait of a Generation," *Rolling Stone,* April 1988, 28–64; May 1988, 44–71.
7. Ibid.

## Chapter 2: The Baby Boomer Cultural Ethos

1. Bertrand Russell, *Unpopular Essays* (New York: Simon and Schuster, 1950), 99.
2. Reginald Bibby, *Mosaic Madness* (Toronto: Stoddard, 1990), 1–2.
3. John Hick, *God and the Universe of Faiths* (London: Fount, 1977), 131.
4. John Hick, *An Interpretation of Religion: Human Responses to the Transcendent* (London: Macmillan, 1989).
5. Ibid., 246–47.
6. *Nostra aetalt: The Declaration on the Church's Relation with Non-Christian Religions* (1965), 2.
7. Karl Rahner, "Christianity and the Non-Christian Religions," in *Theological Investigations,* vol. 5. (Baltimore: Helicon, 1966). See also related essays in vols. 6, 9, 12, and 14.
8. Cheryl Russell, *One Hundred Predictions for the Baby Boom: The Next Fifty Years* (New York: Plenum, 1987), 45–46.
9. Doug Murren, *The Baby Boomerang* (Ventura, Calif.: Regal, 1990), 141–42.
10. Eric D. Hirsch, Jr., *Innocence and Experience: An Introduction to Blake* (New Haven: New York Univ. Press, 1964), 258–59.
11. Reginald Bibby, "The State of Collective Religiosity in Canada," *The Canadian Review of Sociology and Anthropology* 16 (1979): 105–16.
12. Allan Bloom, *The Closing of the American Mind* (New York: Simon and Schuster, 1987), 25.
13. Ibid., 25–26.
14. Ibid., 26.
15. Ibid.
16. Ibid., 39
17. Hans Finzel, *Help! I'm a Baby Boomer* (Wheaton, Ill.: Victor, 1989), 26.

18. Ibid., 39.
19. Joseph Fletcher, *Moral Responsibility: Situation Ethics at Work* (Philadelphia: Westminster, 1967), 38.
20. Ibid., 34.
21. H. Richard Niebuhr, *Moral Man and Immoral Society: A Study of Ethics and Politics* (New York: Scribner's, 1952), 170.
22. Paul W. Kurtz, ed., *Humanist Manifestos I and II* (Buffalo: Prometheus, 1981), 17–18. The "Humanist Manifesto I" first appeared in *The New Humanist* 6 (May/June 1933); The "Humanist Manifesto II" first appeared in *The Humanist* 32 (September/October 1973).
23. Reginald Bibby, *Fragmented Gods: The Poverty and Potential of Religion in Canada* (Toronto: Irwin, 1987), 140.
24. Ibid., 142.
25. Henri de Lubac was an erudite and prolific French Jesuit theologian. For a good example of his work see *Catholicism: Christ and the Common Destiny of Man,* trans. Lancelot Sheppard and Elizabeth Englund (San Francisco: Ignatius, 1988).
26. Calgary Herald, n.d.
27. Thomas E. Power, *Invitation to a Great Experiment* (New York: Doubleday, 1979), 4.
28. See *The Coming of the Cosmic Christ: The Healing of the Mother Earth and The Birth of a Global Renaissance* (San Francisco: Harper and Row, 1989); *Creation Spirituality: Liberation Gifts and the Peoples of the Earth* (San Francisco: Harper and Row, 1991); and *Whee! We, Wee All the Way Home: A Guide to Sensual Prophetic Spirituality* (Santa Fe, N.M.: Bear and Company, 1981).
29. Augustine and a number of other patristic commentators convincingly indicated that Scripture deals with Genesis in metaphors, figures of speech, and narratives—not to answer the question of "how," but rather to deal with the question "what" and "why." The fact is that the Bible does not wish to instruct us on the empirically knowable genesis of the world nor of the different species of organism. It is therefore not a matter of faith that God created the world in six days, nor that in the beginning God created everything such as we find it today.
30. Murren, *Baby Boomerang,* 148.
31. A. Clark, *Aubrey's* "Brief Lives," vol. 1 (Oxford: Clarendon, 1898), 352.
32. Alexis de Tocqueville, *Democracy in America,* vol. 2 (New York: Vintage, 1960), 121.
33. Robert N. Bellah et al., *Habits of the Heart* (Berkeley: Univ. of California Press, 1985), 142.
34. Ibid., 146.
35. Ibid., 285.
36. Christopher Lasch, *The Culture of Narcissism* (New York: Norton, 1978).
37. Bellah, *Habits of the Heart,* viii.
38. Bloom, *Closing of the Mind,* 86.
39. Ibid., 85–86.
40. Lasch, *Narcissism,* 51.
41. Herbert Schlossberg, *Idols for Destruction* (Nashville: Thomas Nelson, 1983), 166–67.
42. Lasch, *Narcissism,* 31
43. James Hitchcock, *What Is Secular Humanism?* (Ann Arbor, Mich.: Servant, 1982), 72.
44. Paul Vitz, *Psychology As Religion: The Cult of Self-Worship* (Grand Rapids: Eerdmans, 1977), 32, 80, 115.

45. David Watson, *I Believe in the Church* (London: Hodder and Stoughton, 1978), 333.

46. The Cultural Information Service, 15 October 1989.

47. John Stott, *Issues Facing Christians Today* (London: Marshall, Morgan, and Scott, 1984), 226.

48. Bellah, *Habits of the Heart*, 22.

49. John Garner, *Leadership* (New York: Free Press, 1990), 186.

50. Russell, *100 Predictions*, 47–48.

51. Michael Green, *I Believe in the Holy Spirit* (London: Hodder and Stoughton, 1975), 176.

## Chapter 3: Jesus and the Jewish World

1. H. Richard Niebuhr, *Christ and Culture* (New York: Harper, 1951), 32.

2. "On Prescription Against Heretics," in *The Ante-Nicene Fathers* (Grand Rapids: Eerdmans, 1957), vol. 3, 7, 246.

3. Hawking observes, "If we do discover a complete theory, it should in time be understandable in broad principle by everyone, not just a few scientists. Then we shall all, philosophers, scientists, and just ordinary people, be able to take part in the discussion of why it is that we and the universe exist. If we find the answer to that, it should be the ultimate triumph of human reason—for then we would truly know the mind of God" (Stephen Hawking, *A Brief History of Time* [London: Bantam, 1988], 175). Note that Hawking does not include theologians in his first category, only philosphers and scientists.

4. Clement of Alexandria (ca. 150–ca. 215) serves as another example of one who was astutely able to incorporate aspects of the current thought in his presentation of Christ to his fellow Greeks. In his writings, Clement made use of the writings of Philo and other Hellenistic, Jewish allegorical methods of biblical interpretation. He also made use of Plato, Aristotle, Homer, and extensive stoic literature in his formulation of such doctrines as the transcendence of God and the divine nature of Christ. See his "Stromata" and "Exhortation to the Heathen" in *The Anti-Nicene Fathers: Translation of the Writings of the Fathers Down to A.D. 325*, ed. Rev. Alexander Roberts and James Donaldson (New York: Scribner's, 1899), vol. 2; also, see "Christ the Educator," in *The Fathers of the Church. A New Translation*, ed. Roy J. Defarrari (Washington, D.C.: Catholic Univ. of America Press, 1948). vol. 23.

5. John Stott, *The Spirit and the Church in the Message of Acts* (Grand Rapids: Eerdmans, 1990), 286.

6. St. Augustine, *City of God* (London: Penguin, 1984), 877.

7. Niebuhr, *Christ and Culture*, 229.

8. F.D. Maurice, *The Prayer Book* (London: James Clarke, 1966), 60.

9. Martin Buber, *I and Thou*, trans. Ronald Gregor Smith, 2nd ed. (New York: Scribner's, 1958).

## Chapter 4: Theological Perspectives on Baby Boomer Culture

1. John R. Taylor, *God Loves Like That! The Theology of James Denny* (London: SCM, 1962), 83.

2. St. Augustine, *City of God* 14:13, 571.

3. Henry Bettenson, ed., *Documents of the Christian Church* (Oxford: Oxford Univ. Press, 1963), 51–52.

4. John Hick, *An Interpretation of Religion* (New Haven, Conn: Yale Univ. Press, 1989), 377.

5. Geoffrey Parrinder, *Encountering World Religions: Questions of Religious*

*Truth* (New York: Crossroads, 1987), 205.

6. Walter Kasper, *Jesus the Christ* (New York: Paulist, 1976), 189.

7. Lesslie Newbigin, *The Gospel in a Pluralistic Society* (Grand Rapids: Eerdmans, 1989), 174.

8. Ibid., 183.

9. Ibid., 182–83.

10. Stephen C. Neill, *Christian Faith and Other Faiths* (London: Oxford Univ. Press, 1961), 17ff.

11. Peter T. Forsyth, *The Person and the Place of Jesus Christ* (London: Independent Press, 1909), 346.

12. Donald M. Baille, *God Was In Christ* (London: Faber and Faber, 1956), 173–74.

13. Samuel Butler, *The Note-Books of Samuel Butler* (New York: Dutton, 1912), 298.

14. Clement of Rome, "Letter to the Christians," in *The Fathers of the Church. A New Translation,* vol. 1, ed. Roy J. Deferrari (Washington, D.C.: The Catholic Univ. of America Press, 1948), 42.

15. Clement of Alexandria, "Exhortation to the Heathen," in *The Anti-Nicene Fathers. Translation of the Writings of the Fathers Down to A.D. 325.* vol. 2, ed. the Rev. Alexander Roberts and James Donaldson (New York: Scribner's, 1899), 195.

16. Augustine, "The Harmony of the Gospels," in *Nicene and Post-Nicene Fathers of the Christian Church,* vol. 6, ed. Philip Schaff and Henry Wace (New York: Scribner's, 1904), 101.

17. St. Augustine, *Confessions,* Bk. 10, chap. 43.

18. Reginald Bibby, *Mosaic Madness* (Toronto: Stoddart, 1990), 144.

19. Leith Anderson, *Dying for Change* (Minneapolis: Bethany, 1990), 144–46.

20. Ibid., 145.

21. Ibid., 146.

22. Reginald Bibby, *Fragmented Gods* (Toronto: Irwin, 1987), 111–36.

23. Mark S. Hoffman, ed., *The World Almanac 1993* (New York: Pharos, 1993), 67. For a Christian response to issues of economic justice, see Stephen Hart, *What Does the Lord Require?* (Oxford: Oxford Univ. Press, 1992); and Joel Blan, *The Visible Poor: Homeless in the United States* (Oxford: Oxford Univ. Press, 1992).

24. Dick Westley, *A Theology of Presence* (Mystic, Conn.: Twenty-Third Pubs., 1988), 60–70.

25. Jean Vanier, *Community and Growth* (New York: Paulist, 1979), 6.

26. Dietrich Bonhoeffer, *Life Together* (London: Harper and Row, 1954), 54.

27. Alan Richardson, *A Theological Word Book of the Bible* (London: SCM, 1957), 82.

28. Hans Finzel, *Help! I'm a Baby Boomer* (Wheaton, Ill.: Victor, 1989), 141.

## Chapter 5: Biblically Relevant Teaching in Today's World

1. The Greek word *apostolos* literally means "a person sent." The Book of Acts reflects a situation in which the Twelve are recognized as apostles in a unique sense. Luke emphasizes both the significance of the number twelve and their role as authenticating witnesses of the life, teaching, and resurrection of Christ.

2. C.H. Dodd, *The Apostolic Preaching and Its Developments* (New York: Harper, 1936). See also, Robert H. Mounce, *The Essential Nature of the New Testament Preaching* (Grand Rapids: Eerdmans, 1960), and Alan Richardson, *A Theological Word Book of the Bible* (New York: Macmillan, 1950).

3. Ibid., 84.

4. It is believed among some scholars that those "sayings of Jesus" had proba-

bly been collected and written down in a Logia, such as Q. This would contain much of the teaching of Jesus such as the Sermon on the Mount and the Parables. It is also believed that some of these sayings can be seen in the New Testament, especially in the letters of Paul where there are some striking parallels with much of what is recorded in the synoptic Gospels. When one considers and contrasts the following examples, it would seem that there is solid evidence for primary source in a collection of dominical Logia: Rom. 12:21, cf. Matt. 5:39; Rom. 13:8ff, cf. Matt. 22:34ff; Rom. 14:10, cf. Matt. 7:1; 1 Thes. 4:15-16, cf. Matt. 24:30-31; 1 Thes. 5:3, cf. Matt. 24:42; 1 Thes. 5:16, cf. Luke 6:23, 10:20. See also, 1 Peter 2:13-17; 5:5-9; James 4:6-10.

5. Dodd, *Apostolic Preaching*, 11.

6. C.H. Dodd, *Gospel and Law: The Relation of Faith and Ethics in Early Christianity* (New York: Columbia Univ. Press, 1933), 77.

7. Tertullian, chap. 39, in *Ante-Nicene Fathers*, vol. 3, 46.

8. See Joachim Jeremias, *Jerusalem at the Time of Jesus* (London: SCM, 1969), see chap. 8.

9. Anderson, *Dying for Change*, 17.

10. Jill Bell and Margaret Inkpen, "When the Cock Crows" (1978), "These are the Words of Jesus" (1979), and "The Kingdom" (1983). The scripts and musical scores for these musicals are currently distributed privately by Bell/Inkpen. They have been used to incorporate members at a parish level as well as members of many parishes at a diocesan level. Scripturally based, these musicals can be performed in part or in their entirety depending on the appropriateness of the setting and the time frame. A full range of musical styles from blues and honkytonk to calypso and gentle rock, are incorporated in each musical enabling all ages to culturally identify with specific parts. A narrative prior to each song adequately prepares the relevance of each song allowing portions to be used in a variety of settings (e.g., to support a particular Scripture reading during a Sunday service, to reinforce the theme of a festival day, to celebrate a social or seasonal special event, to educate at retreats, or to entertain as an outreach ministry).

11. See Appendix 1 for a suggested One-Year Preaching Plan.

12. See Appendix 2 for suggested outlines for small group study.

13. See Appendix 3 for suggested outlines for Adult Catechumenate/Discipleship Classes.

## Chapter 6: Transcendent Worship

1. For an interesting discussion of changing trends within the worship life of Protestant denominations see Robert Webber, *Signs of Wonder* (Nashville: Abbott Martyn, 1992), particularly pp. 54–55.

2. Blaise Pascal, *Penseés* ed. with an introduction and notes by Louis Lafuma, trans. John Warrington (New York: E.P. Dutton, 1960), 59–60.

3. Bryan Appleyard, *Understanding the Present: Science and the Soul of Modern Man* (New York: Doubleday, 1993).

4. James F. White, "The Missing Jewel of the Evangelical Church," *The Reformed Journal*, June 1986, 13.

5. Ralph Martin, *Worship in the Early Church* (Grand Rapids: Eerdmans, 1976), 122.

6. Joachim Jeremias, *The Eucharistic Words of Jesus* (London: SCM, 1966), 120.

7. Justin Martyr, in *Ante-Nicene Fathers*, vol. 7, (Grand Rapids: Eerdmans, 1951), 378.

8. Ibid., 15.

9. Hans Küng, *The Church* (New York: Search, 1971), 233.

**237**

10. Doug Murren, *The Baby Boomerang* (Ventura, Calif.: Regal, 1990), 188.
11. Ibid., 194.

## Chapter 7: Healing in the Contemporary Church

1. I believe the first author to call Jesus a physican was Ignatius of Antioch in a letter written to the Church at Ephesus, *Ignatius to the Ephesians* 7:2. Furthermore, he spoke of the eucharist as the medicine of immortality.

2. E.g., the essayist David Hume who maintained that truth was not verifiable, showed extreme skepticism to the idea of miracles. His argument is documented in his book *Enquiries Concerning Human Understanding and Concerning the Principles of Morals* ed. L.A. Selby-Bigge, 3rd ed. (Oxford: Clarendon Press, 1975).

3. One can trace a dialogue on the subject that extends over 150 years in the following works: Conyers Middleton, *A Free Inquiry into the Miraculous Powers* (1749; reprint, New York: Garland, 1976); John H. Newman, *Two Essays on Biblical and on Ecclesiastical Miracles* (1870; reprint, Westminster, Md.: Christian Classics, 1969); Benjamin B. Warfield, *Counterfeit Miracles* (1918; reprint, London: Banner of Truth Trust, 1973).

4. Augustine's writings contain many insights which are foundational to an understanding of miracles. His major contribution in this area is probably his discussions of the relationship between the special activity of God in performing miracles and the divinely established universal order of nature. In *De Utilitate Credendi,* he defines a miracle *(miraculum)* as "whatever appears that is difficult or unusual above the hope or power of them who wonder" (16.34). And in *The City of God,* he explains that a miracle *(portentum)* "happens not contrary to nature but contrary to what we know as nature *(contra quam est nota nature)"* (21.8). In other words, Augustine is saying that a miracle is an unusual event. The above translations are from *Nicene and Post-Nicene Fathers of the Christian Church,* vols. 2 and 4, ed. Philip Schaff and Henry Wace (New York: Scribner's, 1904). For a brief but interesting discussion on the theory of miracles from Augustine to the twelfth century, see Benedicta Ward, *Miracles and the Medieval Mind* (Philadelphia: Univ. of Pennsylvania Press, 1978).

5. Morton Kelsey, *Psychology, Medicine and Christian Healing* (San Francisco: Harper and Row, 1988), 54.

6. For a longer historical account of the tradition of prayer for healing from biblical through rabbinic, patristic, medieval, Reformation, and post-Reformation traditions, see Morton Kelsey, *Psychology, Medicine and Christian Healing* (San Francisco: Harper and Row, 1988).

7. See Dennis Guernsey, "Healing of Memories" in *Dictionary of Pastoral Care and Counseling* (Nashville: Abingdon, 1990), 501.

8. See e.g., John J. Heaney, *The Sacred and the Psychic: Parapsychology and Christian Theology* (New York: Paulis, 1984); Jeffrey R. Burton, *The Devil in the Modern World* (New York: Cornell Univ. Press, 1984); Morton T. Kelsey, *The Christian and the Supernatural* (Minneapolis: Augsburg, 1976); and *Discernment: A Study in Ecstacy and Evil* (New York: Paulist, 1978); Walter Wink, *Unmasking the Powers: The Invisible Forces That Determine Human Experience* (Philadelphia: Fortress, 1986).

9. For an interesting discussion on possession and exorcism from the psychological viewpoint, see M. Scott Peck, *People of the Lie: The Hope for Healing Human Evil* (New York: Simon and Schuster, 1983), 182–211.

10. David Martin and Peter Mullen, eds., *Strange Gifts? A Guide to the Charismatic Renewal* (New York: Basil Blackwell, 1984), 98.

11. E.g., see Michael Perry, *Deliverance* (London: SPCK, 1987), 113.

# SELECTED
# BIBLIOGRAPHY

Anderson, Leith. *Dying for Change*. Minneapolis: Bethany, 1990.

Appleyard, Bryan. *Understanding the Present: Science and the Soul of Modern Man*. New York: Doubleday, 1993.

Augustine. *City of God*. London: Penguin, 1984.

Bellah, Mike. *Baby Boom Believers*. Wheaton, Ill.: Tyndale, 1988.

Bellah, Robert N., Richard Madsen, William M. Sullivan, Ann Swidler, and Steven M. Tipton. *Habits of the Heart: Individualism and Commitment in American Life*. Berkeley: Univ. of California Press, 1985.

Bibby, Reginald W. *Fragmented Gods: The Poverty and Potential of Religion in Canada*. Toronto: Irwin, 1987.

————. *Mosaic Madness*. Toronto: Stoddart, 1990.

Blan, Joel. *The Visible Poor: Homelessness in the United States*. Oxford, Great Britain: Oxford Univ. Press.

Bloom, Allan. *The Closing of the American Mind*. New York: Simon and Schuster, 1987.

Bonhoeffer, Dietrich. *Life Together*. New York: Harper and Row, 1976.

Briggs, John. "From Christendom to Pluralism." In *Essays in Evangelical Social Ethics*, edited by David F. Wright. London: Paternoster, 1978.

Brown, Colin. *Miracles and the Critical Mind*. Grand Rapids: Eerdmans, 1984.

————. *That You May Believe*. Grand Rapids: Eerdmans, 1985.

Buber, Martin. *I and Thou*. Translated by Ronald Gregor Smith. New York: Scribner's, 1958.

Cohen, Bernard I. *The Birth of the New Physics*. London: Penguin, 1987.

Dayton, Donald W. *Discovering an Evangelical Heritage.* New York: Harper and Row, 1976.

Dodd, Charles H. *Gospel and Law: The Relation of Faith and Ethics in Early Christianity.* New York: Columbia Univ. Press, 1933.

_____. *The Apostolic Preaching and Its Developments.* New York: Harper, 1936.

Finzel, Hans. *Help! I'm a Baby Boomer.* Wheaton, Ill.: Victor, 1989.

Fox, Matthew. *The Coming of the Cosmic Christ.* San Francisco: Harper and Row, 1989.

_____. *Creation Spirituality.* San Francisco: Harper and Row, 1991.

Fuller, Reginald H. *Interpreting the Miracles.* London: SCM, 1963.

Grant, Robert M. *Miracles and Natural Law.* Amsterdam: North Holland, 1952.

Green, Michael. *Evangelism in the Early Church.* Grand Rapids: Eerdmans, 1970.

Greidanus, Sidney. *The Modern Preacher and the Ancient Text: Interpreting and Preaching Biblical Literature.* Grand Rapids: Eerdmans, 1988.

Hart, Stephen. *What Does the Lord Require?* Oxford, Great Britain: Oxford Univ. Press, 1992.

Hawking, Stephen. *A Brief History of Time.* London: Bantam, 1988.

Hestenes, Roberta. *Using the Bible in Groups.* Philadelphia: Westminster, 1985.

Hick, John. *Christ and the Centre.* London: SCM, 1968.

_____. *God and the Universe of Faiths.* London: Fount, 1977.

_____. *An Interpretation of Religion: Human Responses to the Transcendent.* London: Macmillan, 1989.

Hick, John, Don Cupitt, Michael Goulder, Leslie Houlden, Dennis Nineham, Maurice Wilts, and Frances Young. *The Myth of God Incarnate.* London: SCM, 1977.

Hitchcock, James. *What Is Secular Humanism?* Ann Arbor, Mich.: Servant, 1982.

Jones, Landon. *Great Expectations: America and the Baby Boom Generation.* New York: Ballantine, 1980.

Kasper, Walter. *Jesus the Christ.* New York: Paulist, 1976.

Kelsey, Morton T. *Psychology, Medicine and Christian Healing.* San Francisco: Harper and Row, 1988.

_____. *The Christian and the Supernatural.* Minneapolis: Augsburg, 1976.

_____. *Discernment: A Study in Ecstacy and Evil.* New York: Paulist, 1978.

Küng, Hans. *The Church.* New York: Search Press, 1971.

Lasch, Christopher. *The Culture of Narcissism.* New York: Warner, 1978.

Martin, David, and Peter Mullen, eds. *Strange Gifts? A Guide to the Charismatic Renewal.* New York: Basil Blackwell, 1984.

McNutt, Francis. *Healing.* Notre Dame, Ind.: Ave Maria, 1974.

Miller, Craig. *Baby Boom Spirituality.* Nashville, Tenn.: Discipleship Resources, 1992.

Moberg, David O. *The Great Reversal: Evangelism and Social Concern.* New York: J.B. Lippincott, 1977.

Moule, C.F.D. *Miracles: Cambridge Studies in Philosophy and History.* London: Mowbrays, 1965.

Mounce, Robert. *The Essential Nature of New Testament Preaching.* Grand Rapids: Eerdmans, 1960.

_____. *Preaching and Teaching in the Earliest Church.* Philadelphia: Westminster, 1967.

**241**

Murren, Doug. *The Baby Boomerang.* Ventura, Calif.: Regal, 1990.

Naisbitt, John and Patricia Aburdene. *Megatrends 2000.* New York: William Morrow, 1990.

Niebuhr, H. Richard. *Christ and Culture.* New York: Harper, 1951.

_____. *Moral Man and Immoral Society: A Study of Ethics and Politics.* New York: Scribner's, 1952.

Newbigin, Lesslie. *The Gospel in a Pluralist Society.* Grand Rapids: Eerdmans, 1989.

Parrinder, Geoffery. *Encountering World Religions: Questions of Religious Truth.* New York: Crossroads, 1987.

Peck, M. Scott. *People of the Lie.* New York: Simon and Schuster, 1983.

Perry, Michael. *Deliverance.* London: SPCK, 1987.

Power, Thomas E. *Invitation to a Great Experiment.* New York: Doubleday, 1979.

Rahner, Karl. *Theological Investigations.* Baltimore: Helicon, 1966.

Roof, Wade Clark. *A Generation of Seekers.* San Francisco: HarperSan Francisco, 1993.

Russell, Cheryl. *One Hundred Predictions for the Baby Boom: The Next Fifty Years.* New York: Plenum, 1987.

Seamands, David A. *Healing of Memories.* Wheaton, Ill.: Victor, 1985.

Scanlan, Michael. *Inner Healing.* New York: Paulist, 1974.

Schlossberg, Herbert. *Idols for Destruction.* Nashville: Thomas Nelson, 1983.

Snyder, Howard. *The Problem of Wineskins.* Downers Grove, Ill.: InterVarsity, 1975.

Stott, John R.W. *Issues Facing Christians Today.* London: Marshall, Morgan, and Scott, 1984.

_____. *The Spirit and the Church in the Message of Acts.* Grand Rapids: Eerdmans, 1990.

Suenens, Joseph-Leon. *Renewal and the Powers of Darkness.* Ann Arbor, Mich.: Servant, 1983.

Tocqueville, Alexis de. *Democracy in America.* Translated by George Lawrence. Edited by J.P. Mayer. New York: Anchor, 1969.

Vanier, Jean. *Community and Growth.* New York: Paulist, 1979.

Vitz, Paul. *Psychology as Religion: The Cult of Self-Worship.* Grand Rapids: Eerdmans, 1977.

Ward, Benedicta. *Miracles and the Medieval Mind.* Philadelphia: Univ. of Pennsylvania Press, 1978.

Watson, David. *I Believe in the Church.* London: Hodder and Stoughton, 1978.

_____. *Discipleship.* London: Hodder and Stoughton, 1981.

Webber, Robert. *Signs of Wonder.* Nashville: Abbott Martyn, 1992.

Wink, Walter. *The Bible in Human Transformation: Towards a New Paradigm for Bible Study.* Philadelphia: Fortress, 1973.

_____. *Unmasking the Powers.* Philadelphia: Fortress, 1986.

Yankelovich, Daniel. *New Rules: Searching for Self-Fulfillment in a World Turned Upside Down.* New York: Random House, 1981.

# Index

## C

## D

## E

## F

## J

## K

## L

## M

Murren, Doug, 47, 61
Music, 77, 99, 104, 157–58, 165–67, 173, 189–92

## N

Narcissism, 64–66, 92, 113, 205
Narcissus, 67
Neill, Stephen, 119
New Collar Workers, 139
Newbigin, Lesslie, 118
Niebuhr, Richard, 56, 92, 96–98, 100–101

## O

O'Connor, Flannery, 169

## P

*Paraklesis,* 150–51
Parrinder, Geoffrey, 11
Pascal, 69, 182
Paul, the Apostle, 91, 98–101, 120, 153
Pike, James A., 22
Plato, 40
Pluralism, 34–37, 39, 41, 44–48, 50–51, 53, 55, 78, 99, 105, 111–12, 116,
    118, 155, 221, 223, 225
Christian perspective, 38–41, 44–51
    philosophical, 35–36
    religious, 41–44, 116–18
    social, 36–37
Prayer, 173, 175, 181–83, 186, 195, 198, 200, 203
Proclamation, 157, 197, 199
Prosperity Gospel, 72–74, 78, 130–31, 133
Protagoras, 62
Pythagoras, 35

## R

Rahner, Karl, 43–44, 118
Redemption, 120, 175, 193, 222
Relativism, 51–57, 60–61, 122, 126, 128, 175, 225
    cultural, 54, 60–61
    ethical, 55–57
    religious, 58, 60